What People Are Saying About
Chicken Soup for the Veteran's Soul . . .

"Accounts of America's past wars are necessarily geared to the actions and decisions of high level officials—generals, admirals and statesmen. That limitation keeps military writers from doing justice to the heroism and sufferings of the actual participants. *Chicken Soup for the Veteran's Soul,* concentrating entirely on the human side of our conflicts, is both a refreshing and moving book."

John S. D. Eisenhower, Brig. General
USAR (Retired) and former U.S. ambassador to Belgium

"I had tears in my eyes from the first story to the last! And this is what American's seem to have forgotten—the pain and torture that our American soldiers went through, in order for us to enjoy the liberty and democracy we have today! 'Lest We Forget'—that should be our motto for all time, for all our veterans!"

Ernest Borgnine, Academy Award-winning actor
and World War II Navy veteran

"It is important for the nation, and for generations to come, that veterans' stories are told. This book is so important not only for veterans' souls but for our children's who are only learning about war from their textbooks. I applaud the authors of *Chicken Soup for the Veteran's Soul* and wholeheartedly recommend this book for all Americans young and old."

Rep. Leonard Boswell, Iowa, Third Congressional District
and two-tour Vietnam helicopter pilot

"*Chicken Soup for the Veteran's Soul* lets you see that every veteran is truly the heart and soul of this great country. As an organization of military widows, we know firsthand the sacrifices made for all of us. Our sincere thanks to everyone who made this book possible."

Rachel A. Clinkscale, board chairman
Gold Star Wives of America, Inc.

"Those who serve in the military understand the bond created by the warrior ethic. In *Chicken Soup for the Veteran's Soul,* the reader gains an appreciation for that bond and the selfless sacrifice to which that ethic gives rise. These stories will touch veterans and non-veterans alike, helping those who did not serve to better understand what that bond and the warrior ethic are all about."

James G. Zumwalt, LtCol, USMCR (Retired)

"The stories are both humbling and inspiring: humbling, in that I was forced to consider whether I could have responded to such adversity with the valor these men and women demonstrated; inspiring, in the sense that I now, more than ever, feel the need to live a more giving life."

Terry M. Murphy, son of Audie L. Murphy,
most decorated American combat soldier of World War II

"So many times our veterans come home from horrendous wars and quietly live their lives. Thanks for affirming courageous Americans who have served our country well."

Commander Frances Omori, U.S. Navy, author,
Quiet Heroes: Navy Nurses of the Korean War, 1950–1953, Far East Command

"*Chicken Soup for the Veteran's Soul* is a book for every veteran's family and extended family. This book helps us all better understand that it is humankind that fights wars. Glory, blood and guts must be respected and honored. I believe this book contributes to that heroic legacy. Please buy this book and give it as a gift to all who love freedom."

Dannion Brinkley, author, *Saved by the Light*
and chairman of the board for Compassion in Action (CIA)

"I was overwhelmed by emotion while reading this marvelous collection of veterans' stories. As a combat veteran and veteran's advocate, no book has touched me the way *Chicken Soup for the Veteran's Soul* has. It provides a poignant and personal insight into the experiences of veterans during their military service."

John F. Gwizdak, commander-in-chief, 2000–2001
Veterans of Foreign Wars of the United States

CHICKEN SOUP FOR THE VETERAN'S SOUL

Chicken Soup for the Veteran's Soul
Stories to Stir the Pride and Honor the Courage of Our Veterans
Jack Canfield, Mark Victor Hansen, Sidney R. Slagter

Published by Backlist, LLC,
a unit of Chicken Soup for the Soul Publishing, LLC. www.chickensoup.com

Front cover design by Andrea Perrine Brower
Originally published in 2001 by Health Communications, Inc.

Back cover and spine redesign by Pneuma Books, LLC

Distributed to the booktrade by Simon & Schuster. SAN: 200-2442

Publisher's Cataloging-in-Publication Data
(Prepared by The Donohue Group)

Chicken soup for the veteran's soul : stories to stir the pride and honor the courage of our veterans / [compiled by] Jack Canfield, Mark Victor Hansen, [and] Sidney R. Slagter.

p. : ill. ; cm.

Originally published: Deerfield Beach, FL : Health Communications, c2001.
ISBN: 978-1-62361-103-3

1. Veterans--United States--Anecdotes. 2. United States--Armed Forces--Anecdotes. 3. Anecdotes. I. Canfield, Jack, 1944- II. Hansen, Mark Victor. III. Slagter, Sidney R.

PN6071.V45 C48 2012
810.8/02/0921/355 2012944878

PRINTED IN THE UNITED STATES OF AMERICA
on acid free paper

21 20 19 18 17 16 15 14 13 12 01 02 03 04 05 06 07 08 09 10

CHICKEN SOUP FOR THE VETERAN'S SOUL

Stories to Stir the Pride and Honor the Courage of Our Veterans

Jack Canfield
Mark Victor Hansen
Sidney R. Slagter

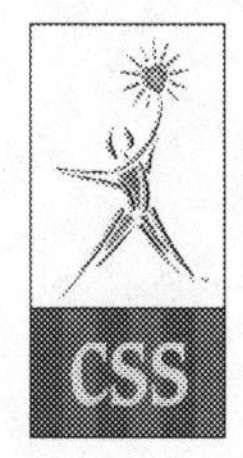

Backlist, LLC, a unit of
Chicken Soup for the Soul Publishing, LLC
Cos Cob, CT
www.chickensoup.com

Reprinted with permission from Jim Willoughby.

Contents

3. ABOVE AND BEYOND

4. ON THE FRONT LINES

5. THE HOME FRONT

6. BROTHERS IN ARMS

7. COMING HOME

8. HONORING THOSE WHO SERVED

9. HEALING

10. REMEMBRANCE

Introduction

Everyone knows a veteran. Take a quick look around your circle of family, friends and coworkers, and you will undoubtedly find someone who served in the Armed Forces. In millions of homes across the country, there are fading brown-and-white photos of family members in uniform, military awards and citations packed away in old boxes in the attic, and stacks of letters—old and new—sent from military bases and battlefields around the world. In the workplace, it's not unusual to overhear conversations about time spent overseas. These are just a few of the many common instances that identify the veterans who surround us.

And everyone has heard a veteran's story. These stories are passed down through families: Grandfather's exploits during World War II, accounts of the aunt who nursed the wounded and still remembers those she couldn't help, tales of a cousin who was drafted and did his year in Southeast Asia.

The stories contained in *Chicken Soup for the Veteran's Soul* come directly from the veterans and their families, people who witnessed these events as they unfolded and who will always be the best custodians of our nation's history. The retelling of their experiences will keep the memory of service, sacrifice, honor and duty alive in the minds of present and future generations.

The outpouring of support for this book has been overwhelming. When we put out the call for veterans' stories, letters, e-mails, faxes and phone calls came in from all over the world. We received over four thousand contributions and enjoyed reading every one of them. Every day brought amazing and powerful stories: firsthand accounts of parachuting behind enemy lines, descriptions of the predawn preparations for the coming day's battle, recollections of the weariness and loneliness of a young man or woman thousands of miles from home.

We also had the good fortune to personally meet and interview hundreds of veterans, from buck privates who saw the war from ground level, to the retired generals who commanded those fine soldiers, to the women who left comfortable homes to treat the wounded. Prisoners of war, Congressional Medal of Honor recipients, USO volunteers who entertained the troops and thousands of ordinary—no, extraordinary—GIs all generously shared of themselves to make this book a success.

It is a difficult task to write about war and the misery and suffering associated with it; yet sometimes, harsh circumstances can bring out what is best in us. The war stories in *Chicken Soup for the Veteran's Soul* are filled with compassion, respect, brotherhood and love, especially love for one another. The love and reverence that veterans hold for each other is second to none. In some cases, the memory of a fallen comrade stays with a veteran for the rest of his or her life. And for many, the admiration that veterans share remains one of the most meaningful experiences of a veteran's life.

It has been our great privilege to personally interview

hundreds of veterans and hear their stories directly. Many veterans have told us that their time spent in the service was one of the best experiences of their lives, a time of camaraderie, of being in top physical condition and feeling the pride that comes with serving one's country. Not many would wish to repeat those times, but they unanimously agree that the memories are priceless.

Chicken Soup for the Veteran's Soul has been an honor to write. For the coauthors, it has fulfilled a longtime desire to give something back to those who gave so much through service to their country. It has been a true labor of love and a journey into the personal history of our nation's finest citizens, our veterans.

It is the hard training, discipline, courage and sacrifice that stand out in the telling of all of these stories. Clearly, because of the great sacrifices made by so many men and women in the past, we are able to live in a time and a place where freedom is taken for granted.

We offer this book to our veterans as a small payment toward a debt that can never be fully repaid. You are our best, and we owe you our full support and our sincerest thanks. It is our hope that these remarkable stories will offer inspiration and insight to those unfamiliar with your tales, and rekindle the pride and admiration in those who have heard them before. In the retelling of these stories, we all share in the promise of freedom hard won by the young men and women of America who fought and died in its name.

1

THE WARRIOR SPIRIT

Bravery never goes out of fashion.

William Makepeace Thackeray

Freedom Village

My most vivid memory associated with the American flag flashes back to Korea and a gray, clammy day in early August 1953. The Korean War had come to an end a week earlier, on July 27 at precisely 10 P.M. I remember lying in a rice paddy and suddenly experiencing the thunderous, deafening silence of peace. The Chinese and North Koreans, surely as joyful as I, were singing and raising their flags less than two hundred yards away from where my platoon sergeant and I sat smoking celebratory cigars.

A military spotlight, affectionately referred to as "Moonbeam Charlie," played along the valley floor and crept up the scarred hills, catching the Chinese and North Koreans in spirited dancing around their outpost flagpole. Their flags seemed to mean something to them, and at that time, I wasn't sure what my flag meant to me.

But that changed dramatically a week later, when I was a part of a contingent sent to represent my regiment at "Freedom Village."

"Operation Big Switch" was on. Our prisoners of war were to be returned to American hands, as the Chinese and North Koreans were to be returned to their people.

Through the dim half-light of fading memory, I recollect that Freedom Village was in a scooped-out hollow with hills brooding over it from four sides. A few dwellings leaned into the village amid taut canvas hospital tents.

We representatives of the United Nations stood at attention as ambulances and beat-up buses arrived from the north. The UN, American and Korean flags hung limply in the humid August air. Photographers, Army and civilian alike, scurried about for good vantage points.

The Chinese and North Koreans were the first to cross over "Freedom Bridge." They were surly, healthy looking and well fed. Some carried signs decrying capitalism. Members of a Republic of Korea regiment scowled, and one of them sent a spray of saliva in his former opponent's direction. The exchange had a tone of tense and bitter antagonism, and as young as I was, I wondered how long the newly inked truce would last.

When the remaining Chinese and North Koreans had been herded off to their own vehicles, the UN prisoners were ushered from the trucks and buses and sent across the bridge to our side. The UN Honor Guard, combat veterans and observers gasped when they saw the condition of their returning comrades, who struggled, hobbled and staggered, gaunt and emaciated, toward friendly faces.

One after another they came. The next one was in worse condition than the one before. Long lines of dull-eyed soldiers of the "Forgotten War" inched their way to freedom, and out of their number, a gray-faced stick figure of a boy-turned-old-man dragged himself along the bridge. His bony arms were held out like a sleepwalker. He staggered and swayed, and one time fell into the wooden railing. Every eye in that village was suddenly trained on that one figure. Even those on the northern side watched the gallant physical effort of the wasted soldier.

Each tried, inwardly, to help, to urge him on, until

finally, when he lurched forward, an MP major, a giant of a man, came up to help. The soldier waved him off with his skeleton hands and arms.

Looking around at the grim faces, he caught sight of the three color bearers and shuffled toward them. When he reached the American flag bearer, he knelt on trembling knees before the flag as though it were an altar. He reached up and tugged at the flag. The color bearer, either by instinct or by some infinite wisdom, lowered the flag, and the soldier covered his face with it, sobbing and shaking uncontrollably.

Other than the clicks of cameras, the village was cemetery-quiet. Tears streamed from all of us. Cotton replaced saliva in our throats. After several moments, the stillness was broken by the sound of the heavy boots of the MP major, who came crunching across the gravel, his cheeks moist and glistening. He bent down and tenderly scooped the soldier up in his muscular arms and carried him off to a waiting ambulance, much as a father would carry a baby.

There wasn't a dry eye in that silent village, thousands of miles away from Main Street, USA.

James F. Murphy Jr.
Submitted by Harry Feltenbarger

A group of American POWs are given a royal welcome at Freedom Village, Munsan-ni, Korea, during the UN POW exchange.

Credit: National Archives.

The Code Talkers

During World War II, U.S. Marines storming Pacific beaches used a unique kind of code machine. Each Marine Corps cryptograph had two arms, two legs, an M-1 rifle and a helmet. Their code name was *Dineh*—"the People." In English, they were called the "Navajo Code Talkers," and theirs is one of the few unbroken codes in military history.

Like all Americans of his generation, Keith Little, who is a Navajo, remembers exactly where he was when he heard the news of Pearl Harbor. Little, then sixteen, was attending boarding school on the reservation in Arizona.

"Me and a bunch of guys were out hunting rabbits with a .22," he recalls. "Somebody went to the dorm, came back and said, 'Hey, Pearl Harbor was bombed!'

"One of the boys asked, 'Where's Pearl Harbor?'

"'In Hawaii.'

"'Who did it?'

"'Japan.'

"'Why'd they do it?'

"'They hate Americans. They want to kill all Americans.'

"'Us, too?'

"'Yeah, us, too.'"

Then and there, the boys made a promise to one another. They'd go after the Japanese instead of the rabbits.

The next morning, the superintendent of the reservation looked out his office window and saw dozens of ponytailed young men carrying hunting rifles, ready to fight. But the Navajo volunteers were sent home. No official call to arms had been issued, and besides, most of the men spoke only Navajo.

When the war broke out, a man named Philip Johnston had an extraordinary idea. Johnston, the son of missionaries, also grew up on the reservation and was fluent in Navajo. Early in 1942, he visited the Marine Corps's Camp Elliott, north of San Diego, and proposed to use the Navajo language as an up-to-date code, guaranteed unbreakable.

The Marines were skeptical at first. At the time, military codes were encrypted by high-tech black boxes that used rotors and ratchets to shroud messages in a thick alphabet soup. Still, Johnston returned with a few Navajo friends. For fifteen minutes, while the iron jaws of Marine brass went slack, messages metamorphosed from English to Navajo and back.

In the spring of 1942, Marine recruiters came to the Navajo Nation in the mile-high Southwest desert. There, among the sagebrush and sandstone, they set up tables, called them enlistment offices and began looking for a few good men fluent in Navajo and English.

Fewer than eighty years had passed since the Navajos had fought against the U.S. military. Kit Carson's scorched-earth campaign had broken their resistance in 1864. Why would men volunteer to fight for a nation that had humbled their ancestors, killed their herds and wouldn't even let them vote?

Soldiers enlist for reasons of jobs, adventure, family

tradition—and patriotism. Says one Navajo who fought in World War II, "This conflict involved Mother Earth being dominated by foreign countries. It was our responsibility to defend her."

Few Navajos had ever been off the reservation. Mostly, they had only met "Anglos" on trading posts. Soon they would fight across an ocean they had never seen, against an enemy they had never met. Yet they proved to be model Marines. Accustomed to walking miles each day in the high desert, they marched on with full packs after others buckled. When training was finished, the first group of Navajos became the 382nd Platoon, USMC, and was ordered to make a code.

On the reservation, the language was primarily oral, and the Code Talkers were told to keep it that way. There would be no code books, no cryptic algorithms. Navajo itself was puzzling enough. Germans deciphering English codes could tap common linguistic roots. Japanese eavesdropping on GIs were often graduates of American universities. But Navajo, a tonal language, was known to few outsiders. Its vowels rise and fall, changing meaning with pitch. A single Navajo verb, containing its own subjects, objects and adverbs, can translate into an entire English sentence.

To devise the code, the Navajos turned to nature. They named planes after birds: *gini*—chicken hawk (dive bomber); *neasjah*—owl (observation plane); *taschizzie*—swallow (torpedo plane). They named ships after fish: *lotso*—whale (battleship); *calo*—shark (destroyer); *beshlo*—iron fish (submarine).

To spell out proper names, the Code Talkers made a Navajo bestiary, turning the Marines' *A*ble *B*aker Charlie . . . into *Wollachee Shush Moasi* . . . (*A*nt *B*ear Cat . . . They also played word games. "District" became the Navajo words for "deer ice strict," and "belong" became "long bee."

The finished code was a hodgepodge of everyday Navajo and some four hundred newly devised code words. As a test, Navy intelligence officers spent three weeks trying, and failing, to decipher a single message. New Navajo recruits untrained in the code could not break it. Yet it seemed too simple to be trusted. And while codes normally took hours to translate, these Indians were encoding and decoding sensitive military information almost instantly. What kind of magic was this?

"In Navajo, everything—songs, prayers—is in memory," said William McCabe, one of the code's designers. "That's the way we was raised up. So we didn't have no trouble."

Two Code Talkers stayed behind to teach the next group; the rest were shipped to Guadalcanal. There, Code Talkers met skepticism in the flesh. One colonel agreed to use the Navajos only if they won a man-versus-machine test against a cylindrical gizmo that disguised words and broadcast in coded clicks. The Code Talkers won handily. Still, officers were reluctant to trust lives to a code untested in combat.

More than 3,600 Navajos served in World War II, but only 420 became Code Talkers. In boot camp, Keith Little was just another Indian, and few cared from which tribe. Then a drill instructor took him aside and asked, "By any chance, are you a Navajo?" He was sent to Code Talkers' school.

Eventually, Marine commanders came to see the code as indispensable for the rapid transmission of classified dispatches. Lent to the Navy, the Code Talkers kept the Japanese from learning of impending air attacks. On Saipan, an advancing U.S. battalion was shelled from behind by "friendly fire." Desperate messages were sent, "Hold your fire," but the Japanese had imitated Marine broadcasts all day. Mortar crews weren't sure what to believe. The shelling continued. Finally, headquarters asked, "Do you have a Navajo?" A Code Talker sent the same message to his buddy, and the shelling stopped.

During the first two days on Iwo Jima, six networks of Code Talkers transmitted more than eight hundred messages without error. On the morning of February 23, 1945, the Stars and Stripes were hoisted on a mountaintop. The word went out in Navajo code. Cryptographers translated the Navajo words for "mouse turkey sheep uncle ram ice bear ant cat horse intestines," then told their fellow Marines in English that the American flag flew over Mt. Suribachi. A signal officer recalled, "Were it not for the Navajos, the Marines would never have taken Iwo Jima."

When the war ended, the Navajos headed home to their reservation. But the code itself remained top secret. Asked about the war, Code Talkers simply said, "I was a radioman." Finally, in 1968, the code was declassified, and the secret was out.

In 1992, Keith Little was invited to the Pentagon, where he translated a prayer for peace phoned in by a Code Talker in Arizona. Then, Little and other Navajo vets helped dedicate a permanent exhibit on the Code Talkers.

"Most of us are common men," Little once said. But in school, all young Navajos learning native studies read about the Code Talkers. The students all agree that without them, "We could have lost the war."

In code, the Talkers spoke of snipers and fortifications, but their real message needed no interpreter. These heroes spoke of overcoming stereotypes and past conflicts for a higher cause, about blending tradition into the modern world. They spoke Navajo.

Bruce Watson

That Old Man Down the Street

We can't all be heroes. Some of us have to stand on the curb and clap as they go by.

Will Rogers

Back in the early 1920s, when I was growing up in Seneca Falls, New York, Memorial Day was known as Decoration Day. It marked the beginning of summer, although its true purpose was to bring the village together to honor the memory of those people who had fought the nation's battles—in the War to End All Wars, the Spanish-American War and the War Between the States.

The main event of the day for us kids was the mid-morning parade, which formed in the park in front of the high school. As the marchers gathered there, so did a swarm of bike-riding small boys to approve the lineup before racing ahead to lead the procession. We pedaled in front of the parade through the heart of Seneca Falls and over the Seneca River via the Ovid Street Bridge. Only then did we pull to the curb and fall in behind the colors with everyone else as the marchers moved toward Restvale Cemetery at the eastern edge of town.

The goings-on at the cemetery always made my spine tingle. Even now, seventy-odd years later, I can still smell the flowers under the morning sun, beat time with the brass band playing "The Star-Spangled Banner," wince at the crack of the rifles firing the salute and choke up listening to the last mournful note of "Taps."

Central to my memories of that day is the figure of Abraham Lincoln, which sat in the shadows at the edge of the cemetery, his head bowed in sorrow over the adorned graves. I especially remember Mr. Lincoln because in those parades of my boyhood, the main figures were the town's surviving veterans of the Grand Army of the Republic.

These few old men—they were fewer every year—spent 364 days rocking on front porches, sitting by windows overlooking the street or shuffling downtown to buy a plug of chewing tobacco at Sullivan's Cigar Store. Normally, no one paid them any mind.

But come the Decoration Day Parade, in the vestiges of their Union Army uniforms, the old soldiers walking proudly through the streets made me think through the words of "The Battle Hymn of the Republic" as those of a prayer. Even though I was only a boy, the veterans stirred in me visions of Bull Run, Chickamauga, Chancellorsville, the Wilderness and, especially, Gettysburg. *These,* I marveled, *were the same men who had saved the Republic.*

One of them lived on our street, about halfway downtown. He was a friend of my grandfather. Grandpa Billy always spoke of his contemporary as "Old Jimmy Barton."

Old Jimmy Barton had fought at Gettysburg, and my father, who had heard his war stories many times over the years, decided it would be interesting to take the old man back to that battlefield. So a few weeks after the 1924

Decoration Day parade, he loaded Old Jimmy, Grandpa Billy and me into the car for the day's drive to the south. The next day, with an official guide leading the way, we set off on a tour, following the day-by-day course of the bloodiest battle ever fought in North America.

The first day, we saw where Confederate strength smashed the Yankees north and south of Gettysburg to take the city, forcing the Union forces to the high ground to the south. On the second day, we followed the flag to the Peach Orchard, the Wheat Field and Devil's Den. Then we saw where Union troops secured Little Round Top, lost Culp's Hill and Spangler Springs, and attacked Cemetery Hill, losing at first, and then regaining its crest.

Old Jimmy Barton had little to say as we walked through the sites of the first two days of the bloody battle. He nodded sometimes as the guide read the commemorative plaques aloud, now and then looking puzzled. He would stand facing the Confederate lines, then the Union emplacements, looking around him, then his gaze seemed to go inward and, I figured, backward in time as well.

A change came over him when we moved down Cemetery Ridge to brood over the location of the battle's third day. From a point opposite Pickett's position, we looked across to where 138 Confederate cannons had stood wheel-to-wheel blasting the Yankees on the heights before fifteen thousand proud and brave Southerners launched their incredible assault.

Then the old survivor of those three days of carnage walked with all the briskness he could muster, up and down the Union line. Finally, he nodded his head decisively and seated himself on the remains of an old stone fence.

"Right there," he said, pointing behind the stones on which he sat.

Right there was where he had spent the longest day of

his life. There he had lain, fired, loaded, fired, until the muzzle of his rifle was too hot to touch.

There he had trembled, sweated, prayed, laughed, wept, loaded and fired, loaded and fired, over and over again.

"The Rebels kept on a-coming up that slope, right over there," he said. Then, all of a sudden, they were either sprawled out on the ground or running back down the side of the ridge.

When he saw that, he told us, he climbed up on this stone fence, waving his cap in one hand and his weapon in the other, cheering with his comrades until he had to sit down to be sick between his trembling legs.

The next day—the Fourth of July he said it was—the rain fell on the Yankee and the Rebel dead who were scattered everywhere. The old man recalled how the burial details dug thousands of shallow graves to contain the fallen until a proper cemetery was provided. When he spoke next, his voice was low with reverence. He described how Mr. Lincoln himself came to that very same battlefield only four months later and spoke, inaugurating the cemetery there, and calling this nation to a new birth of freedom under God.

After Cemetery Ridge, he was never Old Jimmy Barton to me again. After seeing him sitting on his very own piece of battlefield, and listening to his account of that terrible day, even now, long after his death, I can only think of him as Mr. James Barton, the fine man who fought at Gettysburg.

Emerson D. Moran

At the entrance to Devil's Den, Gettysburg battlefield. Left to right atop the boulder: Civil War veteran James Barton, attorney Daniel Moran (author's father) and their battlefield guide. Standing is William Moran (author's grandfather).

Credit: Emerson Moran.

The Postcard

The ambush came out of nowhere and everywhere. My platoon members and I were strung out and moving through the bush near Hiep Douc in the Que San Valley of South Vietnam. It was August 20, 1969, and, as always, it was hot and wet.

All at once, the distinctive angry staccato of the enemies' AK-47 assault rifles filled the air. It was mixed with a different sound, that of a heavier machine gun. The incoming rounds slapped and tore through the foliage. Adding to the din were the shouts of the platoon sergeant to return fire. Company C of the 196th Light Infantry Brigade was in trouble.

Suddenly, it felt as if someone had smacked me—hard—with a baseball bat on the left thigh. I had been hit by one of the incoming rounds! I tried to scramble out of harm's way, but there was no escape from the withering fire. Then I heard the ear-splitting "ruuump!" of a grenade explosion, and the baseball bat smashed down hard again, this time pounding onto my right leg and foot.

My memory after that is of crawling—for what seemed like forever. I later calculated that over the course of six hours, I had dragged myself across two miles of ground. I did a lot of thinking and remembering in that time.

At one point during my slow and painful journey, it occurred to me that I'd had the peculiar fortune to have been "drafted" twice. In January 1968, I was a late-round draft pick for the Pittsburgh Steelers, and in November of that year, the U.S. Army drafted me. In my weakened condition, I found this double-draft thing infinitely amusing.

But the joke soon faded, and my mind once again tried to grasp the reason that I was in Vietnam at all. The political reasons for the U.S. being there were easy to understand. The difficult part for a soldier like me to comprehend was my role in this conflict. I had been over all this in my mind many times before, and I always came back to an incident that had happened early on in my tour.

We had come across a village—not even a village, really, but just a couple of hooches inland. There was a family there—kids, an old man and an old lady. I saw that they didn't have anything—except for an old tin can. They had filled the tin can with water and put it on an open fire to boil. When I looked inside the can, I saw a buffalo hoof. That pathetic soup was their sustenance. I decided right then that if I could help these people take a step forward, then my time in the country would be worthwhile.

As it happened, my opportunity to follow through was cut short. My wounds got me evacuated to Tokyo, where the docs told me I had nearly lost my right foot and that I would never play football again. They informed me I was getting discharged with 40 percent disability.

This was not good news. Football was my whole life and dream—a dream that had started in Appleton, Wisconsin, at Xavier High School and matured at Notre Dame, where I had been voted the captain of the Fighting Irish in 1967. There wasn't anything else in my life I wanted to do. Football was something I identified with and that defined me.

It was a black time for me. Wounded and depressed, I tried to contemplate a future without football. Then I received a postcard from Art Rooney, the owner of the Steelers. He had written only, "We'll see you when you get back."

Such simple words, but their impact was immediate. It was then that I determined that I *would* be back—I would fight this thing with everything I had. The first thing on the program was learning to walk again on what remained of my right foot.

With more patience and resolve than I knew I had, I succeeded. In 1970, I returned to the Steelers and was placed on injured reserve. By the following year, I was on the taxi squad. In 1973, I made special teams. That year, I began running. In 1974, I was still running—but now I wore the Steelers' number 20 jersey.

We won the Super Bowl that year. We won again in 1975, 1978 and 1979. Franco Harris and I ran and ran, setting some modest records along the way.

In 1980, I retired from football, having—against all probability—lived my dream. I have tried to thank providence for my exceptional second chance by serving as a board member of the Vietnam Veterans Memorial Fund and being involved with charities for disabled children. I've also done a lot of professional motivational speaking, hoping to inspire others to overcome any obstacles that may bar their way.

In my talks, I always tell people about Art Rooney, whose faith in me was contagious. As long as I live, I don't believe that I will ever experience more inspirational words than the simple sentence written on that long-ago postcard: "We'll see you when you get back."

Rocky Bleier with David Eberhart

The Harbinger

It wasn't noon yet, but the temperature was already approaching ninety-five degrees on the morning I started my flight training at Fort Wolters. It was warm for May, even for Texas, and since the base was intended to be a training ground for Vietnam, the heat just made the experience all the more authentic. We knew that the lucky few who made it through the grueling nine-month warrant officer flight-training course would soon be off to a destination even hotter than Texas.

As nearly two hundred of us stood at attention, we were flushed with excitement. On this day, we would finally begin the "hands on" portion of flight school. We had been through nine tough weeks of basic training in Louisiana and four weeks of continuous harassment from our tactical officers while we began the ground school portion of our classes. The purpose of the harassment, we knew, was to shake out anyone from the program who couldn't handle the pressure of intimidation and confusion. The ability to remain focused during combat is critical to survival.

That morning, however, no amount of harassment

could have taken away from the excitement of climbing into the cockpit of the TH-55 training helicopter to actually begin learning to fly. Although it was common knowledge that only a portion of those who began flight school would actually end up with wings, each of us was convinced that we would soon fly "above the best." Lunch, and our tactical officers, were all that stood between us and our first flight. We knew from experience that the tac officers could be brutal, so we wondered, uneasily, what they would throw at us during this portion of our training.

As we stood rigidly facing the tac officer, waiting for instructions, a tiny robin hopped out in front of our formation. It seemed confused and a little frightened. Suddenly, its mother flew a low swoop across the lawn, as if encouraging her youngster to take to the air. Despite our efforts to remain focused on the men in command in front of us, everyone's eyes followed the birds. Even our officers turned to watch, mesmerized by the scene.

Over and over, the tiny bird ran as fast as its little legs could move, taking off after its mom. But despite its best efforts, gravity kept it tethered to the earth. Again and again, the little ball of feathers raced across the grass, flapping its wings, only to hop up on a stone at the end of its long run.

Completely ignoring the crowd of staring bystanders, the mother robin swooped down after her baby's attempts to fly, cajoling and chiding it. "Like this," she seemed to be saying. "Try again." All two hundred of us watched breathlessly, silently praying for the little bird to succeed. Each time it flapped and hopped its way across the lawn in front of us, we'd groan at its failure.

Finally, after we had stood at attention for what seemed like hours just watching, those tiny wings took hold of the air, and the baby bird became airborne for a few feet. You could almost see the little bird swell with pride. Then, on one last run across the front of our formation, the gray piece of fluff rose into the air. Two hundred would-be warrant officers burst into wild cheers. We watched, ecstatic, as the little bird followed its mother to the horizon.

Our tac officers turned back to us, smiling. What could they add? It had been the ultimate flight lesson.

Bill Walker

The Final Battle

Italy, 1945. As the first and second platoons of E Company of the Japanese-American 442nd Regimental Combat Team closed on the perimeter of the German defenses, we could hear the crackle of rifle fire and an occasional machine gun off to the right.

Then it began, machine-gun fire and grenades going back and forth in fierce volleys. I took a slug in the gut, but kept on moving, leading my men and continuing to throw grenades.

As I drew my arm back, all in a flash of light and dark I saw him, that faceless German, like a strip of motion picture film running through a projector that's gone berserk. One instant he was standing waist-high in the bunker, and the next he was aiming a rifle grenade at my face from a range of ten yards. And even as I cocked my arm to throw, he fired and his rifle grenade smashed into my right elbow and exploded. I looked at my dangling arm and saw my grenade still clenched in a fist that suddenly didn't belong to me anymore.

Time passed and finally the medic came and gave me a shot of morphine. Then they carried me down off that hill.

It was April 21. The German resistance in our sector ended on April 23. Nine days later, the war in Italy was over, and a week after that, the enemy surrendered unconditionally.

I had another war to fight. When they became reasonably convinced that I wasn't going to die, I was transferred to the general hospital at Leghorn. And it was there, on May 1, Lei Day in Hawaii, that they amputated my right arm. It wasn't an emotionally big deal for me. I knew it was coming off and, in fact, had stopped thinking of the arm as belonging to me for some time. But acceptance and rehabilitation are entirely different things. I had adjusted to the shock before the operation. My rehabilitation began almost immediately afterward.

I was staring at the ceiling in the afternoon of my first day as an amputee when a nurse came by and asked if I needed anything. "A cigarette would go pretty good," I said.

"Yes, surely." She smiled and walked off, returning in a few minutes with a fresh pack of Camels. "Here you are, Lieutenant," she said, still smiling, and neatly placed the whole pack on my chest and went on her merry way.

For a while I just stared at it. Then I fingered it with my left hand, trying to decide how I'd go about it if I did decide to have a fling at opening it with one hand. I sneaked a look around the ward to see if there was anyone in shape to help me, but everyone seemed to be at least as badly off as I was: this was obviously not the ward reserved for officers afflicted with athlete's foot and charley horses. Then I began pawing at that cursed pack, holding it under my chin and trying to rip it open with my fingernails. It kept slipping away from me and I kept trying again, sweating in my fury and frustration as freely as if I'd been on a forced march. In fifteen minutes, I'd torn the pack and half the cigarettes in it to shreds, but I'd finally gotten one between my lips. Which is when I realized that the nurse hadn't brought me any matches.

I rang the bell and she came sashaying in, still smiling, still trailing that aura of good cheer that made me want to clout her one. "I need a light," I said.

"Oh," she said prettily. "Of course you do." She pulled a pack of matches out of her pocket—she had had them all the time—and carefully put them in my hand. And she strolled off again!

If I had obeyed my first instinct, I'd have bellowed after her with rage. If I'd obeyed my second instinct, I'd have burst out crying. But let's face it, I was a big boy now, an officer, and I just couldn't let some nurse get the best of me. I just couldn't.

So I started fooling around with the matches. I clutched them and pulled them and twisted them and dropped them, and I never came remotely close to tearing one free, let alone getting it lit. But by this time I had decided that I'd sooner boil in oil before asking her for anything again. So I just lay there, fuming silently, and having extremely un-Christian thoughts about that angel of mercy.

I was on the verge of dozing off when she came around again, still smiling.

"What's the matter, Lieutenant?" she purred. "Have you decided to quit smoking? It's just as well . . . cigarettes make you cough and. . . ."

"I couldn't get the damned thing lit."

She tsk-tsked at her thoughtlessness and sat gracefully on the edge of my bed. "I should have realized," she said, taking the mangled matches from me. "Some amputees like to figure it out for themselves. It gives them a feeling of—well, accomplishment. But it doesn't matter. There'll be lots of things you'll be learning for yourself. We only give you the start."

I just gaped at her. I didn't even know what she was

talking about. *A start on what? Who needed her?* "Look," I growled, "just light the cigarette, will you? I've been three hours trying to get this thing smoked."

"Yes, I know." Nothing ruffled her. Absolutely nothing. "But you see, I won't be around to light your cigarette all the time. You can't depend on other people. Now you have only one hand with which to do all the things that you used to do with two hands. And you have to learn how. We'll start with the matches, all right?"

She opened the cover, bent a match forward, closed the cover, flicked the match down and lit it—all with one hand, all in a split second.

"See?" she said.

"Yes," I whispered.

"Now let's see you do it."

I did it. I lit the cigarette. And all at once her smile wasn't objectionable at all. It was lovely. I wish I could remember her name—I'll never forget her face—but all I remember is that she came from Eagle Pass, Texas, and as far as I was concerned she was the best damn nurse in the United States Army. In a single moment, she had made me see the job that lay ahead of me, and in all the weeks that followed she found a thousand subtle ways to help me master it. And in the year and a half that it took me to become a fully functioning citizen again, no one ever did anything more important for me than that nurse did on that afternoon when she showed me how to light a cigarette, the afternoon my rehabilitation began.

Senator Daniel Inouye

Wiggle Your Toes!

My childhood years of varied sports, including chasing a homemade wooden puck on roller skates up and down Cantrell Street in South Philadelphia, had given me strong legs and a healthy body that were prepared to endure and respond quickly.

When I was wounded seriously in action, I didn't accept my condition of paralysis as permanent—although it did make life more complicated. But I wondered how to explain this condition to people back home, especially Mom and Dad, who only knew me as a happy-go-lucky, smiling kid who was nonstop on my pins. What about telling Grace, brother John and his wife Jeanne, and a lot of friends and relatives back in the States? And was there any solution to the problem of depending on others to do everything? Thoughts like these were another set of challenges to add to my new physical weaknesses.

Charlie was one of the first to ease the situation. He had a friendly smile on his face all day long, and frequently came across the aisle to talk with me. Charlie was the source of most information and always knew what was going on in the ward.

Charlie was the first who told me about the patient who was five or six beds from me. By twisting and turning my head and trunk, I could see the mass of bandages that Charlie said was Captain McCarthy. They kept McCarthy close to the nurses' station, where he could get special attention when it was needed.

Charlie explained that the captain was a tank commander who had survived a fiery explosion when his tank was hit by the enemy. The captain climbed out of the tank with two broken legs and literally ran, on fire, thirty to fifty yards from the burning vehicle. His body and head were severely burned.

Something about that still, white-bandaged form made me count my blessings despite my lifeless legs. Charlie seemed to know everything about everyone in the ward.

But even Charlie was surprised to see an unfamiliar, pretty and smiling young nurse enter the ward early one morning. The lady smiled as she proceeded along the center aisle, unruffled by the patients' whistles and greetings. I pushed myself up on my elbows as high as I could and stretched my neck to see what the commotion was all about. By the time I could see the nurse, she had steered right toward my bed.

She carried what looked like an elongated birdcage with no bottom and an electric bulb rigged inside its top. The nurse lieutenant introduced herself as Penny, a physical therapist, and placed a carefully folded sheet at the foot of my bed.

It didn't take Charlie long to find his way to my bed. After all, what are ward buddies for? He greeted the attractive nurse, then told her I was not the one who needed therapy but that he, Charlie, was in dire need. "Anyway," he said, "I outrank him!"

Penny laughed this off and, turning to me, said she would come in every day at about the same hour to spend some time helping me "get those legs working again." This was the first time anyone had suggested such a possibility. While I had no idea what physical therapy was, I was delighted, especially with the thought of this new friend coming to see me, at her own invitation. I especially relished the idea of Charlie standing by, green with envy, watching her in action.

The first "treatment" began immediately. Nurse Penny uncovered my legs and placed the birdcage contraption over them. She covered it with the sheet and plugged it in, lighting the bulb. It wasn't long before I felt the warmth. Penny told me she would be back in about twenty minutes. Once again, she flashed her pretty, therapeutic smile and left. What a morale builder—and I was responsible for it. Things were looking up!

Penny's visits and birdcage applications were always followed by hand massaging that began with my feet, followed by my legs. This kind of treatment both overwhelmed and embarrassed me at first. I was always the center of attention in the ward as long as Penny was there.

Next Nurse Penny touched each toe, or pointed to it, as she coaxed me to work hard at thinking about moving it. "Think Scotty! . . . Move!" she'd urge. Eventually, she was joined by the rest of the ward, Charlie's raspy voice generally in the lead. The battle cry was "Wiggle your toes, Scotty!"

It seemed the whole ward, myself included, was fully devoted to talking my toes into moving. This was a battle not unlike combat, where mind and will joined together against the enemy—a motionless pair of big toes.

Penny was there the day I first wiggled my left big toe! She watched eagerly as the toe slowly bent downward under its own power, then moved up. As word spread around the ward about the victory, Charlie led those nearby in a big cheer.

I have no doubt that Penny's coaching and unfailing cheerfulness were a big part of my recovery. Her presence in the ward did wonders for us all. I learned before leaving England that Penny's sweetheart was a young pilot "missing in action," but if she was down, she never let it show.

Once the challenge of the big toe had been met, it was followed by major improvements in moving my left foot and leg. The right foot proved more difficult; my right toes were obstinate (and still are, fifty-five years later).

Even so, after a month of help with learning to walk again, I was able to shed my crutches. But I have never shed my memory of the lovely nurse whose dedication to her work inspired my recovery and turned a group of wounded soldiers into an unlikely cheerleading section. I still have to smile when I picture them all, shouting loud enough to shake the walls, "Wiggle your toes, Scotty!"

Walter W. Scott

"Go, Gunfighter, Go!"

When the last bugle is sounded, I want to stand up with my soldiers.

General John Pershing

My new commanding officer, Major General Henry E. "The Gunfighter" Emerson, had taken over the Second Division at Camp Casey just a few months before I arrived in Korea in September 1973. When I went to division headquarters to report to the general, he came bursting out of his office and seized my hand, which he pumped like a well handle.

The man was about fifty, tall, rangy, with a great eagle's beak of a nose, craggy features, a hot-eyed gaze and a booming voice. He never stopped pacing as he welcomed me. He had earned his nickname in Vietnam by carrying a cowboy-style six-shooter rather than a regulation forty-five-caliber pistol. I was also aware that he had won a reputation there as a fierce fighter.

General Emerson had scheduled a commanders call for this morning, and I stayed on to attend. As my fellow officers came in, the general introduced me, and we seated ourselves around the conference room. Emerson continued to pace. "Today's subject," he announced, "is marksmanship." He started off in a reasonable tone. As he went on, however, he warmed to his subject. Marksmanship was important! The pacing quickened. If marksmanship was neglected, soldiers would be unprepared! The eyes began to blaze. And if soldiers were unprepared, they would not win. And what the hell kind of leadership was that? Fists now pounding.

The pattern was never to change all the while I served under the Gunfighter. A modest premise, mounting fervor and an apoplectic windup. I observed his accelerating excitement on every subject from deploying helicopters along the DMZ to soldier correspondence courses. And his punch line was always the same, a vein-popping "If we don't do our jobs right, soldiers won't win!"

His performance before the troops was no different. The first time I witnessed it, we had assembled the entire division on the Camp Casey parade field. Gunfighter started off calmly. "Our mission in Korea is to maintain the armistice agreed to on July 27, 1953, between the United Nations and North Korea. Further, our mission is to come to the aid of our South Korean allies should that armistice be violated." As he spoke, Emerson's voice took on velocity. I heard one of the sergeants whisper, "Here he goes." Pretty soon, Gunfighter was shouting, his eyes were flashing and the veins throbbed on his neck. The troops caught the spirit and began shouting, "Go, Gunfighter, go!"

Emerson had inherited a tough command. Morale in the Second Division when he took over was not high, and discipline was slack. Today's all-volunteer Army has high standards. It was not the case then. We were in transition from the draft to the all-volunteer force. Close to

50 percent of our troops, in Army shorthand, were "Cat Four," Category IV, soldiers possessing meager skills in reading, writing and math. They were life's dropouts, one step above Category V, those who were considered unfit for Army service. I found it heartening to hear a leader sound off with spirit and show a will to change. This division could stand a little gung-ho.

General Emerson was determined to turn around the slack, demoralized operation. He had begun a program for remaking the Second Infantry Division, which he called "Pro-Life," not to be confused with the antiabortion movement. Emerson's Pro-Life program, as he put it, "was to provide the soldier opportunities to become a winner rather than a loser in life." Given Army conditions in Korea, I favored "pro" anything, within reason, though reasonableness was not always Gunfighter's long suit.

Gunfighter, nevertheless, was determined to lift morale. "You see, gentlemen, if you play football, you've only got twenty-two men on the field. Baseball, nine men plus the runners. Basketball, ten." General Emerson had brought us together one fall morning, and I was not sure where this commander's call was headed. "But we've got eighteen thousand men in the division," he continued. "And we want all of them to play. We want all of them to feel like winners. Pro-Life!" His solution was "combat sports."

Gunfighter went on to explain. We would start with combat football. Instead of conventional eleven-man teams, we would field whole units—first platoon against second platoon, maybe eighty men at once. We would play on the soccer field, and the objective was to get the football into the opponent's net. How? Any way you can, the general explained. Run it, throw it, kick it, pass it. And, to liven up the action, we would use two footballs at once. The rules? None. You can tackle, block, clip, blindside, anything. Referees? No rules, so you don't need any referees. And no penalties.

It sounded crazy to me, but it fit General Emerson's athletic philosophy. Conventional team sports, with their rigid regulation, favor stars. But in anything-goes, no-holds-barred sports, finely developed skills become marginal. The ninety-six-pound weakling can trip the all-county six-footer as easily as anyone else. In combat football, everyone's a quarterback. In combat basketball, everyone's a forward, a guard, a center. Gunfighter's goal was maximum participation.

As soon as we started combat football, the division doctors were in an uproar. They were being flooded with orthopedic cases, some serious. They threatened to blow the whistle on Gunfighter. We instituted minimal rules. We put in a referee to stop play at least when both balls went out of bounds. We replaced combat boots with sneakers. We banned kicking, clipping and punching. The troops loved combat football, at least the spectators did, and Gunfighter Emerson adored it.

Yet, I can easily put that man's occasional excesses into perspective. In the end, results are what matter. While I served under General Emerson, AWOLs in the division dropped by over 50 percent. Reenlistments jumped by nearly 200 percent. And while impetuous youths might occasionally punch each other out, racially related brawling practically disappeared. He had an instinct for knowing what gave soldiers pride, especially the rank and file who had rarely tasted any in their lives.

One day years later, I got a call from Gunfighter's staff telling me that the old soldier was about to retire, and the Eighteenth Airborne Corps was going to put on a big show. Emerson had personally requested me to command the troops for the parade. I begged off. Fort Bragg was the home of the Eighty-second Airborne. Even though my division was part of Emerson's corps, the paratroopers of the Eighty-second would not appreciate having someone outside their division come over to lead their troops. Ten minutes later an aide was on the phone again. "The general said, 'Tell Powell to get the hell down here.'" It sounded like the Gunfighter to me.

I went to Fort Bragg and started whipping these brawny paratroopers into marching trim. On the appointed day, thousands of people were in attendance and Gunfighter stood on the reviewing stand, shaking every hand in sight and slapping every back. I was standing before the troops at parade rest when I saw him gesture for me to come over. He thanked me for taking charge of the parade and said he had something special he wanted me to do. When he gave the word, I was to order the officers to do an about-face, so that they would be facing the troops from about eight inches away. I started to question him about this novel command, but he told me not to worry. I went back and managed to get the word passed along to the other officers on parade.

The ceremony began with speeches and awards honoring Emerson. When the time came for Gunfighter to speak, he could barely compose himself. He began weeping, repeating himself, and summoning the names of long-dead comrades. He paused at one point, looked straight at me and shouted, "Now!"

"Officers—and officers only," I ordered, "about face!" There we stood almost nose-to-nose with the soldiers, wondering what was supposed to happen next.

Then Gunfighter bellowed from the reviewing stand, "Officers, salute your soldiers!"

It was a moving gesture, pure Gunfighter Emerson, and in its simple symbolism said everything that had to be said about armies and about who, in the end, most deserves to be saluted.

General Colin L. Powell

2

UNDER FIRE

Courage is resistance to fear,
mastery of fear—not absence of fear.

Mark Twain

Against the Odds

It was the summer of 1942. I was nineteen years old and a signalman third class on the USS *Astoria* stationed in the South Pacific.

One hot night in August, we found ourselves skirmishing with the Japanese for control of Guadalcanal, gearing up for the bloody battle that soon followed. At midnight, I finished my duty on watch. Still wearing my work detail uniform of dungarees and a T-shirt, and only pausing long enough to unstrap my standard-issue life belt and lay it beside me, I fell into an exhausted sleep.

Two hours later, I was awakened abruptly by the sound of an explosion. I jumped to my feet, my heart pounding. Without thinking, I grabbed my life belt and strapped it on. In the ensuing chaos, I focused on dodging the rain of enemy shells that were inflicting death and destruction all around me. I took some shrapnel in my right shoulder and leg, but by some miracle, I avoided being killed.

That first battle of Savo Island lasted for twenty minutes. After the enemy fire ceased, the men left standing helped with the wounded, while others manned the guns.

I was making my way toward a gun turret when suddenly,

the deck disappeared. My legs windmilled beneath me as I realized that an explosion had blasted me off the deck. My shock was immediately replaced by a stomach-clenching fear as I fell like a stone—thirty feet into the dark, shark-infested water below.

I immediately inflated my life belt, weak with relief that I'd somehow remembered to put it on. I noticed between ten and thirty men bobbing in the water in the area, but we were too far away from each other to communicate.

I began treading water, trying to stay calm as I felt things brushing against my legs, knowing that if a shark attacked me, any moment could be my last. And the sharks weren't the only danger: The powerful current threatened to sweep me out to sea.

Four agonizing hours passed this way. It was getting light when I saw a ship—an American destroyer—approaching. The sailors on board threw me a line and hauled me aboard.

Once on the ship, my legs buckled and I slid to the deck, unable to stand. I was fed and allowed to rest briefly. Then I was transported back to the *Astoria,* which, though disabled, was still afloat. The captain was attempting to beach the ship in order to make the necessary repairs.

Back on board the *Astoria,* I spent the next six hours preparing the dead for burial at sea. As the hours passed, it became clear our vessel was damaged beyond help. The ship was taking on water and finally, around twelve hundred hours, the *Astoria* began to roll and go under.

The last thing I wanted to do was to go into that water again, but I knew I had to. Filled with dread, I jumped off the high side of the sinking ship and began swimming. Although I still had my life belt on, it couldn't be inflated a second time. Luckily, I was soon picked up by another destroyer and transferred to the USS *Jackson.*

Against all the odds, I had made it—one of the lucky men

to survive the battle of Savo Island. We were issued Marine uniforms, and I spent my time, in between visits to the ship's doctors for treatment of my wounds, sitting on the deck of the *Jackson,* waiting for our transport to San Francisco's Treasure Island and the leave that would follow.

Though it felt odd to wear the unfamiliar uniform, I wasn't sad to lose my old dungarees and T-shirt. The one thing I found I didn't want to give up was my life belt. I hung on to the khaki cloth-covered rubber belt, studying it sometimes as I sat around on the Marine ship.

The label on the belt said it had been manufactured by Firestone Tire and Rubber Company of Akron, Ohio, which was my hometown. I decided to keep the belt as a souvenir, a reminder of how lucky I'd been.

When I finally took my thirty-day leave, I went home to my family in Ohio. After a quietly emotional welcome, I sat with my mother in our kitchen, telling her about my recent ordeal and hearing what had happened at home since I went away. My mother informed me that "to do her part," she had taken a wartime job at the Firestone plant. Surprised, I jumped up and grabbed my life belt from my duffel bag, putting it on the table in front of her.

"Take a look at that, Mom," I said. "It was made right here in Akron at your plant."

She leaned forward and, taking the rubber belt in her hands, she read the label. She had just heard the story and knew that in the darkness of that terrible night, it was this one piece of rubber that had saved my life. When she looked up at me, her mouth and her eyes were open wide with surprise. "Son, I'm an inspector at Firestone. This is my inspector number," she said, her voice hardly above a whisper.

We stared at each other, too stunned to speak. Then I stood up, walked around the table and pulled her up from her chair. We held each other in a tight embrace, saying nothing. My mother was not a demonstrative woman, but the significance of this amazing coincidence overcame her usual reserve. We hugged each other for a long, long time, feeling the bond between us. My mother had put her arms halfway around the world to save me.

Elgin Staples

The Rescue

In a cruel jungle in Vietnam, a country that fiercely punishes its foreign inhabitants, a small group of men fought for survival. The sweltering heat tormented the soldiers with every step they took. Surrounded by the enemy, their losses astronomical, they wanted to hold their dying comrades, but they could only watch helplessly as the fallen men's bodies writhed from the mortal wounds. Screams filled the air, "I'm hit, I'm hit. Oh, God."

Bullets whistled by them as the group gathered to form a strategy. Their chances were grim. They were trapped, the ammunition was gone, and the only thing left to do was pray. They were no longer at home, where war was fought in the halls of Congress. They were in Vietnam, in combat.

"Ben, what are we gonna do?" a young soldier named James asked, his voice shaking with fear.

"Somebody will come get us. It shouldn't be long now," Ben replied, but he was filled with doubt. He felt in his heart that it was over, but maybe if he didn't say it out loud, it wouldn't happen. He grabbed the cross that hung from his aching neck and prayed to be anywhere but there. "God, please help us. I'm not ready to go," he pleaded quietly as he dived for cover from the enemy fire. Blood and death surrounded him. He was sure that hell existed because he was in it.

At the same time, approximately twenty kilometers away, I was playing a game of gin with a group of fellow pilots. The winner would be rewarded with a bottle of gin. *Quite fitting,* I thought. From looking at my hand, it seemed I might have a good chance at sampling that bottle, but in the next instant, I threw down my cards as our flight commander came in shouting, "On your feet! Second Platoon's pinned down by VC. Reported seven left. OPS has the grid coordinates. Get in, get 'em and get out!"

I ran to the UH-1 Huey, my adrenaline rushing. My door gunner, a Texas cowboy named Eric, raced toward the plane, hollering war yells, "Let's rock 'n' roll, boys!"

"Just don't slam your privates in the door," yelled Garret, my copilot. He quickly boarded the bird, ready to go. And off we went, over the deceptively beautiful jungles of Vietnam, wondering what we would find when we reached our destination. We were hoping for the best and fearing the worst.

As we approached the coordinates, we could see the tracer rounds of the VC weapons. Eric released the safety, pulled the gun stock of the weapon tight against his armpit, drew a bead on the closest enemy soldier and opened fire. He continued to fire, struggling to keep the muzzle of his raging machine gun from firing high of its mark. The enemy scattered for cover. We could see the flash from the weapons of the VC as they returned fire.

I spotted a place where it looked like I could touch down, bring the soldiers on board and take off again. I landed the bird, but our soldiers were nowhere in sight. Eric kept up a rack of fire that seemed endless. He was crazy but good—very good.

Finally, we saw a band of six U.S. soldiers running toward the door; they were being shot at from every direction. We saw one take a shot to the gut, and he was gone. Then, just as another reached the tail of the bird, he was hit in the head. The remaining four soldiers safely reached the bird, and as quickly as I could, I flew up to the treetops and skimmed across them, hoping to remain hidden.

In the back of the helicopter, one of the soldiers clapped his buddy on the back, "You were right, Ben."

"Of course I was," Ben told him. Turning to the soldiers who'd saved the group, he said, "I can't thank you guys enough. We were on a routine mission, walked straight into the middle of an ambush! There were forty-seven of us, and they got most everybody within the first five minutes. It was brutal. I really didn't think we'd make it. Sent the transmission and lost the radio, bullet right smack through it. I just didn't know what to do. But we're here, thanks to you. By the way, I'm Lieutenant Ben Brooks." He was still shaking—both from the terror of his ordeal and the shock that he was safe.

"Brooks? We got a Brooks flying the plane. Where ya from, pardner?" Eric asked.

"Iowa."

Eric turned and called to me, "Hey, Bob, ain't you from Iowa?"

"Yeah. Why are you asking me that at a time like this?"

"This guy back here's from Iowa. Name's Ben Brooks."

Ben? I couldn't believe it. Was it possible that I had just saved my own kid brother from the worst kind of combat situation in the middle of a war, what seemed like a million miles from home? It wasn't the first time I'd saved his skin. Growing up, I'd pulled him out of neighborhood fights where he'd stuck his foot in his mouth, but this situation was unbelievable. It couldn't be my Ben. But as the soldier maneuvered his way toward the front of the bird, I turned my head, and sure enough, there stood Ben.

"Well, I'll be damned," I said, shaking my head in sheer astonishment.

"No, I thought I was damned," Ben grinned at me. "You saved our butts back there."

"I only wish it could have been more," I said and watched his smile fade.

"I lost the whole platoon, Bob. We didn't have a chance."

"I know, Brother. I know."

We finished the remainder of the flight in silence, each thinking what might have been, what was. I landed the bird, and we all stepped off. Ben walked over to me. I reached out my hand; he grabbed me and pulled me against him. I patted his back, reassuring him that he was safe.

"Bob, um . . . I . . ."

"Yeah. I know."

"Thanks, Bob."

Ben and the other remaining soldiers from his platoon disappeared into the barracks, where they were interviewed and extensive reports were taken.

That fateful day in Vietnam had started out like any other day, and had ended like no other. I'd simply been doing my job. Yet, I didn't just save my little brother's life that day; I saved my own as well. I know if I'd lost Ben, part of my soul would have been lost that could never have been found.

From that day on, whenever I went out on a rescue, I always carried something extra with me. Never again did I go up as though it was another day at the job. I went up with the thought that I was saving somebody's kid brother. I went up knowing I was making a difference.

Robert E. Brooks Jr.
As told to Kimberly D. Green

Sergeant Mills

Mercy to the vanquished is the brightest gem in a soldier's character.

Duke of York, order of the day
during the campaign in Flanders, 1794

Sergeant Gary Mills was a bulldozer operator from North Pole, Alaska (really), serving with Bravo Company, 299th Engineer Battalion as part of the 24th Infantry Division.

During Desert Storm, he was escorting a military dozer north into Iraq on a flatbed truck when soft sand caused the rig to go off the road. The flatbed—dozer and all—toppled over. Sergeant Mills wasn't hurt, but the convoy he was following moved on without him. Mills decided the best thing he could do is stay with the downed vehicle, guarding it until more U.S. Armed Forces came along, or his convoy missed him and sent someone back.

While he waited, a sandstorm began to blow and visibility became very poor. To get relief from the stinging, blowing sand and to get away from the dozer in case it got hit by traffic (or worse), Mills took shelter in a foxhole he found nearby. When at last the storm began to die down, Sergeant Mills could hear voices. They weren't speaking English.

He peeked out of the foxhole and saw seven Iraqi soldiers. They were armed. He ducked back into the hole. His position wasn't easy to spot and chances were good they would pass by without noticing it. Outnumbered seven to one, hiding seemed like a reasonable thing to do, but as he crouched in the foxhole, Sergeant Mills didn't feel good about it.

He almost let them walk by. But then he thought about their AK-47s. *If someone gets hurt,* he thought, *it will be my fault. I won't be able to live with myself.*

Gathering his courage, he popped up out of the foxhole and said the only Arabic word he knew, "*Qif!* (Stop!)" The seven stopped. Apparently, it didn't occur to them that there would be just one American soldier all alone in the middle of the desert. Surely, there must be at least a platoon. They put down their weapons and raised their hands.

The American was now faced with a tricky situation. It wouldn't take long for the Iraqis to figure out he was alone. In fact, the next minute, the leader of the group said something in Arabic and raised his thumb, as if to say "There's just one of you?" The American kept his M-16 pointed at them and his finger on the trigger. Using his left hand, he raised his thumb, smiled, and nodded yes.

The dumbfounded look on the Iraqi's face was almost comical.

But Mills had no time to laugh. One soldier with seven prisoners is awkward, at best. In the movies, this would never happen. There would be a fight and all seven of the enemy would shoot at him, but miss. The American would gun down six of the soldiers, then fight the last guy (the leader) hand to hand. Right. But this was no movie.

Using gestures, Sergeant Mills had them move away from their weapons and ordered them to empty their pockets. He discovered that the Iraqis had pilfered his lunch and his water bottles from the overturned dozer. The seven looked frightened when he discovered the theft. The Iraqi Army had been thoroughly indoctrinated about the heartlessness and barbaric actions of the infidels from the West. The soldiers expected he would kill them.

What they had taken from the dozer didn't amount to much: a few partial MREs (meals ready to eat: the standard Army ration) and a couple of bottles of water. Not much of a feed for seven soldiers. As Sergeant Mills took a closer look at the men, he saw what a pitiful lot they were. Their uniforms didn't match and weren't complete. They didn't even have on helmets. Their gas masks were cheap and flimsy. They were thin and looked tired and hungry.

At gunpoint, Sergeant Mills marched them to his dozer, opened a locked compartment, and took out the rest of his MREs and water. These he gave to his prisoners.

One of the soldiers was so moved by this gesture, he slowly got up and walked over to Mills, who had his M-16 leveled and his finger on the trigger. Walking right up to the muzzle of the M-16, the Iraqi slowly reached out, took Gary Mills's face in his hands and kissed him on both cheeks.

It didn't take the convoy long to realize they were missing a vehicle. The radios were alive with talk about a guy who had been left behind, and help was sent back immediately. The sandstorm slowed things up, but soon an Airborne colonel leading an armed force arrived. They could only shake their heads in amazement that one guy, a dozer operator, had captured seven prisoners.

In the distance, some medical evacuation helicopters had landed and the Americans turned the captives over to them. Smiling and waving good-bye, the Iraqis climbed into the choppers to be flown to a prisoner-of-war camp. As Mills watched them board, one of them turned, put his hands together, gave a slight bow, and in heavily accented English, said, "Thank you."

No, it definitely hadn't gone like it would have in the movies—and for that, Sergeant Mills was grateful and relieved.

John D. Governale

The True Face of Humanity

All right, they're on our left, they're on our right, they're in front of us, they're behind us. . . . They can't get away this time.

Lieutenant General Lewis B. "Chesty" Puller
(when surrounded by eight enemy divisions)

The 1950s and 1960s were interesting times, especially for a white boy coming of age in the South. The Selma marches, the Woolworth lunch counter sit-ins, Rosa Parks refusing to give up her seat on the bus, Governor Wallace openly defying the law and federal troops—these events weren't just stories on the six o'clock news; they happened in places we knew, to people we knew.

I understood what was going on around me, why there were "civil disobediences" and why the civil rights movement gained strength and momentum. I understood why certain segments of our society didn't feel included in the benefits of that society. The only thing I couldn't understand was why the situation existed in the first place.

Being unable to comprehend bigotry and hatred wasn't due to any moral superiority on my part, and had nothing to do with my being smarter or wiser. In fact, it had nothing to do with me at all but, rather, had everything to do with the clear-sighted example my father set.

And what made a boy like my father, raised in rural, depression-wracked Texas, defy his own racist upbringing and teach his children to accept every person on his or her own merits? Maybe that had something to do with a summer night long ago, a night that opened the eyes and heart of a born and bred Southern boy.

The Allied Army fought its way across France and Belgium, liberating Europe foot by bloody foot in the summer of 1944.

The Third Armored, the Spearhead Division, was in its customary spot at the head of the advance. Out in front of the rest was a big Sherman tank with the ace of spades—the death card—arrogantly painted on its turret, and stenciled under that, "In the Mood," the title of the Glenn Miller hit.

Hanging half out of the turret, as was his habit, rode Staff Sergeant L. G. Pool. He had been—before the war—a bull rider in rodeos around South Texas. Riding this particular thirty-ton bull that same way seemed only natural.

As the day wound down and the fighting slacked up, the column turned and began to regroup for the night. Pool's crew wanted to take just one more field, liberate one more farm before turning back. Everybody knew that was Pool's way.

While Pool was frequently chewed out for not staying in formation, everyone knew that his kind of soldier didn't come along very often. Certainly, General de Gaulle had recognized that trait when he made Pool one of only a handful of American GIs whom de Gaulle would personally decorate with the French Medal of War.

Sergeant Pool was the first acknowledged ace of tankers. After the war, major studios would vie to make a film of his exploits. When the tank commanders would assemble the night before an attack and draw straws to see who would lead, Pool would grab the entire bunch of straws and drawl, "I'm leadin' this one." Then he would grin and look around, daring the others to take the straws from him. That was also Pool's way. So, no one seemed particularly surprised that Pool's tank hadn't turned with the rest of the column.

This night, however, would be different from the rest. Darkness was settling in when the radio crackled in the headquarters tent. Pool's tank was five miles from bivouac, five miles behind a heavily fortified enemy line, out of fuel.

Consternation was the best word to describe the reaction at division headquarters. One of the top fighting men in the entire European theater of war was stuck with his crew in a totally untenable situation, and sending the column back out to rescue Pool and his men was unjustifiable.

For Sergeant Pool and the others, the same bitter realization dawned as they grimly calculated that by hoarding their shells and choosing their targets wisely, they might live to see reinforcements, to see morning.

The tank's big gun split the night with its thunderous roar; the fifty-caliber machine gun mounted on the turret chattered to life every now and then—all in an attempt to keep the German Army from claiming what looked like an easy prey. Hours passed in this deadly standoff.

Then, in the glaring daylight of the muzzle flash, Pool's men thought they saw movement near their vehicle. Sighting down the barrel of the fifty-caliber, Pool challenged the intruders. Softly, he growled the day's password, "Brooklyn." Softly, across the darkness, came the correct response, "Dodgers."

Two men from the division had volunteered to crawl

those five treacherous miles through enemy territory in the dark. Two men crept with exquisite care, dragging five-gallon cans of petrol with them, guided only by the sight and sound of gunfire from Pool's tank. They crawled toward a team of men they didn't know. They knew only that fellow American soldiers were in need of fuel.

They saved the lives of five men that night, including Staff Sergeant L. G. Pool, my father.

I don't believe Dad knew the names of the young men who had risked everything for total strangers. If he did, he never told us. We only knew one of them was Native American and the other was African-American.

Thomas Lafayette Pool

One Hell of a Plan

The movie *2001: A Space Odyssey* had been playing for about twenty minutes when my gunner tapped me on the shoulder and told me my ACs (Aircraft Commanders) wanted me at OPs (the operations hut).

I was a member of a helicopter team from the 176th AVN, a company of Hueys based out of Chu Lai. Our two-ship team worked with Special Forces units, taking them into and getting them out of often risky places.

When I got to OPs, the two ACs, Warrant Officers Connors and Rodriguez, were listening to a distress call from a three-man Special Forces team, code name Montana, deep in the A Shau Valley, "The Valley of Death."

The SF team was in deep trouble. Exhausted and with one wounded, they were under heavy pursuit by the Viet Cong and North Vietnamese army. The voice on the radio was tense, whispering coordinates and asking for help. They needed an extraction, through a triple-canopied, three-hundred-foot-high jungle—*now*.

My ACs turned to me as if to ask, "Do we go?"

What the hell, I thought, *I didn't understand that movie anyway.*

The A Shau was called the "Valley of Death," because it is thick jungle about a half mile wide with six-thousand-foot mountains along each side. If you flew at treetop level to evade small arms fire from below, you were fired upon from both mountainsides. If you flew at altitude, you were a target for the radar-controlled thirty-seven-millimeters stationed throughout the valley. It was a bad place to be, especially in the middle of the night.

We lifted off into a moonless sky. The sky, the trees, everything was black. Using a treetop zigzag search pattern, we instructed the SF team to use only single-word directions like "west" and "north" to indicate where we were in relation to them. They were on the run, trying to evade the enemy and find an open hole in the sky where we could get to the ground and pick them up.

Communication was difficult. The enemy was so close that the Special Forces team couldn't speak above a whisper, if at all. They couldn't pop smoke or flash a light.

Finally locating them, we hovered around over their heads looking for a place to land when the radio voice warned, "Pull away, you're bringing them in on us. PULL AWAY!"

We flew off quickly as small arms fire erupted below. In our attempt to rescue them, we had marked their location for the enemy.

The beleaguered team moved fast, escaping the enemy and letting us know they were still alive. Then my AC instructed them, "Key your mike twice when we are over you." (Keying a microphone means pushing the button but not speaking; it makes no sound on the transmitting radio, but makes a "click" in the receiving radio.)

We pinpointed the team once more, flew a few hundred yards away from their position and hovered, as if that were their location. It worked; the enemy moved in our direction, away from the team.

"Minuteman, you are about three hundred yards to our south," a voice whispered over our headphones.

"Roger that, we're going to make some noise over here while our sister ship comes in for you. Can we land?"

"Negative. We're in a small crater," came the whispered reply. "There is a hole in the canopy, but not LZ [landing zone] room."

"Can you move to an LZ?"

"Negative. They are all over us."

AC Connors clicked his mike button twice, to signal: transmission received. He did not have words to respond. We were close, but couldn't get to them; we couldn't help.

"We have a rope," came over the radio from our sister ship.

"Say again?" asked Connors.

"We have a rope on board," repeated Rodriguez. A quick conversation ensued between the two ACs.

Our ship would fake a rescue and draw enemy fire, while our sister ship dropped a rope through the blackness of a narrow, three-hundred-foot long shaft of jungle canopy in an attempt to pull three men straight up from the jungle floor.

It was a foolish plan; we all knew it couldn't work. Even if they found this small hole in the jungle and lowered a rope—if we weren't shot all to hell in the attempt—the weight of the three men would be too much for a UH-1C to lift straight up at such a high hover.

Yeah, it was a hell of a plan—but it was all we had.

"Montana, we are dropping you a rope," Rodriguez transmitted. "Give us a vertical light flash when we are over your location." Our ship hovered in the distance in an attempt to draw the enemy, while Rodriguez did a slow zigzag over the area. "I have three red flashes," Rodriguez said.

"Roger, three red," the SF leader replied.

Rodriguez's crew chief secured one end of the rope to the floor of his ship, then tied an empty five-gallon water can to the other. The Montana team flashed another quick signal and the can was tossed into the darkness.

Ditching their heavy radio, the SF team gripped the lifeline as Rodriguez started lifting them up and out through the narrow throat of jungle forest. Suddenly, small arms fire erupted everywhere. The thick night air was full of green tracers and the sound of chopper blades.

Then the rope snapped. The SF team fell back through the trees into the darkness, their lifeline becoming a death sentence for Rodriguez's ship. The rope had wrapped itself around their main rotor and the ship was shaking itself apart.

"We lost them!" yelled Rodriguez over the radio. "I'm losing power! I'm going down!"

Somehow, Rodriguez kept his ship in the air and headed toward the nearest airfield. "Tower, this is Minuteman Two Niner, we have a bird in trouble. We are coming in maximum, running landing, clear the airfield. Stand by emergency."

Helicopters have skids, not wheels. A running landing is a very dangerous maneuver. You have no control. You hit the ground at one hundred knots, slide, flip, roll, crash and burn—or don't. And if his main rotor stopped turning before Rodriguez got his ship on the ground, he would simply fall out of the sky.

They hit the ground, hard. The skids spread under the strain of the impact. The helicopter slid across the ground as the main rotor locked up, almost flipping their ship over.

We landed about thirty yards away just in time to see Rodriguez and his crew run from their smoldering UH-1C. They were safe!

No one said much during the flight back to our home

base. Our crew was alive and, for that, we were grateful. But we'd lost the Special Forces team. We had picked them up and then dropped them through three hundred feet of trees. Rodriguez had been going down; we had to go after him. No one talked about it, but we all knew. They were dead.

But what else could we have done—stayed looking for them? Once the rope had broken, we'd lost contact with the SF team. If the fall hadn't killed them, then our hovering around would only have brought the enemy in. Plus, there had been no place to land, no more rope, no more options.

Some rescue.

This one was hard, the kind of thing that you stuff deep inside. You can't have feelings and survive a war. "It don't mean nothing," as they say. But it did.

Several days later, I heard someone calling to me from across the flight line. It was Mike, my AC, coming toward me.

"They walked out!" he yelled.

"What?"

It was true. Three days after we'd dropped them through the trees, the Special Forces team had walked out of the A Shau—one with a broken arm from the fall, but all three alive. By pulling them out of the crater by rope, we had managed to move them a few hundred yards from where the enemy had believed them to be. They had fallen back into the jungle and hid. Our departure had fooled the enemy into thinking the team had been rescued, so they'd called off the search.

And they'd walked out of the Valley of Death!

Yeah, it had turned out to be one hell of a plan.

Ronald C. Williams

The Altar Boy

We had made a rapid advance across Northern France from the Normandy beachhead. (Historians say it was the fastest opposed advance in the history of modern warfare.) Now, our 105-millimeter howitzer battalion was bivouacked in an abandoned castle on the outskirts of a small Belgian town. The exact locations of occupied and unoccupied territory were not well known, and due to an error in map reading, we learned at daybreak that we were close to a German infantry unit. Watching our artillery battalion attempting to act as infantry was laughable, but we had no choice. Using our pieces at close range with time bursts, we caused the enemy to retreat.

Later that morning, I ventured away from the castle and observed the local townspeople walking to the center of the village to the sound of church bells. I realized that it was Sunday and people were on their way to a Catholic mass. I followed them.

Inside the church, when the priest appeared from the sacristy, I saw that he was without an altar boy. I was only nineteen years old, not too far away from my own altar boy days in Philadelphia. So almost by rote, I went into the sanctuary, knelt down next to the priest and, still in my uniform, started to perform the normal functions of an acolyte:

"Ad deum qui laetificat juventutem meam" [To God, the joy of my youth];

"Qua to es Deus fortitudo mea" [For Thou, O God, art my strength];

"Confiteor Deo omnipotenti" [I confess to Almighty God].

The priest and I went through the whole mass as if we had done it together many times before: water and wine; *lavabo* (the ritual of washing hands after the offertory); changing the book; *suscipiat* (a five-line prayer of acceptance); and the final blessing.

As prescribed, I preceded the priest into the sacristy and, as is the custom, stood apart from him with my hands in the prayer position while he divested. He removed the chasuble, then the cincture. When his arms lifted the alb, I saw that he was wearing a German uniform. My heart stopped: The priest was a German officer!

The man was a German chaplain and though he had realized immediately that he had an American sergeant as an altar boy, during the entire twenty minutes of the mass, he had given no outward sign of recognition.

My German was rather rudimentary, and the only thing I could put together was, *"Gut Morgen, Vater"* ("Good morning, Father"). Evidently, his English was nonexistent, for somewhat flustered, he only smiled at me. Then, we shook hands, and I left.

I walked back to the castle strangely exhilarated. Two strangers, enemies at war, had met by chance and for twenty minutes, without any direct communication, had found complete unanimity in an age-old ritual of Christian worship.

The memory of this incident has remained with me for over fifty years. It still brings the same elation, for I know firsthand that, even in war, our common humanity—under the same God—can triumph over hatred and division.

Richard H. Kiley

The Vision

I thought being raised in a devout Roman Catholic family would give me the faith and courage to face any hardship a young man of nineteen would be asked to bear, but I quickly realized that nothing can prepare a young man for war.

Originally assigned to a supply division during World War II, I found myself at the front when the generals began stripping the rear units for more replacements to cover their heavy losses. As part of Patton's Third Army, I joined up with a squad that spearheaded the American advance through France. Our job was to probe the front line, looking for the enemy. Hitching rides on the back of tanks and armored vehicles, we drove through many French towns, all the time pushing back the German troops. When we made contact, my squad would deploy on the flanks, setting up a fifty-caliber machine gun, and wait for our infantry to close in. The German soldiers were first rate; well trained, highly disciplined and unwilling to give up their conquered territory, they fought viciously in retreat. We were always a prime target, and German artillery fire was deadly accurate. Many buddies, as well as guys I barely knew, were hit. I lived moment to moment, always in fear of being the next GI carried out. This pattern persisted day after day. Village after French village was leveled in our effort to push the enemy out, towns and cities reduced to smoldering rubble. Witnessing all the destruction—seeing guys like me, getting killed or wounded—I despaired that I would ever see my home and family again. The ruined French towns were also filled with civilians looking for lost loved ones, digging through debris for anything that might help them live. Through all of this chaos, I prayed constantly for the strength to continue. Dog-tired, constantly on the move, alert every minute to the possibility of enemy fire and numb to the violence surrounding me, I was drained of all hope for my survival.

As we approached the German border after endless months of fighting, one last nameless French village lay ahead. A recent artillery exchange had left the town another smoking wreck, and we probed cautiously forward. Riding in the back of a half-track, my vision obstructed by the haze from still-burning fires, I caught a glimpse of a bombed-out Catholic church. There, on the only standing wall, was a crucifix, the body of Christ, arms still outstretched, eyes lifted to the heavens, untouched by the destruction around it. I could see the wounds Jesus had received at the hands of a different enemy, but he had been left perfectly safe from this battle. I instinctively made the sign of the cross, tightened my helmet strap another notch and gripped my rifle even firmer. If he had made it through, I could make it through. Although almost destroyed by the harsh reality of war, now I was able to continue. I carried this sight within my heart and mind into many more battles through the war, and then safely home. The image has never left me.

Paul Charlillo

Boom Boom

In Vietnam, I served as a helicopter pilot with the A Company, Helicopter Assault Battalion, 101st Airborne Division. During the summer and fall of 1968, we spent an inordinate amount of time in an area called the A Shau Valley. We had two basic missions: performing combat assaults and resupplying the troops in the field. The days following a combat assault were known as "log days": logistics missions where our helicopters brought supplies to the field troops. We carried out all the essentials needed to conduct a war. During these resupply missions, we also brought back the wounded and the dead.

The first thing we did on log day was land at the logistics point and load the aircraft with the material to be taken to the field positions. One memorable day, as we were being loaded, a small dog jumped into the back of the helicopter and settled among the boxes and bags as if he owned the place.

"What's with the dog?" I asked the officer in charge of the loading detail. He explained that the dog was the mascot of the unit I was assigned to, and he always took the first log bird that went out to the troops in the field. He did, however, always manage to return on the last flight from the field to the base camp. Apparently, he didn't want to spend his evenings in the A Shau Valley. I thought to myself that this dog had more sense than a lot of people. I asked the logistics officer what the dog's name was, and he replied, "Boom Boom."

As soon as we landed at our first site in the A Shau Valley, the dog leaped from the aircraft and was treated like a celebrity. There were smiles all around from the troops as they played with Boom Boom, and I felt that I had really done these people a favor. The dog was a definite morale boost.

As evening approached, we received a call from one of our units that they had a trooper who had been injured in an explosion and the resulting fire. This man needed an immediate medical evacuation. We proceeded to the location at our best speed. I felt quite calm at the time, because after nearly a year of doing this sort of mission, you learn not to become too involved emotionally with the wounded. My job as a pilot was to transport the injured soldiers to medical help as soon as possible, and not be distracted by their distress.

Since this young soldier's injuries were quite severe, I had to take him to the nearest medic, who was in a forward base in the mountains bordering the A Shau Valley. Berchtesgaden was a difficult place to get into, mainly because of the updrafts and windy conditions. But the injured soldier needed immediate treatment. If he didn't receive it, he might not survive the thirty-minute trip to the nearest hospital.

Just as we were loading our patient into the helicopter's empty cargo bay, in jumped Boom Boom for the trip back to the rear area. I paid little attention to him since my thoughts were on the task at hand; I just knew Boom Boom was in the back with the wounded soldier.

Just before beginning the approach into Berchtesgaden, I looked back at our patient. The man was burned quite badly, and his arms and chest were blackened; but he was conscious, so, I motioned back at him to grab onto something, knowing that the trip was about to get very rough. He grabbed onto a support in the rear of the helicopter, and I started our descent.

I was having a very tough time controlling the aircraft. At one time, the collective control was bottomed out, which should have had us dropping like a rock, but instead of descending, we were climbing at five hundred feet per minute. I took a quick look at our patient. The burned trooper seemed to be doing okay. But, then, I caught sight of Boom Boom, and I was horrified: The little dog was slowly sliding toward the open cargo door! He was frantically trying to stop himself by digging his claws into the metal floor, but it wasn't doing any good. He couldn't hold onto anything.

I was powerless to save him. This friendly dog was going to go out the door of my helicopter and fall five hundred feet to his death in the jungle below. Instead of flying my aircraft with total concentration, I was staring at little Boom Boom, this dog that had done nothing but make people happy. I thought of the joy I saw on the faces of the men that morning when I brought their dog out for a visit. *How could I face these people again?* For me, this incident would probably be the last straw. After nearly a year of missions, in which I had heard the cries of the wounded and looked into the unseeing eyes of the dead, I was going to be emotionally destroyed by a small dog's death.

Boom Boom was whining with fear and still struggling to save himself, but it was no use. Nothing he or I could do would prevent disaster.

Then, at the very moment Boom Boom was about to go flying out the cargo door, I saw a blackened arm reach out.

The arm grabbed the flailing dog firmly and pulled him back from the edge.

I breathed an immense sigh of relief. "Thanks, trooper," I whispered as I focused my mind back on the task of landing the helicopter. For the remainder of that roller-coaster landing, Boom Boom was held close to the blackened chest of a badly injured man who still had it in him to save a small but precious life.

As soon as we landed, the young trooper received medical attention from several skilled people. I was informed that he would remain at the forward base until the next day; he needed a lot of attention before he could make the ride back to a hospital. Boom Boom stayed with him. I guess the dog wasn't about to risk another ride in my chopper, and I can't say I blamed him.

James R. Morgan

Prepare to Ditch

Flak took out the number-three engine of our newly delivered B-24 Liberator and badly damaged two others as we made our run on Ludwigshafen, Germany, April 1, 1944. This was my fourteenth mission, leaving the unlucky thirteenth behind me.

Hundreds of bombers—B-24s and B-17s—were on this raid in southern Germany. We were informed the target was heavily defended and warned to expect deadly flak and plenty of German aircraft.

With the number-three engine out and two others barely hanging on, we managed to drop our bombs. The loneliest feeling I've ever had was watching our squadron fly on above us as we lost altitude, alone now and sitting ducks for German fighters. On the intercom, I told the crew, "We're hurt bad. I'll try to make the coast. If you're bailing, bail now while we have enough altitude." No one did. Our only hope now was sinking into an overcast that, hopefully, would shield us from the Luftwaffe.

Nearing the coast of France, down to eight hundred feet with one sputtering engine left, we had only minutes before ditching in the English Channel. The Germans were firing at us from the ground with rifles. We had to make the channel! And we did, barely a mile off the French coast. I hollered into the mike, "Prepare to ditch!"

I had a decision to make and make quickly. Current ditching procedures for the Liberator were "to tail-drag the aircraft onto the water." But too many Liberators had broken apart using this tactic. They'd sunk almost immediately and lost the crew. I decided I would attempt a normal landing—as normal a landing as could be effected on white-capped waves. As our last engine sputtered and died just feet above the water, I hollered into my mike, "We're going in." Then we hit the water—hard.

The copilot was thrown through the Plexiglas over us into the water and was lost. I plummeted headfirst into the instrument panel from the impact, and my legs jackknifed beneath me. Panic hit as I realized that if she sank quickly, I would go down with her. Wrenching my head free, I floated out the awful hole the copilot's body had made.

Our Mae West life preservers were keeping us afloat, but we wouldn't last long in the icy water; we had to get into the dinghies. I didn't realize those dinghies were still hung up inside the bomber. "Thank God. It's still floating," I muttered to myself, realizing the plane hadn't sunk in the presumed five-minute time period.

The radio operator swam back into the plane and released the two dinghies, a courageous act that saved our lives. To everyone's surprise, the plane continued to bob on the water for forty-five minutes. The crew seemed okay, except for the flight engineer. We guessed he had internal injuries, but were helpless to do anything for him. He kept calling his wife's name; hours later, sometime during the night, he fell silent. One of the crew said, "He's gone, Lieutenant." We all joined in saying the Lord's Prayer, and someone said a Hail Mary as we gently slipped him into the black waters of the channel.

Dawn found us surrounded by heaving water, no land in sight. We took turns paddling, hoping we were headed toward England. Allied aircraft flew over, but didn't see us; fortunately, neither did the German planes.

Huddled under our parachutes, we were miserably cold and soaking wet from the constant spray. One of the crew blurted out, "Pee in the dinghy, guys." It was good advice; the urine was warm, and no one much cared where the warmth came from. Someone found a small bag of hard candy in a survival kit, and we all shared it.

As we drifted aimlessly with no land in sight, I wondered how many nautical miles separated England and France. Too many. But at least the Germans hadn't come out after us.

One fear was constant: We could be swept past the tip of England and out into the Atlantic Ocean. The second dawn showed nothing but endless water. Surely, someone had to see us. An airplane, a ship, a fisherman! We couldn't survive much longer.

We'd had nothing to drink or eat, except for the candy, for almost forty-four hours, and the constant tossing in the waves weakened and sickened us all. *How long can we last?* I wondered.

I was half-dozing when I heard the bombardier cry out. "Hey! Hello! Hello!" Then he shouted to the rest of us, "There's a fishing boat over there." Tying a piece of parachute to an oar, he waved it frantically, screaming, "Hello! Hello!"

The fishermen called back. "Ahoy! Ahoy! Yanks?"

"Yes, yes, Yanks. We're Yanks," we all yelled back as loudly as we could. It was hard for us to believe, almost too good to be true, that we were about to be rescued.

Satisfied we were indeed "Yanks," the fishermen immediately started their engines and chugged slowly through the choppy water to the two dinghies. To a man, we all thanked God in our own way as we watched them approach us.

They gently lifted each one of us onto their boat and offered us food and cigarettes. A cup of steaming hot tea was the best thing I had ever tasted! These men may have been rough-and-ready English fishermen, but they looked like angels to us. Now that our ordeal was over, my mind drifted to my copilot and the engineer. If they'd only made it, our miracle would have been complete.

Two hours later, we landed at Folkestone in southern England. It was a moment none of us would ever forget. The tail gunner knelt and kissed the ground. I think, given the strength, I think we all would have, but as it was, we could barely walk.

The relief of being rescued was so great that only later did we realize something more about these fishermen: They had cut their commercial nets to come to our aid—those nets that were their livelihood. And they had not hesitated for a moment before doing so.

Many times since then, I have thought of those men and the sacrifice they made to rescue an unknown bunch of American airmen. I have often wondered how they managed afterward without their nets—but, then, angels must have a way.

Jack Black
As told to Patricia Black

Christmas in Korea

When North Korean troops stormed across the thirty-eighth parallel in June 1950 to attack the outmanned South Korean forces, they triggered the Korean War, a bitterly fought conflict that lasted more than three years. As a U.S. Army medic stationed there, I witnessed the tiny country battered by bombings, artillery fire and ground fighting.

Some fifty-four thousand U.S. troops died in the fighting, and South Koreans lost their homes by the thousands. But the part of the war that seemed to hit me hardest were the Korean orphans, children who had lost their parents in the bloodshed or who had been separated from them in the desperate rush to safety.

My days were exhausting, a never-ending supply of wounded or sick GIs occupying almost all of my time. Duty was lonely and scary, but whenever we started feeling sorry for ourselves, we needed only to look at those parentless children with confused faces and little hope for the future. It strengthened our resolve to protect them and their country from an enemy that was determined to overtake their homeland, no matter the cost.

Winters in Korea were brutally cold, but as Christmas approached in 1952, we were warmed by the care packages from home that began to arrive. They weren't much—home-baked bread and cookies, candy, chewing gum, reading materials, a few personal items—anything that could survive a trip of a few thousand miles. But just being able to open a package from home and read the letter inside lifted our spirits immensely.

Determined not to let the holiday pass feeling sorry for ourselves, the guys in my small unit made a makeshift Christmas tree out of a winter coat. We decorated the conceptual tree with some of the treats from home, a few knitted hats and gloves, and even some old socks with holes in them. It looked pitiful, but at least it was something, we thought.

Christmas Day arrived, and after our somewhat halfhearted celebration, my thoughts turned to the children in the local orphanage. They had no family or gifts, and though I knew they were in good hands with the apostolic sisters who ran the orphanage, I kept thinking, *Everyone deserves a Christmas, no matter where they live.*

"Let's go visit those kids at the orphanage," I suggested to my buddies. Surely, we could scrounge up something to give them. They agreed, and the four of us rounded up some Spam and crackers from our supplies, and wrapped the cookies, candy and gum we'd been sent from home in old newspapers we found around our hut. We jumped into one of our ambulances and drove to the orphanage—a converted school building somewhere near Chonju. We didn't really know what we were getting ourselves into and hadn't really thought much about it, beyond the fact that we just wanted some kids to be happy on Christmas.

We couldn't call ahead to tell the nuns we were coming, but we hoped they would approve of our surprise visit. Of course, they did. When we finally arrived at the orphanage, they took one look at us with our arms full of presents and began hugging us and crying. Pulling us along, they led us to a large room where boys and girls of various ages—from toddlers to kids about eight years old—were eating a meager meal.

When the children saw us, their faces lit up. Visitors! "GI! GI!" they squealed. They surrounded us, and as we handed out the crudely wrapped parcels, the room filled with their cries of excited delight. Then the nuns asked us to sit down so the children could give us something. The sisters had apparently taught the orphans a few simple Christmas carols, for they began singing with enthusiasm. We sat, spellbound, tears running down our faces as we listened to their sweet singing. Their voices carried us home, far away from the discomfort and hardship that surrounded all of us.

Then it was time to leave, and as we stood, the children crowded around us again, tugging on our pants, hugging our legs and crying, "Thank you, GI! Thank you, GI!" over and over. We were so overwhelmed that we choked back more tears. Gently, we untangled ourselves from the children and made our way to the door.

As we climbed back into the ambulance, I thought that by all accounts, this holiday should have been miserable, offering nothing but loneliness, bitter cold, some ragtag gifts, a few carols. But as we bounced along the road back to our barracks on the cold, long drive, the night seemed warm and full of promise. It seemed like—Christmas.

Larry Ebsch

Help from an Unexpected Source

It was March 29, 1944, and the twentieth mission for our B-17 crew. We were assigned to the 401st Squadron of the "Mighty Eighth" Air Force and flying out of a former Royal Air Force base at Bassingbourne, England. On that day, we were to lead an attack against an aircraft factory near Brunswick, Germany. On previous missions to this area, we had encountered fierce fighter opposition and were briefed now to expect more of the same. At this point in the war, our strategy was to destroy the Luftwaffe—in the air, on the ground and in the factories—in preparation for the planned D-Day landings.

The ten members of our crew had grown accustomed to the nervous tension that built up in our bodies during each mission, because many crews were being shot down during this period. We were given a detailed briefing on the weather, expected opposition from antiaircraft fire and fighter aircraft, survival techniques, etc. Then we gathered up our parachutes, helmets, flak vests and guns before going to our aircraft.

The ball of apprehension in our stomachs grew during this takeoff in our overloaded aircraft. As we climbed up to our bombing altitude of twenty-six thousand feet, the other five planes in the squadron that I was leading joined us. Over the English Channel, the guns were test-fired and radio checks completed. We sped toward our target and dropped our load.

After completing the bombing run, the formation made a sweeping left turn toward home. A crew member called our attention to a group of about fifty fighter aircraft at two o'clock, ahead and to our right, and slightly higher than our formation. We were always suspicious of any fighter aircraft, because our crafty enemy resorted to all types of ruses to draw our gunners' attention while others would then press in with an attack. Some familiar tricks were simulating friendly fighter tactics, mock dogfights, etc., while other enemy aircraft suddenly turned in to attack us.

However, these aircraft had the familiar P-51 black paint with white stripes on the wings and were equipped with the wing tanks for extra range. Suddenly, they dropped their tanks just off to our right, and we looked around for German fighters in the area. We found them, when the whole formation of "P-51s" turned out to be Luftwaffe ME-109s that turned in to us with their cannons blazing! We narrowly missed being rammed by two of them that just barely passed over us.

We couldn't escape being hit, with two ME-109s firing at us point-blank. Looking out the left window, I saw the left wing covered with a sheet of flame from the cockpit to the wing tip. Frank, in the ball turret, called on the interphone, "We're on fire!"

"Get out of there right away," I responded. Then without thinking—and because in the Flemish farm community near Green Bay, Wisconsin, where I grew up, it was the custom to joke under difficult circumstances—I added, "Come up here, and we'll have a wienie roast."

I didn't wait to hear if he was laughing, for I was watching the flames blow off of the back of the wing, except for those around the number-one engine, where they burned brightly around the cylinders. I immediately followed established procedures to extinguish the fire. If we didn't control it, it would mean bailing out—a prospect I didn't want to consider in this particular situation. It seemed to take forever, but the fire did go out. By then, friendly fighters had arrived to chase the enemy away, so we limped along safely behind the returning B-17 formations.

We "sweated out" the trip back home to England. Since our gasoline supply was low, we chose to remain near the surface to conserve fuel. We came over our home field at Bassingbourne at two hundred feet, made a tight pattern and were once again back on terra firma. The crew gave a huge collective sigh of relief.

The popular expression "There are no atheists in foxholes" applied to our B-17 as well. God spared us above Brunswick; I think we may have been the best-praying crew in the Eighth Air Force.

But it turned out that we had other help that day as well.

The flight surgeon grounded our crew for a week, because we had flown seven missions in the last nine days. Some of the crew spent this free time with the mechanics and armament specialists who were repairing our aircraft. They found that four cannon shells had exploded in the airframe, but they also found three more that, strangely, had not exploded. It gave all of us a nasty turn to realize what a truly close shave it had been. If any one of those shells had gone off, it could have been the end of us.

Two of the shells did not contain any explosives in them, but the third had some paper with a message where the explosives would have been. It took a while to find a translator to read the message; it was in Czech and was probably placed in the cannon shell in the Skoda armament plant in Prague, Czechoslovakia. The majority of the Czechoslovakian people resented German control, but many were forced to work in factories supporting the Nazi war effort. The message read, "THIS IS OUR WAY OF HELPING YOU."

Dr. Lester F. Rentmeester
Condensed from an article in Voyageur
December 2000

[EDITORS' NOTE: *The crew of the* Jeannie Marie: *Joe Ashby of Missouri, bombardier; Bob Roberts of Maryland, navigator; Les Rentmeester of Wisconsin, pilot; Bill Behrend of New Jersey, copilot; Elmer "Mickey" Diethorn of Pennsylvania, flight engineer; Ward Simonson of New York, radio operator; Frank Topits of Illinois, ball-turret gunner; Gordon Wiggett of Vermont, right waist gunner; Rudy Malkin of Maryland, left waist gunner; Philip "Flip" Lunt of California, tail gunner.*]

3

ABOVE AND BEYOND

Men who have offered their lives for their country know that patriotism is not the fear of something; it is the love of something.

Adlai Stevenson

Blind and Alone over North Korea

I was blind, stunned, in pain, bleeding profusely and very much alone. At the controls of my Navy Skyraider attack plane over Wongsang-ni, North Korea, I was climbing, dazed and oblivious, toward a solid overcast at ten thousand feet—from which there could be no return.

It was March 22, 1952. I was just twenty-two years old. Earlier that day, dawn found me on the flight deck of the USS *Valley Forge* in the Sea of Japan, warming up my Skyraider. As a pilot in Fighter Squadron 194, the "Yellow Devils," I was the standby in case one of the eight planes scheduled for the morning's flight became inoperative. When my fellow pilot Charlie Brown's plane lost its hydraulic system, and I was launched in his place. It was my twenty-seventh mission bombing North Korea. The targets were enemy marshaling yards, railroad tracks and other transportation infrastructure.

On the ninth of my planned fifteen bomb runs, at twelve hundred feet, an enemy antiaircraft shell exploded in the cockpit. Instinctively, I pulled back on the stick to gain altitude. Then, I passed out. When I came to a short time later, I couldn't see a thing. There was stinging agony in my face and throbbing in my head. I felt for my upper lip. It was almost severed from the rest of my face.

I called out over the radio through my lip mike (which miraculously still worked), "I'm blind! For God's sake, help me! I'm blind."

Lieutenant j.g. Howard Thayer, in his own Skyraider nearby, heard the distress call. He saw my plane, still climbing, heading straight toward a heavy overcast at ten thousand feet. He knew that if I entered those clouds, he couldn't help me. No one could help me.

He called out, "Plane in trouble, rock your wings. Plane in trouble, rock your wings."

I did so.

Then came the order, "Put your nose down! Put your nose down! Push over. I'm coming up."

Again, I did as he said and pushed the stick forward.

He climbed and flew alongside my plane and radioed, "This is Thayer—this is Thayer. Put your nose over farther."

I complied. Howie Thayer was my roommate on the *Valley Forge.* Hearing his name and his voice gave me just the psychological boost I needed.

He continued, "You're doing all right. Pull back a little. We can level off now."

Thayer could see that the canopy of my plane was blown away and that my face was a bleeding mess. The crimson stain on the fuselage behind the cockpit turned dark and blended with the Navy blue of the Skyraider as the blood dried. He was amazed I was still alive.

Without the canopy, the two-hundred-mile-per-hour slipstream and unmuffled engine noise made sending and receiving our radio transmissions exceptionally difficult.

Despite these obstacles, I began to think clearly—in my moments of consciousness—and began to try to help myself. I managed to pour water from my canteen over my face. For a fleeting instant, there was a sight of the instrument panel, which disappeared immediately. I was blind again.

Howard kept up a stream of conversation. "We're headed south, Ken. We're heading for Wonsan [a port and prime target on the Sea of Japan]. Not too long."

The throbbing in my head was getting worse, and the blood running down my throat nauseated me. I hurt, but I was unable to get the morphine from my first-aid kit.

I radioed, "Get me down, Howie!"

"Roger. We're approaching Wonsan. Get ready to bail out."

To which I replied, "Negative! Negative! Not going to bail out."

All too often, our pilots had drowned or died of exposure after their planes had been crippled by enemy antiaircraft fire and they had ditched the aircraft or bailed out into the frigid waters of the Sea of Japan. My wingman, LCDR Tom Pugh, was killed in just this way on our second mission. In my case, I would have had to successfully evacuate the Skyraider and enter the water blind, with the probability of a tangled parachute harness and my rubber immersion suit, pierced by shell fragments, unable to offer protection from the freezing ocean. To my mind, bailing out meant certain death.

I would not bail out. Howie understood my decision. He would get me back behind the front lines into friendly territory—or I would die in the attempt. We turned and headed south.

Thirty miles behind the front lines, on the coast, was a Marine airfield designated K-50. This was our destination. I wasn't sure whether I could make it that far, as I kept drifting in and out of consciousness.

Then Howard spotted a Navy cruiser shelling enemy positions and knew that this was the bomb line. South of the bomb line was friendly territory.

The instructions continued. "We're at the bomb line,

Ken. We'll head for K-50. Hold on, Ken. Can you hear me, Ken? We'll head for K-50. Over."

"Roger. Let's try." It was an effort to speak.

"Can you make it, Ken?"

"Get me down, you miserable SOB, or you'll have to inventory my gear!"

(In case of an aviator's death, a shipmate must inventory his personal belongings before they are shipped home—not a welcome chore. Howard and I had designated each other for this function.)

I continued to follow Thayer's directions. But he could see that my head kept flopping down from time to time, and he doubted I could make it to K-50. He was probably right. He decided to get me down right away.

Immediately behind the front lines was a two-thousand-foot deserted dirt airstrip named "Jersey Bounce" that the Army used from time to time for its light planes that did artillery spotting. Thayer decided to have me land there.

"Ken, we're going down. Push your nose over, drop your right wing. We're approaching 'Jersey Bounce.' We'll make a 270-degree turn and set you down."

"Roger, Howie, let's go."

"Left wing down slowly, nose over easy. A little more. Put your landing gear down."

"To hell with that!" was my instantaneous reply. I had seen this field on earlier missions and could picture it in my mind's eye. It was rough and short, and with wheels down, too many things could go wrong. It was much safer to land on my belly.

"Roger, gear up," Thayer concurred. This was one time when we wouldn't follow the checklist.

Ahead lay the most critical part of the flight—landing, a complex maneuver requiring precision and skill. As challenging as my flying wounded and blind had been up to now, a sightless landing on a tiny dirt strip would be infinitely more difficult. One slip would result in disaster.

From his plane, flying twenty-five feet away from mine and duplicating my maneuvers, Howard's voice was cool and confident, but the underlying tension was palpable. "We're heading straight. Flaps down. Hundred yards to the runway. You're fifty feet off the ground. Pull back a little. Easy. Easy. That's good. You're level. You're okay. You're okay. Thirty feet off the ground. You're okay. You're over the runway. Twenty feet. Kill it a little. You're setting down. Okay, okay, okay. Cut!"

The shock wasn't nearly as bad as I had expected. Some forty-five minutes after the shell blew up in my cockpit, my plane hit the ground, lurched momentarily and skidded to a stop in one piece. A perfect landing. No fire. No pain, no strain. The best landing I ever made.

Thayer elatedly said, "You're on the ground, Ken!"

After cutting the switches, I clumsily climbed out of the cockpit. Almost immediately, an Army jeep with two men came, picked me up and took me to a shack on the edge of the field. From there, a helicopter flew me to the Marine airfield, where doctors at their field hospital started to patch me up and give me painkillers.

Thayer flew back to the carrier. I found out later that when he landed, a crowd was there to greet and congratulate him. He wondered how they knew what had happened and was told that most of our transmissions had been picked up on the USS *Valley Forge.*

Meanwhile, back at the Marine airfield, they felt I needed more expert medical care than they could offer, so I was transported to the Navy hospital ship, USS *Consolation,* where I underwent immediate surgery. Both of my eyes were bandaged for two weeks, during which time I wasn't sure if I would ever see again.

But the possibility of a lifetime of blindness was a minor

issue compared to just being alive. Eventually, however, I regained sight in my left eye. My career as a Navy carrier pilot was over. My life was not—because, although I was blind that day over North Korea, I was not really alone. Howard Thayer had been my eyes. Together we'd created a miracle. Today, still living on "borrowed time," I am thankful for every moment of each and every day.

Kenneth A. Schechter

[EDITORS' NOTE: *Howard Thayer made the Navy his career. In January 1961, while flying a night mission in an A-4 attack plane from a carrier in the Mediterranean Sea, both he and his squadron commander flew into the water while on landing approach. Their remains were never recovered. Thayer was survived by his wife and three small children.*

The new plane that Ken Schechter landed at "Jersey Bounce" was jacked up, given a new propeller, flown back to Valley Forge for repairs and later returned to service.

Ken and Howard's story became the basis for the 1953 MGM movie Men of the Fighting Lady.]

Aboard the *USS Valley Forge,* just returned from Korea, June 1952, in the captain's cabin. Ken Schechter (right) was in the Naval Hospital and came aboard to greet his friend Howard Thayer.

Credit: Kenneth Schechter.

Do Not Resuscitate

It was exciting, yet a little frightening, too. It was 1967, and I was about to graduate as a young registered nurse. There were a lot of social movements taking place in America and a war going on in Southeast Asia. Expectations were high to go out into the world and do something good. Yet antiwar sentiments were also high; it wasn't popular or fashionable to be patriotic. "Why on earth would a woman want to go to Vietnam?" asked too many to count, when I talked about serving my country.

At school, posters begging for nurses for the Vietnam conflict were everywhere. The words "The most beautiful woman in the world, the U.S. Army Nurse" were printed in bold type beneath a picture of a smiling young woman's face—lipstick and all—topped with a steel "pot."

Boys I knew, baby-faced soldiers in crisp, starched uniforms, with Beatles music in their ears, were taking off on jet planes for a scary place called Vietnam.

But as ragged soldiers returned from combat with old eyes in their broken young bodies, antiwar protesters hurled rotten eggs at them and jeered at them. Angry fists were lifted in marches and protests in small towns and big cities across the country. Draft cards and American flags burned. *What is happening here?* I wondered, dismayed and confused by the bitterly conflicting currents around me.

I made my decision and signed on as a U.S. Army nurse. I kissed my mom and dad good-bye and waved to my little sister and brothers. My parents knew too much—it was all in their eyes—and I knew too little.

I was inducted as a second lieutenant in the Army Nurse Corps and sent to the Central Highlands of Pleiku, about thirty kilometers from the Cambodian border. In 1969, our four-hundred-bed evacuation hospital faced unrelenting casualties as we supported the Fourth Infantry Division, which was being overrun by the Vietcong and NVA. The wounded were perhaps ten minutes away from us by medical evacuation "dust off" helicopters. They arrived, wave after wave, in a steady stream.

Fulfilling my romanticized vision of nursing, in a ward full of wounded and burned young men, as well as Vietnamese and Montagnard civilians injured in the cross fires of war, was next to impossible. How could I make their cares lighter in this terrifying, dismal place?

Idealism clashed with the reality of chest tubes, tracheotomies, pit viper wounds, napalm burns, malaria, 105-degree fevers, gaping open wounds, blood transfusions, hepatitis and gangrene. Warned by the sound of mortar thuds, as rockets and shrapnel pierced the roof and walls, we threw mattresses on top of the patients who hadn't already dived for the floor. How could I bring comfort and healing to this? Perhaps the most important thing for our patients was being there with them—offering our words, a smile and hope—as we went about our work.

It was a privilege to work with many wonderful people during my tour of duty in Vietnam. One person who stands out from my time in Pleiku is Fulton, a young hospital corpsman. Like all of our corpsmen, Fulton worked side by side with us. He dressed wounds and admirably performed many duties far beyond his years or training. Once, he helped me admit a little Montagnard girl diagnosed with the plague. All I knew about the disease was that it had wiped out entire populations. I asked the doctor on our unit to tell us what we could do for this precious, sad little child who was feverish and delirious. The doctor said the disease had progressed too far. He explained that plague can be transmitted through the saliva, and gave strict instructions that no one, under any circumstances, should do mouth-to-mouth resuscitation as she succumbed to the disease. I briefed the corpsman and posted a note for fellow nurses: "Do Not Resuscitate." We quarantined her away from the wounded GIs in the ward, and comforted and cared for her as best we could.

At one point, I looked over at her, and I froze, my heart pounding with fear. I rushed to the little girl's bedside, crying, "Noooo! Fulton! Stop! Stop!" He was desperately trying to breathe life back into her. I reached him and grabbed his arm. "You can't help her! Stop, I tell you!" I pulled him away from her lifeless body—from the soul he could not stop trying to save.

I said gently, "Fulton, did you forget what you learned about plague? What if your vaccination doesn't protect you?"

He said, "Lieutenant, I just didn't think about that."

Over the years, I have thought of that little dark-haired girl so often. She came into the hospital so desperately alone. I know she felt Fulton's love and arms around her as she took her last breath. Maybe her life was not saved by his heroic act, but her death was given dignity.

Fulton did not receive a medal for bravery, nor did he receive a hero's welcome when he returned to America. He may even have been called a "baby killer" like so many of our returning GIs.

Fulton? A "baby killer"? Nothing could be further from the truth.

Fulton, I hope you are reading this. I changed your name to protect your privacy, but you will know that this is about you. You are my hero.

Diane Carlson Evans, R.N.

Colonel Maggie and the Blind Veteran

I don't remember exactly when I first met Martha Raye, our Colonel Maggie. Like so many veterans, as soon as I met her, I felt I'd known this woman forever.

One of our later encounters took place at the Bonaventure Hotel in Los Angeles in 1987 at an enormous veterans' convention. Colonel Maggie was there, every day, just "one of the guys." She was the center of attraction in the lounge.

Day after day, I couldn't help but notice a blind man, quietly standing outside the lounge, his dog stoically beside him. Many vets asked if he needed assistance. He always quietly declined. Finally, a group of nervous veterans asked me to intercede.

I walked up to this man and asked what he was waiting for all those days.

"I'm waiting for Colonel Maggie to have a moment to see me, ma'am. I don't care to disturb her." Something about the guy got to me, and I sent Chuck, Maggie's escort, to go get her.

Maggie strode right over to the man. "What's up,

soldier? You wanted to see me?" Even his dog stood at attention as he replied, "Yes, ma'am!"

"Well, I'm here. What is it?"

"I served in Vietnam in . . ." Maggie finished his sentence by providing the place she'd met him—once he'd mentioned the year.

While others standing around us showed pure awe at Maggie's capacity for memory of detail, I only smiled; it's her trademark.

While Maggie and the man (we never asked him his name) reminisced, the blind soldier's face glowed with joy. Finally, he said what he'd waited twenty years to say."Colonel Maggie," he began, "when I was hit, you stayed in that foxhole, holding me, singing to me till the medevac came. I wasn't so scared, with you there and all." They were staring deeply into each other's eyes. Somehow, we knew they were both seeing a time and place they'd shared long ago; in this moment, his blindness was unimportant. It was suddenly quiet enough to hear footfalls sixteen thousand miles away.

"When the doc went to bandage my eyes, you stopped him," he continued, his voice choking. "You looked me right in my eyes and told me, 'Someday we'll see each other again.'

"Well, back in the world, when they unbandaged me, they told me I'd never see anything ever again. I wasn't depressed. I knew I could live with this"—he pointed to his sightless eyes—"because the last thing I ever saw was the most beautiful sight I could ever live to see. You."

Maggie took him in her arms, and we onlookers had a good cry. The veteran? His eyes were glowing with a sight from within. And Maggie? Once again, she gave that man exactly what he needed—when he needed it.

Susan M. Christiansen

The Stuff They Don't Give Medals For

Danny was a tough, street-smart kid from New York City. I knew him as well as anyone in our infantry platoon in Vietnam and liked him a little better than most. Danny didn't make a lot of friends. He operated solely on two principles. One was: Get them before they get you. The second was: Me first.

Danny was out for Number One, and he didn't care who knew it. He took strange pride in announcing to every replacement who came into our unit, "Listen, rookie, I'm a short-timer, and I'm going back to the world in one piece no matter what happens to the rest of you. So just don't get in my way. Understand?"

The newcomer probably did not understand that "the world" meant home, and "short-timer" meant someone who was close to going there. Yet already this guy was telling him that he didn't care if the kid lived or died as long as he stayed out of Danny's way.

Around the Tet holiday in 1968, we were on a mission outside Dong Ha when we saw a little village to our right near the tree line. It was standard operating procedure to search any settlement we encountered. We lined up about five yards apart and swept toward it like a huge, olive-drab push broom, sending everything from animals to rice-paddy workers scattering.

When we reached the edge of the village, our platoon began its move into the random collection of wood huts with their thatched roofs, dirt floors and doorways full of wide-eyed children hiding behind their mothers. There were no men, just the worn-looking women and the curious children.

The sharp crack of shots sounded foreign at first, like they didn't belong in this place of mothers and children. But the shots were real. Reflexes took over, and I found myself on the ground crawling for protection.

My heart was pounding when I reached a tree, but I wasn't the only one who had sought this refuge. Entrenched behind the broad trunk was "me first" Danny.

When I could raise my head to look around, I found the village empty. Soldiers, women and children had all taken what safety they could find. I heard our people shouting about snipers in the tree line, and at intervals the distinctive crack of Soviet-made AK-47s was answered with the roar of our M-16s.

I glanced at Danny and saw him staring at something a few yards in front of our tree. I followed his line of sight, and that's when I spotted her.

She was strikingly small there on the ground. She couldn't have been much more than five or six. I could see that she was crying and terrified. I could also see a small red stain on her shirtsleeve.

At that moment, out of the corner of my eye, I saw Danny leave the protection of our tree and run, crouching low, toward the Vietnamese girl. The rest all seemed to happen at the same instant. Danny reached the girl, took hold of her clothing and, half crawling and half running, began dragging her back toward the tree. I could hear somebody yelling for Danny to get out of the open; then came the snap of enemy fire.

I saw a muzzle flash in the trees and emptied my clip in that direction. But it was too late. Danny was down. Still, he'd managed to push the fragile child close enough for me to reach out and yank her to safety. The others in our platoon began pouring round upon round into the tree line. The snipers, knowing the game was up, fell silent.

I grabbed Danny and hauled him back to the tree; the medic was there when I turned around. He pulled off Danny's flak vest and began trying to patch him up.

I held the child close to me. Her eyes were red from crying, and tears had made muddy paths down her cheeks. As I examined her arm, where a bullet had grazed her, she didn't cry out. She just kept staring at Danny. The girl seemed to realize she had no words he could understand. Finally, she reached out and gently touched the leg of his fatigue pants. Then she ran into one of the huts.

I heard later that Danny, too, was going to be all right. But he was hit bad enough to get his wish—they were sending him back to the world. Our platoon leader gave us all a long lecture about how a soldier's duty to keep himself safe far outweighs any need to help a civilian.

He said, "This is the stuff they don't give medals for."

I imagine he was right, but I do know that in that village one tough kid from New York found out he was much more of a man than he ever thought he could be. And somewhere there's a Vietnamese girl, now in her thirties, who remembers that an American soldier risked everything to save her life. All in all, not a bad exchange for a medal.

Tim Watts

The Valley

One man with courage makes a majority.

Andrew Jackson

April 1951. A cool, somewhat frosty, but clear spring morning. We are "Charlie Company," Sixty-fifth Combat Engineers, attached to the Twenty-seventh "Wolfhound" Regiment, Twenty-fifth Infantry Division.

Our assignment, just handed to us by regimental headquarters: Locate and find a missing heavy tank company, report their location and position, and ascertain their fitness and ability to carry out whatever assignment they had.

Our company commander echoed our thoughts: "How could a company of approximately ten sixty-five-ton 'General Sherman' class tanks and their full complement of jeeps, command vehicles, heavy supply trucks and over ninety GIs become lost?"

We were told they had been "pushing north" into enemy territory—rugged, mountainous and hostile country.

So we set out on a one-way dirt road in the same direction.

We were very uneasy about our prospects, to say the least. We were huddled in "deuce and a half" trucks, dressed in full battle uniforms, and followed by two Caterpillar D-8 bulldozers, two half-tracks with their quad-fifty machine guns, and last but not least, a truck carrying some grave registration boys and their body bags.

After about four hours (the tractors held us back some, because of their relatively slow rate of travel), we rounded a sharp curve on the steep mountain road we'd been negotiating and halted abruptly.

The "panorama" before us was easy to read: ten tanks, large support trucks and jeeps—all black, completely gutted and burned out. The ninety-four soldiers, likewise, were all dead, most burned beyond recognition, some hanging out of tank turrets, others in and outside the trucks and jeeps.

The air was extremely quiet. Only some buzzards circled overhead. There was no sign of any North Korean or Chinese soldiers. Plainly, the element of surprise had been utilized. From a vantage point on the cliffs, the enemy had thrown bottles of flaming gasoline down on the unsuspecting GIs and caught them in a narrow area where tank guns were useless.

We had the miserable realization that these men never even had a chance to fire their weapons at their attackers.

We were turning to make our gloomy way back the way we'd come when someone spotted him. Partway up the hill, off to the left side, was a dirt and rock overhang forming a shallow cave. At the mouth of the cave, kneeling down, was a dead GI. We could see that he had not been burned, but shot numerous times. From his shirt, we could also tell he had been a staff sergeant. In front of him was a Browning automatic rifle. It had been fired so many times, so rapidly, that the barrel appeared warped. That explained why the Koreans hadn't taken it with them.

Shell casings and bandoliers littered the area.

The sergeant, knowing he was likely the only GI still alive, must have run to the cave, firing his weapon at the dozens of Korean and Chinese soldiers, probably killing a number of them until, finally, their bullets found him.

What bravery in the face of insurmountable odds! Staring down imminent death himself, he vowed to take as many of the enemy with him as he could. It was a scene vividly etched in my mind—in all our minds—that day. Indeed, it was all we could think or talk about.

Our company commander found out the sergeant's name, personally put in a recommendation for a posthumous Silver Star and Purple Heart, and requested that the battalion commander write a letter to the sergeant's family in the States.

God bless him—he stood alone in battle, yet in the company of those who gave their all in the name of peace and tranquillity in those terrible times.

Barry Vonder Mehden

The Mitzvah

It was fall 1945, and I returned to Vienna with the first American occupation troops. I had been there three months earlier as an interpreter of German for a special mission assigned to negotiate the division of the city into four allied zones, similar to what had been done in Berlin. I was fluent in German because, only six years earlier, I had emigrated to the United States from Berlin. As soon as I became eligible, I enlisted in the U.S. Army to serve my new country and was proud to wear its uniform.

One Friday night, feeling somewhat homesick, I made my way to the only remaining synagogue in Vienna to attend services. The crowd there was a pitiful sight, about fifty men and women, thin and poorly dressed. They spoke accented Yiddish, and I surmised that they were the remnants of thriving Jewish communities across Europe, now thrown together in this one place and cut off from the rest of the world. When they spotted my American uniform, they all crowded around me to see a friendly soldier in a synagogue. To their surprise, I was able to converse with them in fluent Yiddish.

As we talked, I could tell my initial assessment was

correct. These people were survivors of the Holocaust who had gathered at the synagogue to see if they could find someone, anyone, who might know of a relative or friend who had also survived. Because there was no civilian mail service from Austria to the rest of the world, these gatherings were the only way the survivors could hope to hear news of their families.

One of the men timidly asked me if I would be kind enough to send a message to a relative in England that he was still alive. I knew that military mail service was not to be used for civilian letters, but how could I say no? These people, who had literally been through a living hell, needed to let worried relatives know they had survived. When I agreed, everyone wanted to send a message.

Fifty messages were a lot more than one: I had to think quickly. Standing back, I announced that I would return to services the following Friday night and accept short messages written in English, German or Yiddish and submitted in an unsealed envelope. If the letters met those requirements, I would send them by military mail.

The following week, as promised, I once again made my way to the synagogue. As I opened the door, I was shocked. The place was packed, full of people who rushed up to me, thrusting their envelopes toward me. There were so many that I had to ask someone to find me a box in which to store them. I spent the next week checking each message for security reasons, making sure it contained only the promised announcement. Then I sent mail all over the world. I felt wonderful to know that this would probably be the first news to most of these relatives that one of their loved ones had survived the horrors of the Holocaust. A good deed, I thought, a little "mitzvah."

About a month passed. The whole thing had started to fade from my mind when the military "mailboy" suddenly stumbled into my office, laden with several sacks of packages.

"What's going on?" he demanded. The parcels he set on the floor came from everywhere, addressed to the survivors I had met in the synagogue, in care of me, Corporal Arnold Geier. I had not expected this result. What was I supposed to do now?

Walter, a buddy with whom I worked as an interrogation team, also a former refugee from Germany, laughed when he saw the pile of packages. "I'll help you deliver them," he offered. What else could we do? I had kept a list of the names and addresses of the people who had given me messages, so we requisitioned a closed winterized jeep and filled it with the packages. All that evening and into the night, Walter and I drove through the rubble of Vienna, dropping off parcels to surprised and grateful survivors. Most of them lived in the Soviet zone of the city. We had to drive into that area late at night, and the Soviet patrols often stopped us, suspicious. Still, we were technically allies, so we would explain that we were delivering packages to survivors of the Nazi horror and were allowed to pass unharmed.

The packages kept on coming for another week, and the mailboy grew increasingly annoyed with us. We continued our nightly deliveries all over Vienna, but I was worried that my well-intentioned offer had grown out of control.

Finally, one morning, our commanding officer called me into his office. He demanded to know why I was receiving so many parcels. Knowing that the officer was Jewish and would understand my motivation, I decided to simply tell him the truth. I admitted that I had misused the military mail to help survivors and perform a mitzvah so desperately needed. I did not expect this simple gesture to turn into this. He admonished me sternly and then smiled. "We'll let it go this time," he said, dismissing me.

Sometimes I think back to the path my little good deed

had taken. Yes, it had spun out of control, but only in the way a true mitzvah does: growing and giving back again, until it has fulfilled its purpose. I was the instrument chosen to let anxious families know of the survival of loved ones.

Arnold Geier

Nurse Penny

The period from 1967 to 1968 was a difficult time in Vietnam, especially during the communist Tet Offensive in early 1968, when American soldiers suffered their heaviest casualties of the war. It was during this time that a young U.S. Army nurse named Penny was stationed at the U.S. Army field hospital at Tan Son Nhut airbase. Like most nurses, she worked a multitude of assignments, but mostly she worked in the critical care, or triage, unit.

Triage duty is an emotionally tough assignment: determining who gets what in terms of treatment and in what priority. One group is made up of those soldiers whose wounds are slight and can wait for medical care. They are set aside, to wait until care is given to the serious casualties. The second category is the toughest: those whose wounds are so severe that they cannot be saved. They are given something to deaden their pain and then set aside to die. In the final group are those whose wounds are serious, but who have a chance at survival. These cases are given the highest priority, and every effort is made immediately to save their lives.

The doctors and nurses who have served this country

in all of its wars have always tried to limit the number of Americans they must place into the second category. It is hard to look at your own people, accept the fact that you can no longer help them and then watch them die. I have observed doctors totally break down over the helplessness they feel when they cannot save some young soldier. In Vietnam, knowing they had tremendous medical resources, the doctors and nurses were even more reluctant to place anyone in the second category.

As a result, they made heroic efforts to save even hopeless cases. Many were flown immediately to advanced medical facilities in Japan. Most, if they could be kept alive for this short flight, had a good chance of making it.

Our soldiers knew of this dedication and had great faith in our doctors and nurses. Yet combat veterans, even young boys, learn early on to understand the signs of death. People with life-threatening wounds knew their chances were extremely slim—what kept them alive was hope. Penny understood this, holding their hands as she helped load them onto the hospital-bound aircraft.

Many of them looked her in the eye and asked her, "Am I gonna make it?"

Penny would respond, "Sure, you'll make it. My name is Penny, and I'm going to give you this penny to let you know you will be okay. And, when you get well, I want you to promise to get in touch and give me back my penny."

She then gave each of them a shiny American penny. Many of them did not make it, but I know that her act made their passing less painful.

In 1997, twenty-nine years after Penny left Vietnam, she received a phone call from a stranger.

"Were you ever an Army nurse?" the stranger asked.

"Yes," Penny replied.

"Were you in Vietnam during the Tet Offensive?" he asked.

"Yes," she replied.

"Well, I have a penny for you," he said. "I want to come give it to you. And I also want you to meet my wife and two girls. I have them because you gave me the hope and will to live."

As you can imagine, it was a tear-filled, joyous reunion.

Ernest L. Webb

The Four Chaplains

In November 1942, four men met while attending Chaplain's School at Harvard University. At age forty-two, George Fox was the eldest. The youngest was thirty-year-old Clark Poling, and the other two, Alexander Goode and John Washington, were both thirty-two.

Reverend Fox, from Vermont, enlisted in the Army the same day his eighteen-year-old son Wyatt enlisted in the Marine Corps. During World War I, Fox—then only seventeen years old—had convinced the Army he was actually eighteen and enlisted as a medical corps assistant. His courage on the battlefield earned him the Silver Star, the Croix de Guerre and the Purple Heart. When World War II broke out he told his family, "I've got to go. I know from experience what our boys are about to face. They need me."

Reverend Poling was from Ohio and pastoring in New York when World War II began. He determined to enter the Army, but not as a chaplain. He didn't want to hide behind the church, "in some safe office out of the firing line," he told his father.

But his father, Reverend Daniel Poling, knew something

of war, having served as a chaplain himself during World War I and he told his son, "Don't you know that chaplains have the highest mortality rate of all? As a chaplain, you can't carry a gun." With new appreciation for the role of the Chaplains Corps, Clark Poling accepted a commission.

Alexander Goode's father was a clergyman, too. While studying to follow in his father's footsteps, Alex had joined the National Guard. When war was declared, he wanted to become a chaplain. He chose to do so as a U.S. Army chaplain.

Mild-mannered John P. Washington left one with the impression that he was not the sort of man to go to war and become a hero. His love of music and beautiful voice belied the toughness inside. As one of nine children in an Irish immigrant family living in the toughest part of Newark, New Jersey, he had learned through sheer determination to hold his own in any fight. Like the others, he wanted to serve wherever his country needed him.

Upon meeting at the chaplains' school, the four men quickly became friends. What makes this fact remarkable is the enormous differences in their backgrounds: Reverend Fox was a Methodist minister, Reverend Poling was a Dutch Reformed minister, Father Washington was a Catholic priest and Goode was a Jewish rabbi.

After graduating from Harvard, the friends were assigned to posts in Europe. The four chaplains said goodbye to their families and reported to New York to board the transport that would take them overseas.

The *Dorchester* was an aging, luxury coastal liner that was no longer luxurious. Pressed into service as a transport ship, all noncritical amenities had been removed and cots were crammed into every available space. The intent was to get as many young fighting men as possible on each voyage.

When the soldiers boarded on January 23, 1943, the

Dorchester was filled to capacity. In addition to the Merchant Marine crew and a few civilians, young soldiers filled every available space. There were 902 lives about to be cast to the mercy of the frigid North Atlantic.

As the *Dorchester* left New York for an Army base in Greenland, many dangers lay ahead. The sea itself was always dangerous, especially in this area known for ice flows, raging waters and gale-force winds. The greatest danger, however, was the ever-present threat of German submarines, which had recently been sinking Allied ships at the rate of one hundred every month. The *Dorchester* would be sailing through an area that had become infamous as "Torpedo Junction."

Most of the men who boarded for the trip were young, frightened soldiers. Many were going to sea for the first time and suffered seasickness for days. They were packed head to toe below deck, a human sea of fear and uncertainty. Even if they survived the eventual Atlantic crossing, they didn't have much to look forward to, only the prospects of being thrown into the cauldron of war on foreign shores. They were men in need of a strong shoulder to lean on, a firm voice to encourage them and a ray of hope in a world at war. In their midst moved the four Army chaplains: Fox, Goode, Poling and Washington.

The crossing was filled with long hours of boredom and discomfort. Outside, the chilly Arctic winds and cold ocean spray coated the *Dorchester*'s deck with ice. Below deck, the soldiers' quarters were hot from too many bodies, crammed into too small a place for too many days in a row.

Finally, on February 2, the *Dorchester* was within 150 miles of Greenland. It would have generated a great sense of relief among the young soldiers crowded in the ship's berths, had not the welcome news been tempered by other more ominous news. One of the *Dorchester*'s three Coast Guard escorts had received sonar readings during the day, indicating the presence of an enemy submarine in "Torpedo Junction."

The *Dorchester*'s captain listened to the news with great concern. If he could make it through the night, air cover would arrive with daylight to safely guide his ship home. The problem would be surviving the night. Aware of the potential for disaster, he instructed the soldiers to sleep in their clothes and life jackets . . . just in case.

Outside it was another cold, windy night as the midnight hour signaled the passing of February 2 and the beginning of a new day. In the distance a cold, metal arm broke the surface of the stormy seas. At the end of that arm, a German U-Boat (submarine) captain monitored the slowly passing troop transport. Shortly before one in the morning, he gave the command to fire.

Quiet moments passed as the torpedo silently streaked toward the *Dorchester.* Then the early morning was shattered by the flash of a blinding explosion and the roar of massive destruction. The "hit" had been dead on, tossing men from their cots with the force of its explosion. A second torpedo followed the first, instantly killing one hundred men in the hull of the ship.

Power was knocked out by the explosion in the engine room, and darkness engulfed the frightened men below deck as water rushed through gaping wounds in the *Dorchester*'s hull. The ship tilted at an unnatural angle as it began to sink rapidly. Wounded men cried out in pain, frightened survivors screamed in terror and all groped frantically in the darkness for exits they couldn't find.

In the darkness, four voices of calm began to speak words of comfort, seeking to bring order to panic and bedlam. Slowly, soldiers began to find their way to the deck of the ship, where they were confronted by the cold winds blowing down from the Arctic. One soldier, reeling from the cold, headed back towards his cabin.

"Where are you going?" a voice asked.

"To get my gloves," the soldier replied.

"Here, take these," said Rabbi Goode as he handed a pair of gloves to the young officer, who would never have survived the trip to his cabin and then back to safety.

"I can't take your gloves," the soldier replied.

"Never mind," the rabbi responded. "I have two pairs."

The young soldier slipped the gloves over his hands and returned to the frigid deck, never stopping to ponder until later when he had reached safety that there was no way Rabbi Goode would have been carrying a spare set of gloves.

Elsewhere on the ship, Reverend Poling guided the frightened soldiers to the deck, their only hope of safety on the rapidly sinking transport. As he led the men, he spoke quietly but firmly, urging them not to give up.

Meanwhile, Reverend Fox and Father Washington tended to the wounded and dying soldiers. Somehow, by their combined efforts, the chaplains succeeded in getting many of the soldiers out of the hold and onto the *Dorchester*'s slippery deck.

In the chaos around them, lifeboats floated away before men could board them. Others capsized as panicked soldiers loaded the small craft beyond limit. The strength, calm and organization of the chaplains, so critical in the dark hull, were still urgently needed. Taking charge, they organized the lifeboat boarding, directed men to safety and left them with parting words of encouragement.

In little more than twenty minutes, the *Dorchester* was almost gone. Icy waves broke over the railing, tossing men into the sea, many of them without life jackets. In the last moments of the transport's existence, the chaplains were too occupied opening lockers to pass out life jackets to note the threat to their own lives.

Now water was beginning to flow across the deck of the sinking *Dorchester*. Working against time, the chaplains continued to pass out the life vests from the lockers as the soldiers pressed forward in a ragged line. And then the lockers were all empty, the life jackets gone.

Those still pressing in line began to realize they were doomed; there was no hope. And then something amazing happened, something those who were there would never forget. All four chaplains began taking their own life jackets off and putting them on the men around them.

Then time ran out. The chaplains had done all they could for those who would survive, and nothing more could be done for the others . . . including themselves.

Those who had been fortunate enough to reach lifeboats struggled to distance themselves from the sinking ship, to avoid being pulled down by the chasm created as the transport slipped under the surface. Then, amid the sounds of fear and pain that permeated the cold dark night, they heard the strong voices of the chaplains.

"Shma Yisroel Adonai Elohenu Adonai Echod."

"Our Father, which art in Heaven, Hallowed be Thy name. Thy kingdom come, Thy will be done. . . ."

Looking back, the men in the lifeboats could see the slanting deck of the *Dorchester,* its demise almost complete. Four figures were clearly visible as they stood braced against the railings, praying, singing and giving strength to others by their final valiant declaration of faith. Reverend Fox, Rabbi Goode, Reverend Poling and Father Washington linked their arms together and leaned into each other for support.

Then, only twenty-seven minutes after the first torpedo struck, the last trace of the *Dorchester* disappeared beneath the cold North Atlantic waters, taking with it many men, including the four chaplains of different faiths who had found strength in their diversity by focusing on the love for God—and mankind—they all shared.

The Chapel of Four Chaplains

4

ON THE FRONT LINES

Duty, honor, country: Those three hallowed words reverently dictate what you ought to be, what you can be, what you will be. They are your rallying point to build courage when courage seems to fail, to regain faith when there seems to be little cause for faith, to create hope when hope becomes forlorn.

General Douglas MacArthur

My Most Memorable Christmas

"Raus mit du, Schwine Hund!" ("Out with you, you pig of a dog!") These were the words I remember hearing every morning of the eight months I spent in Stalag 7-A, the German prisoner-of-war camp located in Moosburgh, Germany, fifteen kilometers from Munich.

To discourage escape attempts, we were not allowed shoelaces, socks or belts. Very few of us had underwear. Of my own GI clothing, all that remained were the wool pants and shoes I hit Omaha Beach with on D-Day.

Most of the thousands of POWs in our camp were issued old French flannel Army shirts, woolen trench coats and a woolen blanket with more holes in it than material. The trench coat they gave me must have been made for a seven-foot-tall French soldier. It dragged on the ground, and I could hardly walk in it.

Using a piece of sharp tin from a can received in an American Red Cross food parcel, I cut the coat off between my ankles and knees, and used a piece to make a ski mask, with holes for eyes, nose and mouth. With the material left over, I sewed a pouch into my coat to sneak loot from work details into the prison camp.

The blanket was more like a horse blanket, and the odor seemed to confirm it. Some of the POWs were lucky enough to find or steal burlap and other materials to make extra blankets and clothing.

Thanks to the ingenuity of a British POW, each man made his own miniature cookstove out of tin cans from the Red Cross food parcels.

Our barracks were thin-walled, unheated buildings without water or electricity. We slept in bunks stacked three high, made of salvaged wood, with bug-infested straw mattresses. To take the chill out of the air, we lit candles found or stolen on work details in Munich.

Although the winter of 1944 in Europe was the coldest in quite some time, we were still looking forward to Christmas Day. The word was that we would be allowed to lie around and take it easy with no work details.

On the days we didn't work, the guys mostly played cards, read or talked about going home. During one of those days when we were killing time, I suggested putting on a Christmas play to boost morale. Everyone thought it a good idea, except for one man, whom I'll call Joe.

Joe was more depressed than any man in the barracks. Most of us felt he was suicidal. Maybe the play would give him something to think about, we thought, instead of focusing on the loneliness and despair that was eating at him.

The word spread, and the idea caught on like wildfire. Committees were formed, and our barracks leader—a natural-born catalyst—was chosen as director. We never did find out how he managed to get the lumber to build the stage and benches for the audience.

Everyone continued to scrounge things suitable for making music, decorations or something to eat and drink. When things were brought in, they'd be hidden under mattresses or floorboards, or buried.

As Christmas drew near, the anticipation and enthusiasm

grew more contagious and magical. An ex-stage director was found among the POWs. Choirs were formed, and a magician, impersonators, comedians, actors, writers, ushers and stagehands stepped forward. So many people volunteered, they couldn't all be put to work.

The GIs who smoked chipped in one cigarette each to bribe the guard for a Christmas tree. Ornaments were made of tin, paper, wood and cloth, and someone scrounged several cans of paint to color them.

Raisins, prunes, sugar, chocolate and powdered milk from Red Cross food parcels were hoarded for six weeks. They would be added to several loaves of black bread to make a pudding that would be given to each man as he came to watch the show. The rest of the raisins, prunes and sugar would be brewed into a strong alcoholic drink that would be cut with water and portioned out to each man. By Christmas Eve, all was ready.

The building we used to present the show held one hundred men at a time. We scheduled the show hourly, so all the men in our section of the camp could see it. Where the energy in our weakened bodies came from, I'll never know. I suppose our determination to generate some happiness for our fellow GIs spurred us on. It wasn't only Joe who needed it. We all needed it.

The first show was at 8 A.M. Christmas Day. The opening hymn, "O Come All Ye Faithful," brought so many tears, we thought we'd have to stop the show. And there in the very first row of the choir was Joe, singing his head off.

The music and laughter could be heard throughout the camp. After the audience filed out of our third show, we heard the distinctive thump of German boots coming through the door. In came a German colonel, two majors, three captains, numerous lieutenants and about sixty enlisted men.

We feared they had come to put an end to our Christmas

celebration. Instead, they trooped to the front benches and sat down. The colonel then motioned us to proceed with the show.

The head usher, who spoke fluent German, climbed on the stage and dedicated the opening hymn to the German officers and enlisted men. Then the ushers passed out a slice of pudding and a drink to each German soldier.

The Germans were overwhelmed to see that people in our situation could treat their enemy with such kindness. Some on both sides cried, including me.

After the performance, the German guards shook our hands and thanked us, saying *"Sehr gut"* and *"Danke shöne."* There were tears and happy smiles on their faces, as well as our own. All animosities were put aside that Christmas morning.

The next day, however, things went back to normal. Except with Joe. From that day forward, Joe was a new man. I noticed he smiled more, took part in our conversations and card games and even went out of his way to help other prisoners who were feeling hopeless and depressed.

The show had worked. The spirit of Christmas had entered Joe's lonely heart, as well as ours, and never left.

Gene DuVall

To Any Service Member

During the Persian Gulf War, I was stationed aboard the naval amphibious ship USS *Nassau.* As a senior Marine intelligence analyst, my workdays were routinely twelve to sixteen hours long. Like all the veterans, we looked forward to receiving mail from home.

Unlike the Vietnam War, the Gulf War found support among most Americans. As a result, we soldiers received an enormous amount of "To any service member" mail from the States. I never took any of those letters, since I wrote to my wife and two children on a daily basis, as well as occasionally writing notes to my daughter's classroom, and I didn't feel I had time to write to anyone else.

After five or six months of hearing the mail orderly announcing the availability of "To any service member" mail, I decided to take a few of the letters. I planned, as time permitted, to drop them a line telling them "Thanks" for their support.

I picked up three letters, and placed them in my cargo pocket and proceeded back to work. Over the next week or so, I started responding to the letters. When it came time to answer the third letter, I noticed it had no return address, but a Colorado postmark, which made me think longingly of home. I had missed spending Thanksgiving, Christmas and New Year's with my family, and I was really lonesome for them.

I opened the card and started to read the letter enclosed. About the third or fourth sentence down, it read,"My daddy is a Marine over there, if you see him tell him hi and I love and miss him." This statement really touched me and made me miss my family even more. I looked down to the signature—and sat in stunned silence as tears filled my eyes.

My own daughter Chris had signed the letter.

Nick Hill

Now I Lay Me Down to Sleep

All those soldiers belong to somebody. They got moms, they got wives, they got kids. . . . They got somebody who loves them.

Liz Allen, Vietnam nurse

Growing up, I wanted to be a doctor, but money was scarce, so I went to nursing school. In 1966, during my senior year, an Army Nurse Corps recruiter came to talk to us. It all sounded so exciting: I would have a chance to travel, it paid well and, most important, I was assured that I wouldn't have to go to Vietnam if I didn't want to—which I didn't.

I signed up. After basic training, I was assigned to Letterman Hospital at the Presidio of San Francisco. During my two years at Letterman, I received orders for Vietnam three times. The first two times, I said no. But the third time, I decided that my two years of experience would probably be a huge asset over there.

We landed in Tan Son Nhut Air Base, and when the airplane door opened, I nearly fell backward, overwhelmed by the heat and the stench. Suddenly, all my experience seemed trivial. Being twenty-three years old seemed very young. I was scared, but there was no turning back.

After our debriefing, I was assigned to the Sixty-seventh Evac Hospital in Qui Nhon. When the helicopter landed on the hospital tarmac, they set my things onto the ground. I climbed out, straightening my skirt. The soldiers in the helicopter yelled, "Good luck, Captain" as they took off.

I was in my class A uniform, which meant I was also wearing nylons and high heels. Nothing could have been less appropriate for the surroundings. Miles of barbed wire, topped by concertina wire, encompassed the hospital compound and the large adjoining airfield, along with acres of hot concrete. I squared my shoulders and marched inside the grim cinder block building in front of me. I was told to get some sleep, because I started tomorrow. I gratefully fell into a bed, and in the morning, I donned my hospital uniform—fatigues and Army boots—just like the soldiers.

Because I was a captain, I was made head nurse on the orthopedic ward, which primarily held soldiers with traumatic amputations. I took my role very seriously and had a reputation for strictness.

Being a nurse in the States for two years did not adequately prepare me for Vietnam. I witnessed a tremendous amount of suffering and watched a lot of men die. One of my rules was that nurses were not allowed to cry. The wounded and dying men in our care needed our strength, I told them. We couldn't indulge in the luxury of our own feelings.

On the other hand, I was always straight with the soldiers. I would never say, "Oh, you're going to be just fine," if they were on their way out. I didn't lie.

But I remember one kid that I didn't want to tell. The badly wounded soldier couldn't have been more than eighteen years old. I could see immediately that there was nothing we could do to save him. He never screamed or complained, even though he must have been in a lot of pain.

When he asked me, "Am I going to die?" I said, "Do you feel like you are?"

He said, "Yeah, I do."

"Do you pray?" I asked him.

"I know 'Now I lay me down to sleep.'"

"Good," I said, "that'll work."

When he asked me if I would hold his hand, something in me snapped. This kid deserved more than just having his hand held. "I'll do better than that," I told him.

I knew I would catch flak from the other nurses and Corpsmen, as well as possible jeers from the patients, but I didn't care. Without a single look around me, I climbed onto the bed with him. I put my arms around him, stroking his face and his hair as he snuggled close to me. I kissed him on the cheek, and together we recited, "Now I lay me down to sleep. I pray the Lord my soul to keep. If I should die before I wake, I pray the Lord my soul to take."

Then he looked at me and said just one more sentence, "I love you, Momma, I love you," before he died in my arms—quietly and peacefully—as if he really were just going to sleep.

After a minute, I slipped off his bed and looked around. I'm sure my face was set in a fierce scowl, daring anyone to give me a hard time. But I needn't have bothered. All the nurses and Corpsmen were breaking my rule and crying silently, tears filling their eyes or rolling down their cheeks.

I thought of the dead soldier's mother. She would receive a telegram informing her that her son had died of "war injuries." But that was all it would say. I thought she might always wonder how it had happened. Had he died out in the field? Had he been with anyone? Did he suffer? If I were his mother, I would *need* to know.

So later I sat down and wrote her a letter. I thought she'd want to hear that in her son's final moments, he had been thinking of her. But mostly I wanted her to know that her boy hadn't died alone.

Diana Dwan Poole

Hot Lips

"Loose Lips Sink Ships," the poster warned.

After a week of censorship duties, I was sure that the squadron harbored no loose lips. But we sure had plenty of "hot lips," and I was growing sick of playing censor.

Every night, a pile of mail was plunked down in front of me, and my job was to pore over it for any information that might be useful to the enemy or unnerving to the home front. It was a lousy way to spend an evening.

My eyes blurred, and my brain turned numb as I read the contents: Complete recitations of the daily menus. Wild guesses at when the war was going to end. Complaint after complaint about fellow soldiers. What else was there left to write about after years of war?

Love letters, of course. Boy-girl letters that positively sizzled with passion. I had my doubts about a number of those fiery attestations of undying love. I'd seen some of those "faithful" boyfriends in action in the "rest camps."

But the husband-wife letters—they were different. They were real, and playing Peeping Tom to them was hard. I still remember one particular letter as clearly as if I had read it in this morning's mail, though it's been forty-five years now.

The letter was written by a ground crewman I didn't know, and the separation from his wife had become unbearable for him. "I must meet you tonight," the man wrote his wife. "And tomorrow night. And the night after that."

What was he talking about? We were on Corsica, an island thousands of miles away from her in the States. "Nine P.M.," he reminded her. "Meet me by the light of the moon." He even specified where he would meet her—a little building near the squadron operations office. *That would be a trick,* I thought. Besides, 9 P.M. here was full sun back in the States.

I folded the letter, placed it back in the envelope and finished my pile. *It isn't any business of mine anyway,* I told myself.

But as 9 P.M. drew near, my curiosity got the best of me, and I strolled by the operations office in the direction of that little building. A full moon was out, and I could see everything clearly. I stopped short when I saw the figure outlined in the moonlight. A lone man. His head was bowed toward his shadow on the ground, his eyes closed in disappointment. Surely he hadn't really expected her to be there?

Yet as I studied the husband's face in the moonlight, his eyes tightly shut, I read not disappointment but intense concentration. That's when I realized what was happening. As far as he was concerned, he wasn't standing by an old operations building in Corsica at all. He had transported himself to be with his wife, just as she had done, and was doing whatever it is married lovers do when they rendezvous unnoticed by the world in a private little corner, after long months of separation.

I quickly turned and walked off into the night, ashamed

that I had played voyeur to such an intimate rendezvous. As I walked back to my tent, though, I couldn't help but feel warm inside. I had just seen devotion that defied time and space. It was a love that nothing could censor.

Philip Weiner
Submitted by Rebecca Langston

Lord of the Chinese Flies

In the summer of 1952, we were in Prisoner Camp 5 located in Pyoktong, North Korea. The peace talks were progressing pretty well, and things were going a little better in the camp.

One morning, we noticed a Chinese guard over in the corner with a flyswatter. We watched him swat a fly, pick it up and put it in a little envelope. Pretty soon, he swatted another fly and put that in the envelope. The guards were always doing strange things, so we didn't pay much attention to him.

But the next day, we saw another guard swatting flies and doing the same thing. Now our curiosity got the best of us, so we asked one of the camp instructors what they were doing. He told us that they had launched a fly-killing project: They were going to make China the most fly-free country in the world. He told us it was the duty of citizens, soldiers, students—of *everyone*—to participate.

It sounded like their starling-killing campaign of a few years earlier. When the starlings were eating all the grain in the fields, they killed all the starlings, only to find out that the insects began eating all the grain. They didn't seem to have learned much from that.

Okay, so now they were going to kill flies. Why, we asked the instructor, were they saving the dead flies? He told us that as an incentive, people were awarded points for the number of flies they turned in. They were working to accumulate enough points to receive a Mao Tse-tung Badge from the camp commander.

One of our GIs popped up and asked if the POWs could collect flies. The instructor told us that he would think about it.

A few days later at the morning formation, it was announced that anyone of us who would like to participate in this campaign could volunteer by raising our hands. Those who raised their hands would be issued a flyswatter. He also announced that as an incentive to kill flies, they would give out a factory-made cigarette for every two hundred flies turned in.

Everyone raised their hand. And by the next day, everybody was swatting flies and saving them. The Chinese kept their word, and we started to get real cigarettes in exchange for flies. It wasn't an easy job, though. It was difficult to kill two hundred flies; you could swat for an entire day and have less than fifty.

Some of us, including me, began playing poker for flies. "I'll call your four flies and raise you three." This game went on until we noticed the flies were getting worn out being pushed around the table. Then, one very enterprising soldier raised the stakes.

Recently we had been issued new socks. We really didn't need them, as we had been without them for so long. This soldier took his sock and slowly unraveled it into a long string, and he then made a very finely woven net. He was very talented, designing a net that looked like a minnow trap—where the fish get in through a small opening but can't find their way out.

He took that out to the slit trench latrine and set it over one of the holes. On the first day, he caught over five hundred flies. We doubted that the Chinese could honor their commitment under the circumstances, but to our surprise, they did. They paid him off with cigarettes.

Immediately, everyone was trying to make a fly trap, which created some unusual problems. One day I almost got into a fight. When I went out to use the latrine, all six holes were covered with various types of fly traps. I picked up one, put it aside and sat down. Instantly a man came over and asked me, what did I think I was doing. I told him it was obvious what I was doing. He told me to use one of the other holes and move somebody else's trap.

By this time, we were turning in so many flies that every night we could look up on the hill and see the Chinese nurses up at headquarters, holding chopsticks, counting flies and keeping records.

Apparently, the administrative work became so much that it was announced that they would no longer count flies, they would weigh them. They secured a very fine scale, like a jeweler's scale, and weighed two hundred flies to set the quota. They cheated a bit, but what could we do? Whatever our reward, it was better than nothing.

Then they stopped collecting them from us on the day they were caught, but instead waited till the next day, as flies that are saved overnight tend to dry out and don't weigh nearly as much as a fresh fly. This caused a real dilemma. How were we going to keep the weight on the flies overnight? A lot of things were tried, some worked and some didn't. To retain the moisture level, most of the fellows took a little piece of cloth, wet it and laid it over the dead flies until just before collection.

There was one system that worked unfailingly—and

then some. One of my friends, who was called "Sake" because that was all he drank when he was in Tokyo, had become a real expert at swatting flies. He would swat the blue-green flies, the big ones. He was an artist, for he would hit them just right so they would roll over dead; he didn't squash them. I asked him what he was doing with them, and he said, "Chik, come over to my hut tonight, and I will show you something special."

I went over that night, and he was there, bent over a little bench with his flies. He had a small, flat, sharp piece of metal in one hand. He told me that while he was on a work detail down at the riverbank, he had found a couple of toothpaste tubes—the old kind that were made of lead foil. While I watched, he used the piece of metal as a tool, cutting a thin strip of the lead foil from the tube, rolling it up and inserting it inside the fly. The Chinese never did find out why his flies weighed so much.

After that, I stopped calling him Sake. He'd undoubtedly earned his new title: Lord of the Chinese Flies.

Akira B. Chikami

A Show of Strength

In war nothing is impossible, provided you use audacity.

General George S. Patton

In the spring of 1945, the war was almost over in Northern Italy. My squadron, the Ninety-first Cavalry Reconnaissance Squadron, an armored company consisting of light tanks, was encamped in the Po River Valley.

By this time, the Germans realized the end was near and were surrendering in large numbers.

A German general in our area had indicated that he was interested in talking with an Allied officer. It was assumed he wanted to discuss surrendering, since the German insisted on meeting with an officer of equal rank, a common requirement for surrender negotiations. It was arranged that the two generals would meet in a small village nearby.

The decision to surrender is always a difficult one. To put one's own fate and the fate of the men you command into the enemy's hands is a daunting prospect and needs to be considered carefully.

It seems that someone in authority thought this German general might need a little encouragement and came up with a plan to help him make the right choice.

At the agreed-upon time, a member of the American military police escorted the general to a building along the main street of the village. The streets were narrow, and the building was very close to the street, with only a tiny strip of sidewalk separating them. As the general walked up the street, the first of a line of American tanks began to rumble past him, almost running over his boot, as it passed with only an inch or two to spare. The tanks continued to roll by as he turned into the doorway.

Once he was inside, tank after tank passed by the window of the room where the two generals were meeting. The tanks were so heavy that the floors vibrated each time a tank went by. There was no way anyone could ignore this impressive show of strength.

After almost one hundred tanks went by with no sign of the parade ending, the general must have seen enough. He couldn't wait to get his signature on the papers spread in front of him on the table. He surrendered all the troops under his command, bringing the Allies another step closer to victory and to the end of the war.

What the general didn't know was that on the day of the meeting, our armored company received orders to drive our five tanks up the main street of the village. We were instructed to start our drive at a certain time and proceed north past the meeting location. Once we were three or four blocks past the building, we were to go east two or three blocks, south eight or ten blocks, and west to the main street again, and then we were to repeat the process until we received further orders.

We followed our orders, and after we'd made this loop

about twenty times, the signal came for us to stop. The Germans had raised the white flag!

We went to refuel our nearly empty tanks, feeling that the money for fuel had been well spent and had surely saved more than a few lives on both sides.

Ivan W. Marion
Submitted by Edward Daszynski

Stalag Las Vegas

My buddy Milt Moore and I were part of the 101st Airborne Division, "A" Battery, 321st Glider Field Artillery Battalion and participated in Operation Market Garden, on September 19, 1944. Our glider was shot down, and we were captured. Eventually, we were sent to Stalag 7–A near Munich, where living quarters were less than adequate and the food was poor and limited. Though each man was supposed to receive one Red Cross package a week, this rarely happened. Six of us would split one package, containing among other things, cigarettes.

Milt was a smoker, but I was not. So I did what many other servicemen did—bartered the smokes for candy and other goodies.

During the day, we were sent out of the camp to work. Most of our forced labor was done in Munich or nearby Landshut, usually building or repairing the railroad lines. We would often work for weeks to repair a particular stretch of tracks, only to discover the next day it had been bombed by our planes overnight.

Despite the efforts we put into our repairs, we didn't mind the destruction one bit, because we knew the

Germans couldn't make use of the tracks and roadways we were repairing under duress. Besides, the renewed damage provided more opportunities for us to go into the city to work. We considered our daily work trips into Munich an economic benefit.

Among other things, we used the city as a means to trade our cigarettes for bread and meat. While at our work detail location, we were often approached by black-marketers and ordinary citizens who would ask the guard if anyone had cigarettes to trade for bread. *"Cigareten fur Brot? Cigareten fur Brot?"* they would call out.

Before the barter could begin, we would have to bribe the guard with one or two cigarettes so we could make the trade. Then the bread itself would cost anywhere from five to ten cigarettes. Once in a while, we'd get a guard that wouldn't allow trading with civilians, but that was rare.

One day in Munich, we were working on the railroad tracks outside a machine shop. During our lunch break, a German worker wearing a greasy leather apron came out of the shop and asked me, in broken English, if we were Americans. When I told him we were, he said he had something to show me. Out of his apron, he pulled a grimy letter, obviously handled many times. He said it was from his son, who was at a POW camp in America, in a place called Georgia. His son wrote that he always had fresh fruit to eat and slept in a bed with sheets on it. The machinist wanted to know if this was the truth, or if his son was just telling him that to make him feel better. I told him it was true and that the United States treated all POWs that well or better. The German citizen said he felt badly that we had to work so hard and were given such poor food but, he explained, that was all his country had at present.

Seeing the sincerity in his eyes, I knew he was looking at me not as a captured enemy soldier, but as a man. It was a feeling I hadn't had before in Germany.

Then he asked if there was anything he could do for me to show his appreciation for how my country was treating his son.

For some reason, his simple offer, a gesture of respect and gratitude amid the brutality of war, affected me. For a moment, I did not know what to say. I looked down at the ground and then back at this man's face. *What could he possibly do for me?* I wondered. Then, suddenly, I remembered a makeshift lamp I had fabricated from a tin can and a wick-controlled element (stolen from a railroad signal lantern). I told the man I could surely use some fuel oil to burn in my little lamp.

He left and quickly returned with three soda bottles of fuel. After bribing the guard (I don't remember how many cigarettes I lost on that one), I was able to keep the bottles, which I put under my belt and covered with my thin coat.

Unfortunately, on the ride back to camp, one of the bottles broke, filling my pants with glass shards and fuel oil. I warned everyone around me not to light any cigarettes—I would have gone up like a torch!

Safely back in camp, I now had all the ingredients for a lamp, which we could use after our carbide lights burned out each night. Equipped with the lamp and a deck of cards that I had received back at the German captivity distribution camp, Milt and I had a new source of revenue.

After our official barracks lights went out, we threw a blanket on a table and ran a poker game. Naturally, cigarettes were used for money in this gambling venture. Neither Milt nor I played in the game, but we dragged one "house" cigarette from every pot. And from that day on, I always had cigarettes to trade, and Milt always had as many as he wanted to smoke.

This arrangement lasted for many months, providing a great deal of recreation for our buddies, and kept Milt and me "in the chips." Incidentally, our patrolling guards knew that this clandestine game was going on. About once a week, a guard would come into the barracks, lay his hat beside the table and scoop that pot of cigarettes into the hat. That was his cut for allowing the game. The guard was happy, Milt and I were happy, and the only guys complaining were the ones whose cigarettes were in the confiscated pot!

Our nightly parties boosted morale for everyone, but what helped me most were not the games but the German worker in the greasy apron. He had shown me, a stranger and an enemy, that even war cannot wipe out the simple courtesies of the human heart.

Robert D. Reeves

The Greatest Compliment

My small unit was one of the very first to arrive in Sarajevo after the signing of the Dayton Peace Accords. A day or two after our arrival, I began making the rounds, visiting other units in and around the city.

One of the American communications outfits I went to see had set up in an old Ottoman fort high on a mountaintop overlooking the city. The road to the fort was along a mountain path, barely passable in our humvee. At one point, the road squeezed between a sheer vertical drop on the left and a small village on the right. Absolutely pressed against the road, the tiny community was wedged into a minuscule space between the path and the wall of the mountain.

I was riding in the front side passenger seat of the humvee with my arm out of the window. In the arcane reasoning of the military, because we were part of an international force, the national flag emblem was affixed on the right shoulder of our BDUs (not on the left as was normally the case). Thus, the American flag was showing on the sleeve that was nearer to the open window.

In the United States, there were—and still are—many

mixed emotions about the mission in Bosnia. Some were shared by the troops who were sent there. But whatever our feelings, it became immediately clear that the people who appreciated us most were the very old and the very young. Our presence allowed the old people to live their lives in dignity and the young to play in the sunshine, and both groups were always grateful.

As our vehicle inched through the village, two elderly Muslim gentlemen were drinking tea at a small table set right next to the road. We were so close that as we inched by, one of them reached out and touched the flag on my arm and said something to me in very passable English.

I smiled at him and for the rest of the drive wondered at his words. When I returned to my quarters, I asked about the significance of the expression the old gentleman had spoken. It turned out that he had used an ancient phrase—words with meaning so deep they were reserved for use in his culture only to express the most profound appreciation.

What the old man said when he touched the American flag was, "We will love you for a thousand years."

Thomas D. Phillips

Operation Chow Down

As World War II was winding down, the starvation situation was acute in many parts of Holland. The B-17 fleet, based in Snetterton Heath, England, was designated to drop parcels of food rations in the soccer fields of The Hague, in an action called "Operation Chow Down." All armament was removed from the planes, with the understanding that the remaining German troops should fire no shots on the aircraft. Run after run was made with bomb bay doors wide open to disperse heavy food supplies. Skimming low over the fields, the B-17s dropped their food "bombs" while the hungry survivors scrambled below to seek a share of the needed nourishment. After so many months of empty bellies, the bundles left the field immediately. On the final run of the program, the grateful receivers had fashioned a gigantic display on the raised dike at the end of the field, their most prized tulip plants spelling out in vivid color the words "THANKS YANKS."

Richard Oakley

Amina's Way

East Timor. Kosovo. Chechnya. Every day it seems there's another "hot spot" somewhere in the world—people in some faraway location in a crisis that doesn't touch our lives. I used to think that, too, until 1993, when I deployed as an Army chaplain to Somalia.

The medical group I was with was sent to Mogadishu, the once elegant capital city of Somalia. By then, many houses sat empty or ruined, but it didn't take much imagination to see how handsome the architecture was, how it once must have been a charming coastal city with a Mediterranean flair.

On the main road that ran in front of our heavily guarded compound was a large refugee camp and feeding center. Although it was only half a block away, it took quite an effort for us to get there. The streets were alive with gangs, vandals and sniper fire, so we couldn't go anywhere without full regalia, including flak jackets and helmets—not the outfit of choice in ninety-degree heat!

Tall walls surrounded the feeding center. On my first visit there, I noticed that somehow it managed to be an island of sanity in the midst of a world gone berserk. I would soon discover that the physical and mental health of the people here was due to the director, a woman known only as Amina.

The first time I met her, she responded to my introduction with a smile. After that, I was always greeted with a hug. She was a large-boned, dark-skinned woman, maybe five feet, four inches tall. But what you first noticed about her was the love and concern she had for each person in her camp. The second thing you noticed was her authority. She treated the inhabitants like her extended family, and they in turn gave her great respect. She might have technically been the camp's director, but in fact she was the matriarch of a large clan, one formed by circumstance.

Amina was friendly with everyone, but somehow she and I formed a special bond, even though we had to speak to each other through an interpreter or in broken foreign words and phrases. Maybe part of it was a sisterhood, the coming together of two women trying to help hold lives together in the midst of chaos.

Amina wore brightly colored scarves, as did all the women in the camp, and her hands and arms always had pictures painted on them. The pictures were intricate, made with stains of berries, like temporary tattoos. They were signs of respect and affection from the native artists who drew them.

Shortly after arrival, we were taken back to see the refugee camp section, where families lived together in row after row of igloo-shaped dwellings fashioned out of large sticks covered with anything available: cardboard, corrugated metal, plastic tarps, even basketball hoops fastened down sideways.

I wondered how I—how any of us—would feel if our comfortable world collapsed overnight and we were left living in cardboard, unable to even provide food for our children.

But Amina did not allow a spirit of bitterness in her camp. I saw this in the four overcrowded schoolrooms. The children, crammed three or four to a desk, had no books or notebooks. There were no pencils or chalk, so the teachers taught by having the children recite out loud—English, Arabic and math. Yet there was an eagerness to learn.

We soldiers could tell what the week's English lesson had been because, as soon as we entered the camp, we would be greeted with the day's new phrase: What's your name? Where do you live? The week they asked, "How old are you?" I was chagrined to discover they didn't understand my answer. I guess they hadn't learned to count that high in English!

But most memorable for me was how the children loved to dance. Their lives had been shattered—their homes, toys and clothes taken away—but somehow they all seemed to share Amina's spirit of gratitude: Just to be alive, with food and water, was enough.

By the second or third time I entered the compound, two little girls were bold enough to come up to me. Because I was a woman, they wanted to show me a girls' folk dance. It started with shouts of *"Yupa! Yupa! Yupa!"* and the shaking of the shoulders. When the older girls heard it, they circled around, clapping or shaking empty water bottles, which had become maracas.

When I began to dance with them, they whooped with delight. I couldn't believe it. We were in the middle of a war zone—and the children were teaching me to dance.

After that, I tried to bring my guitar when I came, and I taught the kids some simple American dances like the hokey pokey. My visits there were a happy time.

Then one day, there was a small incident that could have become a crisis.

After a couple of soldiers and I safely reached the

feeding center compound and the doors were shut behind us, I took off my helmet and reached into my back pocket for my cap. It was missing.

An Army cap would be a real prize to kids who had nothing. I knew that anything stolen on the streets of Mogadishu would never be seen again, guaranteed. But I also knew that Amina made sure we were treated as honored guests in the compound. And in civilized Somalia, honored guests are protected, not pickpocketed. It was even more important to Amina to teach these children values than it was to teach them to read or do math. The whole camp would feel its honor had been slighted if I accused anyone of taking my cap.

So I waited until I was off to one side with one of the teachers. "My cap may have fallen out of my pocket," I said. "If anyone finds one lying around, it's probably mine."

I smiled and went on with the visit.

The very next time we came back, the same teacher wordlessly handed me the cap. Even though we never talked about it, I knew that word had gone through the camp that someone had taken something belonging to a guest, and this was not to be tolerated. It had been returned right away.

In March, near the time when our unit's tour of duty was over, I returned to the camp for the last time. The little girls saw us immediately. *"Yupa! Yupa! Yupa!"* came the immediate invitation to the dance.

Amina saw me, too, and came over. She and I knew that I would soon be leaving, going back to a soft bed, a television and grocery stores with shelves stocked full of food. She, on the other hand, would stay here with the families and children she claimed as her own. Who knew what the future held for her, for the children in the camp? For her, this was not somewhere to come for three months to try to help. This was her home. *It would be so easy to resent my going,* I thought.

But that was not Amina's way. She came over to where I danced with the youngest girls, a smile on her face, tears in her eyes. And as the older girls gathered closer, chanting and clapping, she joined me in the middle of the circle, shaking her shoulders, squatting and jumping with all her might, with a powerful joy.

The other girls stopped dancing and stepped back, squealing with delight and clapping in time as Amina and I did a final dance of celebration—for how good it is to have friends and to love God, and for the sheer privilege of being alive.

Chances are good that I'll never see Amina again. After we left, the fighting in Mogadishu intensified at times, to the point that I'm not even sure if the feeding compound still stands.

But for me, Amina put a face on the war. Now I know that most of the people affected by war aren't the warlords or generals or even the soldiers. They are people not much different from us, trying to feed their families, to teach their children right from wrong.

And sometimes, even when there seems to be nothing to celebrate, they can teach us to dance.

Barbara K. Sherer
As told to Sharon Linnéa

Morse Code

Davey and I bent over our task with the earnest concentration of twelve-year-old boys, nailing kitchen towels to two old broomsticks. Davey was trying to earn his Boy Scout merit badge in communications and had asked me to help him learn Morse code. I found the project so interesting that I was able to squelch my feelings of disappointment that were mingled with just a bit of jealousy. My family was poor, and we couldn't afford the twelve-dollar uniform I needed to join the Boy Scouts. There would be no merit badges for me, no need for me to learn Morse code at all. But that wasn't Davey's fault, and Davey was my friend.

Davey lived two blocks away from me in Philadelphia, and each day after school, we would run home from school, grab our broomstick flags and stand in the middle of Osage Avenue, learning to send messages to each other. Dot on the right. Dash on the left. Be careful not to foul the flag. We were soon so good at reading each other's messages over the two-block span that I pretended we were in the line of battle, skillfully communicating crucial, life-saving messages.

Our efforts paid off. Davey earned his merit badge, and I . . . well, I knew Morse code. And even if it hadn't earned me anything, I figured I was the better for it. I kept up my knowledge of it during my teen years, occasionally interpreting coded messages that came over my shortwave radio.

Years passed, and I finally had a uniform—one belonging to the United States Army. Memories of Davey and my old neighborhood in Philadelphia had faded into nostalgia, but for some reason, the Morse code had stuck with me, though I had no more use for it than I did back then.

Until the typhoon hit. My company was stationed at Dulag on the island of Leyte in the Philippines when a tremendous storm blew onto us, wiping out visibility and drowning us in a whipping torrent of rain and wind. Into this churning chaos, a landing ship tank (LST), loaded with equipment, dangerously approached the beach where we were encamped. The ship's officer was clearly lost.

Shrugging on my rain gear, I slipped out into the storm with my lieutenant and stood at the shore beside him. The officer on the LST was shouting through the storm to us, but all we could hear was the howling wind and downpour. Communication was futile. I stood there helplessly watching the officer's dim form as he gestured frantically from a distance. It reminded me of something, something from long ago. Suddenly, I ran back to my tent, grabbed my flashlight and aimed it at the officer on the bridge. "WHAT DO YOU WANT?" I flashed out in Morse code.

The officer, no doubt surprised to find an Army man who knew Morse code, jumped at his signal lamp, a twelve-inch spotlight, and signaled back: "WHERE IS TARRAGONA?"

Topography was my company's specialty: I made maps of the area. Without hesitation, I skillfully dotted and dashed: "TARRAGONA IS FIVE MILES SOUTH OF HERE."

The officer quickly turned away to reroute his ship to the south and deliver the much-needed equipment. As the LST retreated into the dark storm, one final message flashed to the shore: "- -. -..-("TNX")."

Thanks. I grinned like a little boy. I had just earned my merit badge.

Bernard Belasco

The Twelfth Man

It was Friday evening in May 1945, less than two weeks after the end of World War II. *Shabbos* (Sabbath) was being celebrated in a small synagogue in the Golders Green section of London. A man stood in the back of the synagogue, a lonely figure, clad in new, ill-fitting clothes. His face was pale, his body emaciated. After the service, the rabbi greeted the stranger, and invited the newcomer home to share *Shabbos* with the rabbi and his family. At the meal, with the sensitive encouragement of his host, the man began to tell a little about himself.

His name, he said, was Elimelech Kinderlehrer. He was an Orthodox Jew from the Polish town of Sosnoviec. When the Nazis conquered Poland, he and his family members had been rounded up and sent to concentration camps. Transferred numerous times from one labor camp to another, he soon lost contact with his family. As far as he knew, his wife and children were dead.

A little more than two weeks before this *Shabbos* in Golders Green, Elimelech had been among a group of Jews forced to participate in one of the infamous Nazi death marches. His listeners gasped in horror, one question filling every mind: How was it possible that he was here, alive and safe?

The Germans, he continued calmly, battered from the east by the Russian armies and from the west by the Americans and British, realized that the war was going to end soon in a debacle for the Third Reich. The S.S. troops were taking their prisoners from the concentration camps in Poland to slave labor camps in Germany, because they feared the Allies would discover and liberate the captives. The emaciated Jews were marched by the thousands through cities, towns and fields. Those who were not strong enough to maintain the pace were shot. Thousands of Jews were killed this way, only days before the war ended.

Elimelech was among the marchers. At almost fifty years of age, with a history of more than four years in various concentration camps, he was fragile, weak and afflicted with stomach ailments that made it exceptionally difficult for him to keep up. As the walk wore on and his pain became more acute, it was becoming nearly impossible for him to continue.

His particular group was being guarded by eight Nazi soldiers. Desperate, Elimelech pleaded with one of them, "Please let me stay behind and rest for a few minutes. I am in terrible pain."

"You want to rest?" the Nazi soldier roared. "I will kill you and let you rest forever!"

"Please, no," Elimelech begged. "Let me stay here two minutes—then I will run and catch up with you."

For some reason the soldier let him stay behind, but he warned him, "If you don't catch up with us, I will come back and finish you off."

Elimelech hobbled off to the side as the rest of his group continued marching. Hundreds of tired, jealous eyes peered at him. He took but a few steps and noticed a little shed just off the road. Hoping to find some respite from the cold and a place to sit, he opened the door and walked in.

There was just enough room in the shed to sit and relax for a minute or two. As soon as Elimelech entered, he heard a dog barking outside. He stood up quietly, made sure the door was closed and peeked out through the little window in the door. Just in front of the shed was a huge German shepherd, exhaling puffs in the cold air, as he barked fiercely at some people passing by.

Making sure the door was closed securely, Elimelech sat down quietly. In a few minutes he heard some Polish peasants approaching. As they came towards the shed, the dog began barking again. The peasants maintained a distance from the dog and continued walking down the road.

A short time later, with the dog still just inches away from him on the other side of the door, two Nazi soldiers came towards the shed. Once again the dog began barking thunderously. The Nazis stepped back, but Elimelech could hear one of them shouting in fury. "Where is that Jew?" the soldier yelled. "I told him to be back in two minutes."

"I don't see him," replied his comrade.

"Maybe he is hiding in that shed," the first soldier offered.

"Don't be foolish," the second said. "There is no way the Jew could have gotten past that dog."

The first soldier seemed to be convinced. The two soldiers walked away and resumed their vigil on the Jews marching ahead. Elimelech heard them leave and breathed a sigh of relief.

But his relief was short-lived. He had not seen the German shepherd when he walked into the shed and he had no idea where the dog had come from; now he realized he could not possibly walk out for fear that the dog would attack him, or at the least, give away his presence by its barking.

He was so tired that within moments he fell asleep. As he lay slumped over, he dreamt of his father, who said, "Elimelech, do not be afraid. I promise you that either this week or next week you will be sitting at a *Shabbos* table with wine and *challah* (bread)."

Exhausted, Elimelech slept for a few hours. When he woke up, the dog and the Nazis were gone. Could he chance walking along the road? Surely, other soldiers would find him. Unsure of what to do, he stayed in the shed. A few minutes later, he saw a small group of prisoners come walking down the road. They did not look Jewish, and they were more robust and alive than the labor camp inmates. One of them noticed Elimelech looking out of the shed and immediately came running over.

"If you are hiding," the man said with a British accent, "we can save you and you can save us." He explained that his group of twelve British prisoners of war was being taken to an unknown destination, but that one of their mates had escaped. The German guards would soon count them again, and when they realized that one had run away, they might all lose their lives. The British serviceman assured Elimelech that if he would come along, the British prisoners would give him some of their Army clothes to wear and they would claim he was the twelfth man.

Elimelech thought about it and agreed. He reasoned that among the British group he might receive better food and possibly a chance at survival. He could see that the German soldiers treated the British better than they treated the Jews. The prisoners told him that he would have to act shell-shocked, as if he could not speak; otherwise his Polish accent would give him away and jeopardize all of them.

The twelve "Britishers" began their trek together, and a

while later they were ordered to stop and identify themselves. One by one they called out their names: "Gilliam, Reese, Snider, Hodges . . ." and when they came to Elimelech, he just looked straight ahead as the others called out, "He can't talk. He is shell-shocked."

The Nazi soldier didn't seem to care. He just told them to march on. For the next few days, the British soldiers protected Elimelech, their savior. Two days later, the war was over, and they were led to British headquarters and safety. When a British officer found out that his men had taken along this foreigner, he was furious. "He could have been a German spy!" he screamed.

The British prisoners, giddy with freedom and grateful to Elimelech, assured the officer that their "mute" friend could undoubtedly be trusted. For two more days, hundreds of erstwhile British prisoners were interviewed and allowed to return home, while Elimelech was left alone, a man without a destination. Eventually, a British officer asked him where he wished to go, and Elimelech said he wanted to return to Sosnoviec. The officer, out of compassion for Elimelech, discouraged him from going back because of the lack of stability in the area. He assured him that he would be taken to safety in England.

In England, Elimelech was given fresh clothes and asked where he would like to go. Elimelech said he had no relatives in England but would appreciate being taken to an Orthodox Jewish area. The officers made some inquiries and told him that there was a Jewish community in Golders Green. They gave him a ride there and dropped him off on a Friday afternoon. Alone, bewildered and directionless, Elimelech walked a few blocks and then saw the sign for the synagogue. It was the first time in four years he had been in a synagogue.

As he finished his story, he looked around the table at his deeply moved hosts and said, "And here I am at a

Shabbos table, with wine and *challah,* just as my father promised me less than two weeks ago!"

Almighty God, who has made so many miracles, made a miracle for Elimelech as well—from a shed, a dog and eleven British soldiers.

Rabbi Paysach J. Krohn
Condensed from Along the Maggid's Journey

5

THE HOME FRONT

The eyes of the world are upon you. The hopes and prayers of liberty-loving people everywhere march with you.

General Dwight D. Eisenhower,
order to his troops on D-Day, 1944

Bob "March Field" Hope

In 1939, we didn't take World War II seriously. The enemy armies were stalled at the French frontier, daring each other like kids with a chip on their shoulder.

1940 dawned. It was a year in which Hitler's planes and tanks overran France and pushed the British Army into the channel. Still, we weren't too concerned over here.

Then one night, after our weekly radio program "The Bob Hope Pepsodent Show," one of the sponsor's men came up to me and said that Pepsodent wanted to take the program out of its Hollywood studio and visit March Field, one of our military air bases.

I said, "What for? There's no war going on here. Why should we drag the whole show down there? We're doing all right without going out of the studio."

I was resisting an idea that was to change my whole life.

The next Tuesday, May 6, 1941, I found myself on a bus with Jerry Colonna, Bill Goodwin and the rest of the crowd, on our way to Riverside, California, and March Field for our first show for the U.S. Army. We had no idea we were going to discover an audience so ready for laughter. It would make what we did for a living seem like stealing money.

Also on the bus was Frances Langford, who had replaced Judy Garland as our leading singer. I had always thought her fragile and vulnerable, but we were soon to learn Frances was the bravest of us all. She was actually enthusiastic about March Field.

I'll never forget the moment when that bus pulled through the gates and we were mobbed by a bunch of homesick kids in badly fitting fatigues, screaming greetings. I got out my pen to sign a few hundred autographs, and they knocked me aside and went for Frances Langford. Frances, of course, was a real beauty, but it didn't really matter to those guys. After thirteen weeks in basic training, anything female looked good.

Tom Harmon, then one of the biggest football names in the country, was in uniform at the base and helped us control the enthusiasm. Tom told us what we were doing for the United States Army was the biggest thing that had happened to the military since Gettysburg; we had gotten live girls past the sentries at the gate.

In those simple radio days, there were no cameras, no lights, no huge group of technicians; there were just me, the cast, the writers, the band and two guys with a microphone. We didn't even need idiot cards. On radio, we all read from scripts.

We didn't realize that all the rules of comedy were going to be changed. We represented everything those new recruits didn't have: home cooking, mother and soft roommates. Their real enemies, even after war broke out, were never just the Germans or the Japanese. The enemies were boredom, mud, officers and abstinence. Any joke that touched those nerves was a sure thing.

That night, we were in comedy heaven and didn't know it. "Good evening, ladies and gentlemen. This is Bob

'March Field' Hope telling all aviators, while we can't advise you on how to protect your 'chutes, there's nothing like Pepsodent to protect your toots."

The laughter was so loud, I looked down to see if my pants had fallen. I mean, there must have been something funnier going on than that joke. There wasn't.

"I want to tell you that I'm thrilled to be here. But I'm really here on business. I came up to look at some of the sweaters I knitted."

A howl. *What was going on?* I plowed ahead.

"One of the aviators here took me for a plane ride this afternoon. I wasn't frightened but, at two thousand feet, one of my goose pimples bailed out."

I got goose pimples myself from the roar that followed that one. Then I started to understand. What I said coincided with what these guys were feeling, and laughter was the only way they could communicate how they felt to the rest of the country. I was their messenger boy. A ski-nosed Western Union.

In the years that followed, I came to see that we brought them a special message, too. The soldiers all knew us by our voices. When they heard us speak, they were back in the living room, Tuesday night at ten, in front of the Atwater Kent radio, with Mom and Dad and their pesky little brother or sister, although, at that moment, they might really be in North Africa or Sicily or Guadalcanal. That's why, many times when they were laughing the hardest, I could see some of them trying to hide their tears.

As time passed, we realized the reason for our overwhelming welcome from the troops all over the world was that we spelled, more than anything else, "home."

Bob Hope with Melville Shavelson

A Flag of Any Size

Deeds Not Words

Twenty-second Infantry Regiment

Frank Havlik leaned against the wet brick of the Seventh Avenue firehouse and lit a filtered Camel. Frank was one of a group of middle-aged fathers and husbands living in Hudson, New York, who unofficially gathered every Saturday to debate and philosophize. Today, conversations drifted from weather to politics to the war.

The war in the summer of 1968 was in Vietnam. Frank's only son, John Martin Havlik, whom they called Marty, had enlisted six months earlier and was serving his first tour in the jungle. Marty's mother had begged him not to go, and his four younger sisters had all cried the day he left home. The family had already lost a neighbor to the conflict thousands of miles away, but Marty was not deterred. He felt it was his duty as an American to help the less fortunate—a sense of duty Frank had instilled in him at an early age. Frank was proud of his son and respected his decision to enlist.

"How's Marty?" asked one of the men.

"He seems to be all right. We just got a letter this week," Frank replied.

Frank had already read the letter a dozen times. In the back of Frank's mind, a constant worry for his son pulled at him, so reading about Marty's exploits, no matter how dangerous, was always comforting. Maybe it was simply knowing Marty was alive and well at the time the letter was written.

Frank abbreviated a story from his son's latest letter for his listeners. "He complains there isn't enough to drink and that it's too damn hot. After being in the swamps for a few weeks, he was issued a few canteens of water to shower with, but he decided to drink it instead."

The men all laughed. Most had known Marty since his baptism.

"I would sure hate to be bunking next to him," one man called out.

"Especially if he smells like his father," another man remarked.

Frank crushed out his cigarette on the sidewalk. His friends could always make him laugh and forget about his worries—at least temporarily.

As the conversation wound down, the men noticed they were not alone on Seventh Avenue. The nice weather had drawn a crowd to the park across the street, where one man, who was probably only a few years older than Marty, carried a megaphone and seemed to be leading the gathering.

"How many more must die?" the man with the megaphone shouted. "What are they dying for?"

Hudson was not a big town. The men often joked, "You'd have to quadruple the population of the town just to fill up Yankee Stadium." But like many American towns that summer, Hudson had its own Vietnam protests.

Frank had seen these types of unscheduled rallies

before. They mostly consisted of bored teenagers yelling, singing or praying. There was never any threat of violence. Today, however, looked to be different. Frank did not recognize the man with the megaphone. His tall, lanky body and bright red hair would have been easy to remember. The stranger was new to Hudson but not new to protests. He was an electrifying speaker. Soon the crowd was motivated, yelling to a beat and throwing their fists in the air in unison. Frank could not remember a rally ever being so loud. He felt the hair on his arm raise. Standing where they were—just across the street—the men by the firehouse could not help but watch.

"This country is sending its sons to die," the stranger shouted. The crowd agreed with a chorus of boos and obscenities. At the height of the excitement, the leader grabbed a small American flag that was nearby and pulled it out of the ground. It was the kind of flag people line their driveways with on the Fourth of July or place in honor at a tombstone. It was not the six-foot hand-stitched version of Old Glory, but it was an American flag nonetheless. The man held up the small flag and held a lighter flame near its edge.

None of the men had noticed Frank leave the firehouse. But, suddenly, he was there, next to the lighter-toting protester. Without a moment of hesitation, Frank grabbed the flag out of the stranger's hand.

Frank Havlik, son of a Czech immigrant, veteran of World War II and father of an American soldier serving in Vietnam, did not lecture the young man. He simply took the flag and returned with it to his spot, where he again leaned against the firehouse. He did not want to break up the protest; they were Americans, exercising their rights. Frank only wanted to protect the flag he had fought for in France and that his son was fighting for now, in Vietnam.

The chanting ceased, and the fists were lowered. Eyes

darted back and forth between Frank and the red-haired stranger like an audience at Wimbledon. Neither made a move. Five minutes passed before everyone began to realize there would not be a fight. There would not be a martyr—or a bully. A man with long hair from the protesters' group broke the silence with the strum of a guitar. The tense moment passed, replaced by the sound of voices singing antiwar songs. Onlookers began to disperse. The red-haired stranger, no longer the leader, became a participant and joined the peaceful demonstration.

The men at the firehouse resumed their smoking and philosophizing, but no one commented on Frank's actions. Frank held on to the flag; he planned to put it back after the park was empty.

When the singing was done, the would-be flag burner crossed the street and approached the firehouse. The men sitting on the steps started to stand, ready to defend their own, but when they saw the protester's face, they knew his approach was a white flag.

"I would like to put the flag back in the park," was all the young man said.

Frank handed over the small vinyl flag. "Thank you," he replied quietly.

Frank's story spread quickly. A few days later, the Hudson newspaper ran an article about the incident and included a picture of Frank with an American flag. Marty's sister clipped the article and picture and sent them to her brother in Vietnam.

The letter containing the article arrived in early fall. Marty slipped it and a short note out of the envelope. The picture of Frank and the flag immediately caught his attention. He read the article three times in a matter of minutes.

Marty shared the article with a few buddies, who told

others, and soon all the soldiers in Marty's company had heard about Marty's father and the flag.

Frank's act was a simple one, but it affected the young soldiers deeply. They had heard many stories of protests and riots in the States. They were even told not to wear their uniform home because of the negative attention it might bring. But the story of Frank saving one small flag made them realize some civilians supported them.

Marty carried the article in his helmet liner with his cigarettes for the remainder of his time in Vietnam. His father was not an articulate or emotional man, but the story reinforced what Marty already knew: Frank was proud of him and would always be behind him.

Stacy Havlik McAnulty

Too Young to Understand

I sighed and set aside my pen. Writing a letter to a Marine stationed in Cambodia was the last thing I wanted to be doing. Why was Grandma insisting that I be his pen pal?

Posters of Bobby Sherman and David Cassidy adorned the walls of my room, where I was working; my bed behind me was covered with a pink spread. I loved the Partridge Family and stuffed animals—in short, I was a typical, self-absorbed thirteen-year-old American girl. The Vietnam conflict was something my parents and other grown-ups fretted about. I was too young to understand that stuff.

"Dear Corporal Stephen Conboy," I wrote reluctantly. *I don't even know this guy,* I thought. *He won't write back!*

I was wrong. Corporal Conboy not only wrote back, but he sent me letters almost every day. Before long, I was hurrying home from school in the afternoons, searching through the mail for an envelope addressed to me in Steve's bold handwriting. When one was there, I'd flush with excitement, tearing open the letter as if there were a million dollars inside. There was no money; it was his words that were worth so much to me.

Opening each of his letters was like opening a window to gaze into a world I never knew existed. Steve described a war-torn Southeast Asia, completely unlike the safe and sleepy upstate New York town I called home. He told me about his duties there, his friends, his hopes, his concerns. But always, inevitably, Steve's letters turned to the children.

The fierce fighting in Cambodian jungles had orphaned many children, leaving them desperately in need of care. Steve spent much of his free time volunteering at an orphanage run by a group of French nuns, performing various chores and playing with the children. His kindness stirred my awakening conscience.

I filled boxes with chocolate bars and homemade cookies and shipped them to Steve to hand out in the orphanages. (I was only thirteen and a little vague on the nutritional benefits of the care packages I was sending.) But I was sincere. Like Steve, I felt that something about the orphans compelled me to do something—anything—to help.

"Tell me more about the orphans and how they got there," I would beg him in my letters, but no matter how many times I asked, Steve would never write about that.

When his tour of duty ended, Steve was reassigned to another part of the world, and his letters became less frequent, then discontinued altogether. His influence on me, though, had just begun.

Eventually, I abandoned David Cassidy, my pink bedspread and even my stuffed animals. I grew up, married and planned for a family. When, after several years, no children came, my husband and I discussed adoption. Memories of Steve's letters came to my mind. "Let's adopt from overseas," I urged my husband, and so we made a trip to Romania to visit the orphanages. Then I discovered why Steve Conboy had been so drawn to the Cambodian war orphans—and why he was never able to write about their stories.

As we walked through the orphanages, it crushed my spirit to see the neglected children. During our two trips there, we saw them freezing in their cribs in the harsh winters and sweltering in the scorching summers. Many of them were hanging on to life by a thread, with little hope. Their plight moved me beyond words.

Though my husband and I successfully adopted two of the orphans and brought them home to live in comfort and security, far from the neglect they would have known, I was haunted by the innocent, starving orphans who were still over there. I wanted to do something for them.

I began collecting items for care packages to send to the Romanian orphanages. No chocolate bars this time, but crate after crate of formula, medicine and toys. Our basement began to look like a mini-warehouse for a rescue mission.

One day, while I was labeling another care package to send, my mind drifted to thoughts of the young corporal who had been my pen pal twenty-five years before. I wondered if I could reach him now.

After some investigation, I found his current address. I contemplated the best way to contact him and decided I would rely on the connection we'd already established so many years earlier. Eagerly, I sat down to write him a letter.

I glanced at the pictures on my desk of our two smiling, healthy children. Then I picked up my pen. "I am regularly sending care packages to orphans in Romania," I began. "I don't have to describe to you their situation or how it touches my heart; I know you will remember from your own days in Cambodia." I paused, wondering what to say next. I wanted him to know that he had planted a seed that changed the course of my life. "I do want to tell you what your letters did to open my eyes to the world when I was a little girl," I continued. Then I told him about my children and asked him to write back.

When I received a letter addressed to me in his familiar bold handwriting, I ripped it open eagerly. Steve wrote that he was still a Marine and traveled all over the world. In fact, he had been surprised about my Romanian connection, since not long before he'd received my letter, he had requested an assignment in Romania!

Soon after, Steve accepted my invitation to meet our family. I was nervous, but when I finally saw the man who had given my fledgling conscience wings, something in me felt complete.

Since then, Steve and I have continued our friendship through letters, e-mail and the occasional phone call. I have shared my children's growth and progress with him, for in a very real way, they are his children, too—born of the dream he inspired in me when I was too young to understand but old enough to care.

Barbara Sue Canale

John and his crew members run from the North Platte canteen to catch the train. John is in the center of the photo, hatless, looking over his right shoulder.

Credit: Union Pacific Historical Collection.

I Have the Coffee On

John gazed with astonishment at the newspaper in his hands. The picture on the page in his hands had been taken fifty years earlier. He recognized his uniformed body, hatless head and blurred legs in the photo, running from the canteen to the waiting train.

"What's wrong?" his wife asked, afraid that his exclamation and subsequent stillness meant bad news.

He turned to her, showing her the paper. "That's me in the picture."

As she peered at the photo, John recalled the day the picture was taken.

What a stop that had been! John, then a young Air Force gunner, had been en route from Lincoln Air Force Base in Nebraska—where his crew had been formed—to their next destination of Casper, Wyoming. From there, it was on to England to fight the Germans.

As the steam locomotive slowly lumbered along, the servicemen and servicewomen on board looked out the sooty windows. All around were flat expanses of brown and green, fields of wheat, alfalfa and corn. Occasionally, a silo or barn would break the horizon.

During the war, stops on the troop trains were rare. The hard, wooden seats served as kitchen tables and beds. Food consisted of K-rations with an occasional sandwich. Open windows were out of the question, as the billowing ashes from the steam engine coated soldier and food alike with a dusty grime.

But the train, one of the many troop trains chugging slowly across America, did have to stop for maintenance along the way. Water in the engine's tender had to be refilled and the huge driving wheels needed to be lubricated. The stops, which took about ten minutes, were top secret for security reasons.

North Platte, Nebraska, located in the vast, rich farmlands of the Great Plains, with a large Union Pacific railyard, serviced many of the troop trains.

As they rolled into North Platte's huge train yard, the conversations on board had ceased. Everyone was eager to get off the train and maybe, if they were lucky, get a cup of coffee and a snack.

As the train pulled in to the station, the soldiers and sailors were surprised to see teenage girls with baskets of sandwiches and cookies waiting to greet them on the platform. John had gone in to the depot. He had tried to pay for the food, but had been turned down. Smiling broadly, the woman behind the counter had informed him that all of the food was free for the troops. Too soon, the maintenance stop was over and he'd had to run from the depot back to the train. *That's when the picture must have been taken,* he thought.

John recalled what a boost that stop had been for a tired and hungry soldier. For almost fifty years, the canteen at North Platte had stood out in his memory as a special place, but he hadn't known that it had been special for thousands of other enlisted men and women, too.

Now John read the article: The North Platte canteen

began as a spontaneous gesture. During World War II, troop movements were considered a military secret. Ten days after the bombing at Pearl Harbor, North Platte residents learned through the "grapevine" that their own Nebraska National Guard, Company D, was going to pass through North Platte en route to the West Coast. Company D had been training at Camp Robinson, Arkansas, and family members were anxious to see their sons and husbands after weeks of absence. About five hundred residents showed up at the railroad station and waited with cookies, candy and cigarettes as the troop train pulled up.

When the train rumbled into the station, the crowd moved forward in anticipation, only to discover that the troops on board were from Kansas Company D, not Nebraska. Disappointed not to see their own boys, a collective groan went up from the assembled crowd. They stood for a moment with the treats in their hands. Then someone called out, "Well, what are we waiting for? Welcome to our city, sons, and here's a little something for you." The North Platte canteen was born.

From that one gesture grew a tremendous war effort by the people of North Platte. Soon communities in Colorado and Kansas joined other Nebraska communities as coffee, sandwiches, cakes, cookies and magazines were donated to the North Platte canteen. The arrival times of the trains, a military secret, were given only to the head canteen officials. The officials, in turn, notified canteen volunteers by phoning the message "I have the coffee on." Volunteers then spread the word to bring the food and supplies to the depot to meet the coming train.

"Platform girls," usually teenagers, met the trains with baskets of sandwiches and cookies. If the troops were allowed to disembark, they could run into the depot for a quick bite, a friendly smile and welcome conversation.

The platform girls and the North Platte canteen became known for the dedication to the servicemen and servicewomen who stopped there. The numbers tell the story.

The North Platte canteen served the troops from 1941 to 1946. Every day, three thousand to five thousand soldiers, sailors and Marines visited the canteen located in the Union Pacific station. Toward the end of the war, the daily total reached eight thousand.

Wartime rationing didn't stop volunteers from finding needed supplies. Many residents gave up their own supplies to aid the canteen. Other supplies were donated by farmers or came from victory gardens. Even birthday cakes were presented to those among the troops whose birthdays fell on the days the troop train stopped in North Platte. This was especially challenging because of the ration on sugar. One local woman gave up her own birthday cake to the canteen, so a serviceman could celebrate his birthday "in style."

Besides the food and supplies brought in by private citizens, canteen organizers had a daily shopping list that included 160 to 175 loaves of bread, 100 pounds of meat, 15 pounds of cheese, 2 quarts of peanut butter, 45 pounds of coffee, 40 quarts of cream and 25 dozen rolls.

Donations were received from all over the country as word of the canteen spread. Benefit dances, scrap metal drives, school victory clubs and can drives were held to meet costs. Not a single cent came from any city, state or federal government source, unless one counts the five dollars sent by President Franklin Roosevelt himself.

John sat back, musing on the information in the article, his eyes resting on the picture of himself. A smile crossed his lips as he silently thanked the people of North Platte once again: *There sure are a lot of us that are glad you "put the coffee on."*

Susan Grady Bristol

The "Super Gunner"

Until I went into the Army, my only experience with guns had been with a Daisy air rifle or a BB gun. Then I found myself at the Army Air Force gunnery school at Tyndall Field, Florida, where to graduate and win gunner's wings, the student had to disassemble and then reassemble a fifty-caliber machine gun—blindfolded. This act served as the ultimate test of a rookie gunner's mechanical skill. *But,* I wondered, *will I need it for daytime air combat in the months ahead?* It didn't matter—it was part of the training. So for many weeks, we had been taking apart and putting back together the fifty-caliber machine gun—with our eyes open.

I was pretty pleased with myself when I passed the "test" in well under the time allowed. I was so proud that I went to the nearest pay phone and called my folks and sister in Fords, New Jersey, telling them of my achievement. They were pleased, too, although I'm not sure they truly understood what an accomplishment it was.

The story of my outstanding feat was immediately passed on to my grandma, Lena Yedlin, and grandpa, Heiman, who lived a few doors down from us on

MacArthur Drive. Lena, who knew I was now in the Army Air Corps (transferred from the Corps of Engineers), in turn telephoned her cronies, most of whom still lived in Brooklyn, where we'd come from originally, to inform them of my success. Bursting with pride, she told them that Benny, her "sunshine," had taken apart and put together an *airplane* blindfolded. (I don't think she specified single engine or multiengine.)

Looking back now, what amazes me most is that, as far as I know, not a single one of her friends questioned the feat.

Benedict Yedlin

Love Letters

This past Christmas season, my husband, two daughters and I traveled to Spencer, West Virginia, to visit my parents. During this visit, I decided to explore their attic. They have lived in their home in the mountains since 1953, so investigating the attic was a trip down memory lane for me.

I pulled down the folding steps and climbed the unstable ladder to the dusty, cold, wood-planked third floor. I looked around and noticed a very old, barrel-shaped covered basket in the corner. I seemed to remember that this basket was filled with old letters my parents wrote to each other during World War II. I opened the lid of the basket, and there they were, letters piled high, faded and dirty—untouched since the day they'd been tossed there.

It seemed a shame to leave them that way. Deciding to read and organize them by day and month, I asked Mother and Daddy if I could take the letters back to my Illinois home. They agreed, and soon after returning, I started my little project. As I opened each letter, all of them delicate with age, I discovered a new and previously unrevealed page in this private chapter of my parents' lives.

My father served in the Army as a first lieutenant, 117th Infantry in the 30th Division. His letters were full of front-line accounts of landing on Omaha Beach, and they continued all the way through the Battle of the Bulge. He wrote about his daily experiences with civilians, German POWs, refugees, foxholes, helmet baths and more. I was drawn to these letters like a magnet. Each of my mother's letters was sealed with her 1944 magenta lipstick kiss. Daddy wrote that he sealed his return letters by rekissing her lipstick kiss. I thought to myself, *Oh, how they missed each other!* This ritual filled a void in their lonely, war-torn lives.

I finished reading six months of the letters and discovered there were at least eleven months missing. Where could they be? My mother couldn't remember—perhaps, she said, they had been left in her childhood home; she had lived there with her mother while Daddy was overseas. If so, that meant they were lost forever.

Just six weeks after our Christmas visit, Daddy became very ill and was hospitalized. This time, he was fighting a different kind of war. A new prescription for arthritis had been introduced to his system, and it had almost killed him. He was scheduled for kidney dialysis when I decided to fly down to West Virginia to visit him. As I sat by his bedside, we discussed the letters. He told me how much receiving those lipstick-kissed letters had meant to him when he had been so far from home.

As I left, the thought raced through my mind that tomorrow was Valentine's Day. But I quickly dismissed this thought. My father wasn't in any kind of shape to shop for a valentine. My parents had been married for fifty-six years. My mother would understand that her valentine would just have to be skipped this year.

Later that evening, Mother and I revisited the attic in search of the lost letters. "Perhaps they are in my old college trunk," my mother said as she quickly located the keys. She unlocked the large sixty-year-old trunk. Lying on top were old tattered clothes from years gone by. We started digging, and toward the bottom, we discovered an unmarked gold cardboard box. Mother said she had no clue what was inside. We both held our breath as I slowly lifted off the top. Yes! Here were the long-lost letters! They were all separated by month, tightly bundled in aged cotton twine.

We took the letters downstairs, and I began looking through them. Lying separate, on top of the bundled letters, was a large envelope. I opened it up. It was the valentine card my father had sent Mother in 1944!

The next day, Mother and I visited Daddy in the hospital. At his bedside, I joked with him, saying softly, "Today is Valentine's Day, and I know you have been a little busy lately, but I've got you covered." His curiosity was further aroused when I handed him the old envelope. He carefully opened the card, and when he recognized it, his eyes filled with tears.

There was nothing lacking that Valentine's Day after all. My father, in a voice quavering with emotion, read the loving message he'd sent to my mother fifty-six years earlier. And this time, he could read it to her in person.

Sarah H. Giachino

The Gift of Hope

I will be forever beholden to Ray Kusela of Bremerton, Washington, a man I knew for only a few weeks over fifty years ago. He did me the greatest favor of any man I've ever known. . . .

"So long!" we shouted to our friend Ray as he swung his makeshift backpack over his shoulder.

With a big grin, he answered, "So long, you guys! I just wish I could take all of you with me."

It was a cold, gray day in early December 1944 when Ray trudged across the compound of Stalag Luft 4 in northern Poland and out the gate, never to be seen by any of us again.

When Ray's bomber was shot down over Germany the year before, his left arm had been badly wounded. The Germans knew he'd never be able to use his left hand again, and because of that disability, he was being repatriated on a prisoner exchange.

My B-17 had been shot down on November 2, 1944. But back in the States, all that my distraught parents knew was that I'd been classified as "missing in action." It wasn't until February 1945 that they were officially notified I was being held prisoner somewhere in Germany. That same month, my mother read in the *Los Angeles Times* that the War Department was sponsoring meetings across the country for relatives of prisoners of war. Ex-POWs talked to these audiences about life and treatment in the prison camps.

There was to be such a meeting at the Los Angeles Shrine Auditorium. Mom and Dad could hardly wait.

The following week when the big day arrived, they anxiously took their seats in the big auditorium. Half a dozen soldiers and sailors, all ex-POWs, took seats on the brightly lit stage. One by one, they spoke to the silent audience. Among the speakers was Ray Kusela.

When they finished, the officer in charge announced, "The men will now go down into the audience to look at any photos you brought along. Some of them may be recognized."

When the men came down from the stage, the audience crowded forward, extending photos of their missing sons, husbands and sweethearts.

Dad later told me what happened next:

"Your mother and I had been feeling really bad since we got the telegram that you were missing in action. But those boys up there on that stage gave us hope that everything would turn out all right.

"I watched this one fellow pushing his way through the crowd, looking at pictures—hundreds of them—held out to him. He just shook his head and kept saying, 'No. No. No.'

"By the time he made his way to where your mother and I stood, I began to feel dejected again. But I held out your picture, and suddenly that kid's face lit up with a big grin, and he said, 'Hey, that's Bill!'"

Dad said he had to hold back a sob when he asked, "Is he okay?"

"Yes, he's fine," Ray assured them, relieving them of a burden of worry they'd carried since the previous November. Then he pressed his way deeper into the crowd, looking for other familiar faces on the photos clutched tightly in hopeful hands.

Mom and Dad cried on their way home that night, hearing over and over again those wonderful words that filled them with hope, "Yes, he's fine."

Bill Livingstone

6

BROTHERS IN ARMS

But we . . . shall be remembered;
We few, we happy few, we band of brothers;
For he today that sheds his blood with me
Shall be my brother.

William Shakespeare

A Joyful Noise

Make a joyful noise unto the LORD, all ye lands. Serve the LORD with gladness; come before his presence with singing.

Psalms 100:1

From the very first Sunday after my arrival at the Hanoi Hilton, I prayed in my own make-believe church in the tiny courtyard adjoining my cell. I had access to it through the back door of my room, and only when it was open (a few hours in the morning and a few hours in the afternoon).

When the guard I came to call "Stoneface" opened the door of my room, I walked around the enclosed area looking closely at the walls and finding inscriptions of dates going back to 1950. The most recent date was 1960. All the inscriptions on the wall were in Vietnamese, and I could barely make out the dates. How long had these others languished here? I could not see myself physically surviving long if my captors persisted in serving up the foul diet I'd been fed so far. God seemed my only hope.

Clutching a rusty nail found on the ground, I balanced on the edge of the topmost step outside the back door of my cell and reached up to a section of the wall immediately to my right. Laboriously, I scratched about a quarter of an inch through the tinted mortar until I reached the white base. Then I nicked at the wall, straining to keep my foothold as I drew the outline of a cross. After several hours, I stood down and looked up approvingly from the courtyard. The cross was a foot high and eight inches wide.

Over successive days, I busied myself scratching below the cross a statement of my presence: "Lt. j.g. Everett Alvarez Jr., United States Navy. Shot down 5 August 1964, arrived Hanoi 11 August 1964."

Below this, beginning with Labor Day 1964, I scratched the names of every significant holiday as each arrived.

I now held my daily church services before my cross, which I pretended to be above the altar of the church I had attended as a child.

I had never been more in need of prayer. Not long after I created my "church," my captors began a long series of interrogations. Things got tougher and tougher for me mentally. I was anguished and deeply afraid. Their taunts and threats wore me down to such a degree, I didn't know how much longer I could hold out. Would they kill me? Would I disgrace myself and the country I held dear by breaking down?

One afternoon after I was allowed to return to my cell, I collapsed in despair. Praying fervently, I felt an extreme fear I had never experienced before—my agitation seemed overwhelming. Then, from out of nowhere, I felt my whole body relax and a calm come over me. My breathing slowed. Looking up through the bars to a small piece of the sky, I had the clear thought, *Whatever they do to me, I'm ready. If I have to die, I'm ready to go.*

To the same extent I had been afraid, I was now at

peace. Deeply and utterly secure, I knew a comfort I drew from for the rest of my long stay as a POW.

Yet by necessity, this faith was a private affair. We prisoners were not allowed to worship together. As the years went by, we became skilled, whenever we were permitted to be together, at being very, very quiet if we even dared to pray together. It was many years before we reached a collective turning point in this matter.

In December 1970, almost four hundred POWs were brought together in the Hanoi Hilton. As they represented just about every known American captured in North Vietnam, we called the ring of buildings around our courtyard "Camp Unity." The men in my cell named our twenty-five-by-thirty-foot room "Buckeye," after our SRO (senior ranking officer), Air Force Captain Dick "Pop" Keirn, who was from Ohio.

Our room had two long slabs of solid concrete, each two feet high, facing each other along opposite walls. Between the slabs was walking space. Ten men slept on each row, unrolling their straw mats and bedding down beneath two blankets and mosquito nets tied to string stretched along the length of the room.

The American POWs all over North Vietnam had been consolidated in Hanoi after an elite force of American commandos made a daring rescue bid on Son Tay prison in November. The raiders had hoped to airlift POWs to safety. They were forced to go back empty handed, even though they had penetrated North Vietnamese air space undetected and fanned out in search of imprisoned compatriots. By sheer chance, the Vietnamese had transferred the Son Tay inmates to another camp a mere fifteen miles away only about a month before, leaving Son Tay abandoned. The luckless POWs at the new camp had actually witnessed the nocturnal raid, seeing the explosive flashes light up the dark sky and hearing the U.S. fighter cover scream right over their own nearby holding camp. There was little likelihood of a similar raid coming so soon after the abortive one, but the Vietnamese were taking no chances.

It would be much harder for the commandos to scoop us out of enemy territory if we were kept under lock and key in populous Hanoi. It had the best air defenses and none of the rural isolation of Son Tay.

Our swollen ranks in each of the large rooms of the adjacent buildings of Camp Unity did wonders for our spirits and our camaraderie. The unity and solidarity that we had risked so much to preserve seemed to have paid off. Far from being isolated and lonely, we were all caught up in the new euphoria. Among such numbers, it was impossible to feel the misery and sense of abandonment that came with solitary confinement or isolation.

Confidence in our present strength and ultimate fate peaked on Christmas night, 1970. Though the camp authorities had never relaxed the rule against POWs communicating between rooms and buildings, in our current mood, no one gave a damn about the regulation. Christmas gave us the impetus to act.

Suddenly the cold night air was filled with the sounds of a carol sung joyously and assertively by the men in one of the buildings. No sooner had they finished than the inmates of another building sang a different carol. Camp Unity soon resounded with the words and tunes of many a beloved carol, each time sung in a defiant fortissimo. Even though the wall in front of Buckeye prevented us from seeing the other buildings, we could hear our fellow carolers because none of the iron-barred windows had shutters.

The guards scurried to quash our insubordination. Appearing at the windows of each of the buildings, they shouted for silence and obedience. This only served to encourage even more POWs, who joined in singing "God Bless America" and the national anthem with such gusto that it became a challenge our captors could not ignore. Soon the riot squad appeared. Swiftly and forcefully, the Vietnamese hauled senior officers over to Heartbreak Hotel and clamped them in irons. Other guards stood by with fire hoses, ready to turn on the flow if we escalated the unruliness.

But they had no need for them. We had made our point. Then the camp commander appeared. "You are allowed to have church services," he said, "but you must not be disruptive. You must do it in your own rooms. And the senior officers are responsible."

Starting on the very next Sunday, the faithful in each room conducted services, praying and singing hymns together. With fear vanquished, and on the heels of such a significant victory, we no longer spoke in the hushed tones we had become accustomed to over the years. We had wrung this precious concession from our captors by proclaiming our faith, joyously, loudly and—most important—together.

Everett Alvarez Jr.

More Than Brothers

I was seventy-two years old. For over fifty years, I'd had the same nightmares. I'd wake up in a cold sweat, often with tears running down my cheeks to my sweat-soaked pillow. I couldn't forget that last battle and the friend I'd lost to a Japanese shell.

In the late 1930s, I had joined the Civilian Conservation Corps at the age of eighteen. The second of seven children, a six-foot, two-inch lanky boy from the Deep South, I wanted to help my family after the death of my father.

Four years later—a veteran and survivor of Roi Namur, Saipan and Tinian—I found myself basking in the sun on the Hawaiian island of Maui with my unit, the Second Battalion, Twenty-fourth Regiment of the Fourth Marine Division.

I was a machine gunner, first squad. My best friend was Richards, a broad-shouldered boy about an inch taller and a year older than me, who came from a town in the southern part of New York State. We did everything together.

We had been in Maui nearly three months. We played softball and went on trips to the town of Kahulai, but most of our time was spent in the seemingly endless boredom of marching, training and more training—preparing for our next objective.

Then all the boat rides, ball games, sunbathing and training came to an end. We were boarding transports to once again become a part of war, and we had no idea where our ships were taking us.

Our destination turned out to be a sulfur-smelling volcanic island called Iwo Jima. This island was near the end of Nanpo Shoto, a chain of islands in the South Pacific, 750 miles from Tokyo. Twenty-three thousand Japanese soldiers and sailors occupied it.

On D-Day, we left the safety of our transports and boarded the landing craft around seventeen hundred hours. We were to come in on the second wave; a section of the beach designated "Yellow" beach would be our landing zone. We were to take and hold this pork chop-shaped island as an emergency landing field for U.S. bombers and their fighter escorts returning from raids on Japan.

Leaving the landing crafts, we struggled to make our way across the beach. Trying to walk in the black volcanic sand was like trying to walk inside an hourglass—the sand shifted constantly beneath our feet. We made little progress because of the debris, the mines and the constant fire from the enemy. We also had the unpleasant task of wading through our fallen comrades.

We finally arrived at the crest of the beach and went across Motoyama Airfield Number One. We set up our guns and prepared to fight, staying there for what seemed an eternity.

My buddy Richards, who had been in sick bay aboard the transport, suffering from a high fever, finally joined me on the third day. I felt a lot better with him by my side.

Our gun was set up halfway between two airfields near a place called Charlie Dog Ridge. We were under constant fire from snipers, small arms and machine guns. Plus, a never-ending stream of shells came from the dreaded mortars, which were hidden in the jagged volcanic rock of this hell the Brass called an "objective."

Hours passed as Richards watched my back and I watched his. Brothers in arms, we depended on each other totally.

As we repositioned our gun in what we believed to be a safer place, a Japanese shell suddenly exploded near our crater. Many were killed or wounded, including our ammo carriers and some of our riflemen. I was one of the injured. It seemed like hours, but it was only a few minutes until the angels of the battlefield, the Navy corpsmen, were helping me. As the stretcher bearers picked me up and carried me out, I kept reaching for my buddy. I did not want to leave him alone.

We had only gone a few yards when we were hit by another shell. One of the bearers was killed instantly, the other severely wounded, and I was hit for the second time. I lay there all night in the warm volcanic sand, worrying about Richards, trying to ignore the pain from my wounds. Sometime during the night, I lost consciousness.

The next morning, I was picked up and taken to the aid station on the beach. They told me I was the only one to survive the explosion. It was the last thing I remembered about those three awful days.

I woke up aboard a hospital ship headed for Guam. There, I was placed in a body cast and flown to the United States. Before and after my surgeries, I mourned Richards. I kept saying to myself, *I should have been the one who stayed behind.*

I was discharged in December 1945 and went back home to Georgia to be with my family. I had married that August, while on leave, and over the next fifty years, helped raise three sons and a daughter. My life was as full as a man could ask for, yet there was a hollow place in my heart that could not be filled. Not a day went by that I did not think of my best buddy still on that island. And sometimes there were those awful dreams. . . .

In 1995, I attended a "Veterans of Iwo Jima" reunion in Atlanta. At the reunion, I was asked to join several veterans' groups. After talking with other vets, I finally wrote my name on a few different sign-up sheets. A copy of one of these pages ended up in the hands of a retired police detective in Endicott, New York, who immediately recognized my name.

The detective called me the very next day. I answered the phone, and a man asked, "Newton?" For the first time in fifty years, each of us heard a familiar voice—a voice we both thought we'd never hear again. The voices belonged to two Marines who had gone through the hell of war and who had each been told that his best buddy had been killed in action on that bloody island.

To this day, we continue to phone, write and visit each other. The bad dreams are gone, the empty place filled. We are now, as then, closer than brothers.

William C. Newton
As told to Bill Newton Jr.

The Watch

"Is there something wrong with the watch?" my wife asked. I was holding it in my hand, stroking its face with my thumb as I admired the Christmas present she had given me.

"No. It's perfect, and I love it. I was just remembering another watch of mine from a long time ago," I told her.

My family sat around the breakfast table that Christmas morning and watched me expectantly, waiting for me to tell them about that long-ago watch. Smiling, I strapped on my new watch, and I began my story.

In Vietnam, back in 1970, I'd worn a watch that my dad had given me. The watch itself was nothing special—just an old Timex on a wide, black leather band, complete with buckles and brads, which was the fashion of the day. It was always very important to me to be aware of the time, so it was rarely off my wrist.

This was in complete contrast to the attitude of my friend and hooch mate, Bill, who was a breath of fresh air amid the constant military regimen. He never wore a watch, refusing to be a "slave to time." Instead, Bill depended upon the clocks in the aircraft, or on his fellow pilots, to keep him punctual.

We were both pilots with the Lancers, Company B, 158th Assault Helicopter Battalion, 101st Airborne Division. He was an avid reader with a great sense of humor, and we had quickly become friends.

One July morning, Bill had an early mission to resupply a platoon located atop one of the jungle-covered mountains between Firebase Ripcord and the A Shau Valley, a very hostile area. As he was about to land on the pinnacle, Bill's aircraft was riddled by fifty-one-caliber machine gun fire from directly below the landing zone. Even though one of the rounds had almost completely torn off his right leg just below the knee, he and his copilot were able to impale the helicopter on a tree stump to keep it from crashing down the mountainside. Bill's crew pulled him into a crater, and the ground troops provided cover for them until a medevac helicopter could pick him up and take him to the MASH unit at Camp Evans.

We were all stunned by the news of Bill's injury. That same evening, another Lancer pilot named John accompanied me to the field hospital to visit Bill. The hospital was actually a large Quonset hut containing all of that day's injured who were in recovery. The room, with its rounded ceiling, had no windows and was very dimly lit in an attempt to provide comfort for the patients.

John and I wove our way through the hospital beds until we found Bill. Like all the others in the room, Bill had a Purple Heart pinned to his hospital pajamas. His leg had been amputated, and he was heavily sedated. He was to be evacuated to a hospital in Japan later that evening.

While John and I tried to find the right words, Bill commented that he just wished that he knew what time it was. In the Quonset hut, it was always dusk. As he drifted in and out of consciousness, he found it disturbing that he had no concept of how much time had elapsed. When we were about to leave, I took off the watch that Dad had given me and put it on Bill's wrist. We wished him good luck and said good-bye.

When we got outside, John turned to me and said, "That was really nice, what you did with your watch."

Embarrassed, I told him that it was just an old Timex and that I had been planning to buy another one anyway. Now, I said, I had a good excuse to go ahead and get myself a new watch. Besides, Bill was a friend and a Lancer. I was relieved when he let the matter drop.

The following weeks were hectic, with long, perilous hours of flying and little time to rest. I didn't get to the PX to pick up another watch. With all the enemy contact I was engaged in, it was the last thing on my mind.

One evening when I returned from the day's missions, another pilot met me at operations and told me to hurry to our makeshift officer's club because there was going to be a raffle for a watch. *Great,* I thought, *I need a watch.* I ran to the club to buy a chance before the drawing. But when I arrived there, it was too late to purchase a raffle ticket. Another pilot told me not to worry; they had already included my name.

Unbelievably, it was my name that was pulled from the hat. It was the nicest watch that I had ever seen and much more expensive than any I would have considered buying myself. This was amazing, for I had never won anything. That watch was my prized possession for many years.

I hadn't thought about any of this for a long, long time. And suddenly, sitting at my kitchen table Christmas morning, I was struck with a revelation. It had never occurred to me before but, all at once, I knew with certainty that mine had been the only name in the hat. I closed my eyes as the realization settled in, flooding me with emotion. The Lancers had given to me in a way that allowed them to express gratitude without it being obvious. It had worked; it had taken me over twenty years to realize the true value of that watch.

There are some things about that time so long ago that I do not ever want to remember. And there are other things, like the watch, that I pray I will never forget.

Bill Walker

Honor Bound

Wars may be fought with weapons, but they are won by men. It is the spirit of the men who follow and of the man who leads that gains the victory.

General George S. Patton

In September 1943, as a newly commissioned second lieutenant navigator, I was assigned to the 452nd Bomb Group at Moses Lake, Washington. This was a new group being formed for service in the 8th Air Force, and I was attached to a crew headed by Lieutenant Theodore MacDonald.

"I'll call you Murph," MacDonald said when we met.

"Okay," I replied, "I'll call you Mac." We had quite a lot in common and quickly established a rapport. He was from Rochester, New York, and I was from Brooklyn. Both of us had lost our mothers at an early age and had left college to enlist in the Air Corps.

During our three-month training period, our friendship grew. With the New Year in 1944, our group was sent to England, and we began flying bombing missions against

Germany. Losses were heavy at that time. Our commanding officer was shot down on the group's first mission.

On our crew's eighth mission, a daylight raid on Berlin, we were in the lead squadron and were attacked over Hanover by German "Focke Wulfe" fighter planes. Our bomber was struck repeatedly from nose to tail. Two engines were knocked out of commission. I was in the nose of the plane and was hit several times in my right leg. My parachute was shredded by the cannon fire. MacDonald was ringing the "bail out" bell, ordering us to evacuate the plane.

I yelled to him over the intercom, "Mac, I have no 'chute!"

"Come up here and take mine!" he said without hesitation. "Get out now!"

He was my superior, and I did as I was instructed. I took the 'chute, went to the hatch and after the bombardier and copilot had evacuated the plane, I, too, jumped.

Unfortunately for me, after scraping through trees, I landed in the midst of a Luftwaffe antiaircraft battery. I was immediately taken prisoner and placed in a small cell at an air base. Miserable hours went by as I sat alone in the dark, pondering the fate of MacDonald, whom I'd left in the disabled airplane. I knew the man had saved my life and possibly sacrificed his own in the process. I just hoped and prayed he had made it, and I resolved to do everything I could to discover what had happened to him.

After what seemed like forever, I heard footsteps approaching my cell. The door opened, and two German guards appeared. Standing between them was none other than Lieutenant Ted MacDonald, looking a little worse for wear but otherwise unharmed.

We grinned at each other, and I breathed a long sigh of relief. When the guards left, Mac told me he had managed to crash-land the plane, but he hadn't gotten far before being captured.

Soon we were sent to Stalag Luft 1 prison camp for air corps personnel. My wounded leg festered and swelled, and I became feverish. MacDonald, noticing this, called Colonel Hancke, the camp doctor, who was a British officer. He had me transferred to the POW hospital for treatment. I was there for a month.

Liberated by our allies at the war's end, Ted and I both returned to civilian life. Over the years, we maintained our friendship. Our sons went to college near Rochester, and two of his daughters came to New York City. We celebrated weddings and bar mitzvahs jointly.

In early 1992, disturbed at not having received our customary Christmas card, I called Rochester and spoke to Ted's wife, Patricia. She told me that Ted was suffering from terminal cancer and didn't have long to live. In March, my wife, Irene, and I flew to Rochester to see them. Ted was fading rapidly.

There was a question that I felt I had to ask him. It had haunted me for all these years, though strangely I had never mentioned it before, not even in the POW camp. At his bedside, in a moment when I was alone with him, I finally asked, "Mac, why did you give me your parachute?"

Despite his illness and weakness, he replied in a firm voice, "I was your commander—that's what I had to do."

I just nodded and gripped his hand. I think I'd already known what his answer would be. The reply was so typical of him. Faithful to his country. Faithful to his comrades.

Two days later, Patricia called to tell us Ted had passed away. "He had held on for so long. It was as if he was just waiting to see you first," Patricia told me.

That didn't surprise me either. The bond of friendship tempered by the fire of combat is one of the strongest ties men can have. Mac and I had that connection. And always will.

Jack Moskowitz

Combat Boots

Thirty Christmases ago, I was in Vietnam, a place so different from the Kansas prairie where I live now that I find it unreal. Yet, each Christmas, my thoughts go back to that land and to that time.

Lieutenant William Carter* was typical of the lieutenants who led platoons during the Vietnam War. He graduated from a small college in Tennessee, got married and received his draft notice all within two months of each other. Selected for officer candidate school and sent to Fort Benning, Georgia, after basic training, William was in Vietnam as an infantry platoon leader within a year after graduating from college.

At the time, I was the company commander of B Company, First Battalion, Eighteenth Infantry Division. When William stepped off the resupply chopper in early August, I assigned him to command the first platoon. His next four months were spent in the jungle in War Zone C and along Highway 13 near the Cambodian border.

In my experience, the men you fight beside end up being the reason for fighting: You don't want to let them down. There is no self, only sharing what comes with your

**Names have been changed.*

friends, and this bond becomes closer as the intensity of combat increases. In William's case, his platoon was especially close. What his soldiers felt for him went far beyond respect; he wasn't just their leader, but also their protector, older brother and sometimes father.

Every evening after the ambush patrol (bush) and listening posts (LPs) were sent out, I would visit with as many of the men as possible. Almost every evening, I ended up at William's position. We would spend an hour monitoring the status reports from the bush and LPs and sharing our lives. If I didn't make it to his position, he would come by mine sometime during the night, and we would have our talk. I knew his hopes, ideas and failures, and he knew mine.

One night, we talked about the high points in our lives. When William was commissioned a second lieutenant in the Army, his father and wife had attended the ceremony. Afterward, his father had told him, "Son, I spent four years in the Army during World War II and saw less than a dozen black officers. Now my son is a lieutenant. You have made us so proud." I could tell by the tone of William's voice how much that meant to him.

Quiet moments like those stand out in my memory. Most of the time, we focused on survival and the job at hand. In the jungle, infantry moving from one location to the next carried only what they could use: a few C rations, a clean fatigue shirt to sleep in, a couple of ponchos, an air mattress, ammunition for a personal weapon, a mortar round and an extra battery for the radios. We had enough to eat and received mail every day, but there were very few extras.

In November, I sent a request back to our supply sergeant for a new pair of size-eleven boots, as mine were in terrible condition. The laces had long since rotted away, and I had been using commo wire to lace them. Because of the climate and supply shortage, there were no extra boots in the supply line—commo wire or not, I would have to wait.

Late one afternoon, about a week before Christmas, I was having a meeting with the platoon leaders when the supply chopper came in with the evening meal. It brought a new pair of size-eleven boots, which I took gratefully. One of the other lieutenants noticed the new boots and called out, "Hey, look what Santa brought."

William looked over and said, "Hey, maybe he'll bring me a pair, too."

I looked down at William's boots—they were worse than mine. So I stood up with the new boots in my hand and said, "Merry Christmas, William, here is a new pair of boots. You need them even more than I do."

At first, he wouldn't take them, but when I told him that he couldn't refuse a Christmas present and that I would request another pair, he finally accepted. That evening when I stopped by his position, he was wearing the boots. We talked into the night about Christmases past and future.

The next day, we opened our portion of Highway 13 as usual. The engineers swept the area for mines, and every two hundred or three hundred meters, I posted a squad. William left the column with his squad and disappeared into the wood line to set up the last position.

I was dropping off the first squad of the next platoon when I heard the firing: the flat sound of an AK-47 and the sharper reply of an M-16. The three remaining squads and I ran back to where William's squad had entered the jungle, but before we could finish setting up security, I saw William and two of his men emerging from the wood line.

William was walking unassisted but holding his arm above his head. Although his platoon had been in as many firefights as the others had—and he had always been in the front—this was the first time he'd been hit. I ran over to meet him while the radio operator called for a "dust off." By the time I reached William, I could see that although wounded, his injury wasn't life threatening.

He explained he had been securing the position when he parted the undergrowth with his left hand and saw North Vietnamese soldiers less than twenty meters away. Each saw the other simultaneously, but the NVA fired the first shots. William's extended left arm took the first round on the palm side at the wrist, and the bullet traveled up his arm and lodged just below the elbow. It was a nasty place to get shot, but not as nasty as it could have been.

William sat down and started apologizing for getting shot. His platoon members surrounded him, glad he was okay but sad, too, knowing they wouldn't see him again once he went to the hospital. I felt the same way.

The "dust off" landed on the road, its rotor idling, but William made no attempt to get up. He appeared to be playing with his boots. His one good hand was untying them, while the medic tried to stop the bleeding from his wrist and arm.

The medic asked him if he had been hit in the foot, too. William shook his head. Then he looked at me and said, "I'm not going anywhere until I give you these new boots. I was going to wait until Christmas morning, but now I can't do that."

I felt like laughing and crying at once, but I couldn't do either. I just stood there, looking dumb. William, who had probably just lost the use of his left hand, was worried about *me.*

As I walked him to the waiting chopper—me with an extra pair of boots around my neck and William with bare feet—I had the thought, *We must look like quite a pair.* The chopper revved up and lifted off.

That was the last time I saw William. His gift was soon

worn out, discarded for another pair of boots. But the memory of the giver has never been discarded. To me, this is the true meaning of Christmas—that it is the giver, not the gift, that is unforgettable.

And William, I'm thinking about you this Christmas.

Watts Caudill

The Nine Days

On December 16, 1944, in one last desperate attempt to finish the war in the European Theatre, the Germans punched through overextended American lines in southern Belgium. A handful of my buddies and I had a front-row seat at this action, known as the "Battle of the Bulge."

At the time, I was an infantry aid man on detached service with the 106th Division. When the attack came, I was serving as the medic assigned to a reconnaissance patrol. As the fighting increased in fury, the Germans overran our lines, and we were separated from our unit. We were lost with no maps, no one in command. None of us knew where we were, where the enemy was, or which direction to go to avoid capture or to find our unit.

To complicate matters, we soon discovered that as the Germans advanced, they removed clothing from the American dead—anything for additional warmth against the terrible cold. They also made use of captured American vehicles. So in addition to being completely confused about where we were, who might be around the next bend or behind the next tree—we realized that we could not assume that a man dressed in an American uniform riding in an American vehicle was, in fact, an American soldier.

Even the weather did its best to kill us. The winter of '44 was one of the bitterest Europe had experienced in many years. Temperatures seldom rose above freezing. It snowed heavily, and a blanket of fog made every shadow a menace. When we lay down to rest—there was no way we could sleep—we bundled ourselves in our overcoats as best we could and let the snow cover us, insulating us from the worst of the wind and cold. To make matters worse for the whole patrol, I had a hacking cough, which I constantly tried to suppress so as not to give away our position.

The wounded suffered the most. Very soon our supply of morphine was used up, so in one way, the cold was a positive thing: It slowed the seepage of blood and partially anesthetized their pain. In another way, the snow and cold were deadly because the wounded were in greater danger of frostbite and freezing to death than the rest of us who half-carried, half-dragged them through the deepening snow.

We floundered, lost, for nine days, hoping to come across our own troops, trying to avoid capture. We were aware of German patrols passing near us. The only times we didn't curse the snow and fog was during those close calls. The Germans failed to spot us because the weather conditions created a lacelike, billowing curtain between us, providing camouflage when we needed it most.

We struggled through this numbing nightmare, each day expending more of the little strength we had left. We subsisted on a few Army-issue chocolate bars the size of bricks, and about as easy to chew. We counted ourselves lucky to have them. On the ninth day, strain, lack of food and the penetrating cold had worn us down psychologically, as well as physically. Capture seemed only a matter of time.

That evening, as darkness settled in, we found ourselves at the bottom of a slight rise. As we prepared to try to survive yet another night, we heard the sound of moving vehicles.

"Shhh," someone hissed. We listened. The sound of a horn. An engine starting, then stuttering into silence. Voices purposely lowered. It was too far away to know whether English or German. We crawled to the top of the rise and strained to see down onto the road. Watched. Listened. *Americans? Germans in American clothing? American equipment? Germans using captured American equipment?* We waited. No more voices. No clue. We slid back down the rise.

"It's a road," we told the wounded. "It looks like American vehicles and soldiers down there."

"Yeah, but . . . ," someone said, his voice trailing off. Everyone understood the unspoken. If we were wrong, and they weren't Americans, we'd be taken prisoner. More likely, we'd be shot. It was rumored among American troops that the Germans had stopped taking prisoners quite a while ago.

We hunkered down to discuss the situation. The wounded were barely holding on, but none complained of their pain; some of the men suffered with seriously frostbitten extremities; by now, my cough sounded like the whooping kind; all of us were stretched taut with the unrelieved tension.

"Well, what should we do? Play it safe and wait till morning to get a better look?"

"Or take the chance they're us, put our hands up and go over the hill?"

"Maybe we should stay where we are and hope that in the morning, they'll still be there and then, maybe, we can tell if they're Americans or Germans."

"If we do that, the wounded will have to spend another

night in this freezing hell. And what about all the guys who have frostbite? They'll be in worse trouble after another night out here."

"Yeah, but what if they're not our troops? The wounded and the frostbites who can hardly walk will be shot first."

In the end, the wounded, in danger of losing their lives, and the frostbitten, in danger of losing their limbs, refused to jeopardize the rest of us by suggesting we take the risk of showing ourselves this night. The rest of us refused to jeopardize their lives if by waiting a few more hours, we would know for sure.

Impasse. Silence.

Finally, "What's one more night after all of 'em we've been through?" one of the wounded asked.

So it was decided. We would wait until morning.

We prepared for another restless night. I made the wounded as comfortable as possible, then rolled up in my overcoat. We fell quiet, each man weighing the chances of survival, dreaming of home, loved ones. . . .

Suddenly, out of the darkness came a voice from the road, very loud and very clear: "Get those blankety-blank vee-hic-culs moving!" it bellowed, cursing as only an American sergeant can.

Within moments, we had slung the wounded onto our backs, clambered up the rise, over the rise, screaming, "Americans! We're Americans! Americans! Americans!" We slid and fell down the slope, stumbling and crying, toward our countrymen and safety.

I never saw any of those men of the nine days again. I never knew if the wounded lived, if the frostbitten kept their limbs. I can't recall even one name. But the memory of their devotion to their comrades, and their courage in the face of incredible odds, remains with me still—and will forever.

Walter F. Peters

Grandpa's Apple Pie

I can still see the images vividly, as if I were standing right there gazing at the pictures on Grandpa's wall. Black-and-white photos, with heavy black frames and weighty images. The brave smiles on the faces of the men in Grandpa's platoon could not hide the hardship of the war.

I knew by heart the stories that went with the pictures. Grandpa had a gift for description, and when we begged him to tell and retell his war stories, we could see, hear, even smell the front lines of battle.

Just as vivid in my mind are the weekend visits to Grandpa, when my sister and I would sit with him around his kitchen table. The three of us would share an apple pie after supper, savoring the sweet, smooth taste and Grandpa's company. Even today, a taste of apple pie brings back memories of Grandpa and his war stories shared around that table. One story in particular I insisted he tell every time—the story of when he almost didn't make it home.

Right at the end of the war, Grandpa was shot in the back, twice, and would have perished where he fell had it not been for two brave soldiers who carried him out of the line of fire, risking their lives to save him.

My curiosity about those two young soldiers was never quenched. "Who were they, Grandpa? What were they like?" I asked, even though I knew that when Grandpa told me about them, his eyes would fill and his voice waver.

"We ate together, slept together and fought together," he would answer. "A good old apple pie." Dave was a tough apple, strong in body and mind, protective, always making sure they looked out for each other. Ron was the filling, sweetening the mix with high spirits and jokes. And Grandpa, he was the crust, keeping them all together by reminding them, during the hard times, of the things that waited for them at home and the plans of things they would do together then. Their short interval of six months of service together had created the most secure of friendships—the kind of friendship that will lay down its life for another.

What I wouldn't have done to meet the two friends who held my Grandpa's heart and thoughts so securely!

And then, unbelievably, I had my chance. During one of my visits to Grandpa, when I was nine years old, I awakened early one morning and found Grandpa in the kitchen, sipping a cup of coffee. Two other coffee cups, almost empty, were near him at the table, but no one occupied the chairs.

"Why are there three cups here, Grandpa?" I asked.

"Well, you see," Grandpa replied, "on Saturday mornings, my old buddies—my apple pie buddies—come over to drink coffee with me and talk about old Army stuff."

"Really, Grandpa?" I was thrilled! "Why didn't you tell me?"

Those two heroes who had trudged through the war with Grandpa amid hand grenades and gunfire had been sitting here, in this kitchen, while I was upstairs, oblivious.

"Can't I meet them, Grandpa?" I begged. "Please?"

"All right," Grandpa agreed. "But there's one stipulation. You have to wake yourself up at 4 A.M. to meet them. That's when they come, and I won't do it for you."

What a deal! Of course I would get up on my own! I'd stay up all night if I had to!

But I was only a child, after all, and as excited as I was the night before, as unsleepy as I felt, by the time 4 A.M. rolled by, I was dead to the world. Every weekend visit brought the same end: I raced down the stairs, knowing I was too late by the strength of the sun's rays peeping through the kitchen window, to find only Grandpa and three empty cups of coffee.

I got no more chances after that year. The bullets that had been intended to take Grandpa's life during the war eventually succeeded; cancer emerged from the sites where they were still lodged deep in his back. Grandpa died, and I never made it in time for the coffee. And I never met those two Army buddies.

I'm glad, in a way. Perhaps my nine-year-old mind wouldn't have understood if I had made it down at 4 A.M. and seen Grandpa's lone figure sipping from three cups of coffee, two laid out for young men who likely never even made it home from the war. It probably wouldn't have made sense to me then.

But it makes perfect sense to me now, as much as it did to Grandpa. He was, as ever, the crust of that special apple pie, holding together a friendship that had never died and showing me the kind of love that lasts as long as memory and beyond.

Heather L. Shepherd

Fellow Marines

What had been predicted as an easy triumph for the U.S. Marines—the swift conquest of a small remote island—quickly became a nightmare and one of the costliest battles of World War II. But the battle for Peleliu Island was not without its victories, for during this bloody campaign, some of our social and military barriers were changed forever.

In the 1940s, racial segregation in the military was a fact of life. Although hard to understand today, it was part of our routine, and no one questioned it. Some, like me, a young kid from New Jersey, were hardly aware of it—until my experience at Peleliu.

After many weeks of intense fighting, we battle-weary Marines suffered heavy casualties with severe shortages of replacements and supplies.

The fourth day of the battle, I left the hospital ship after being treated for wounds and was returning to my company ashore. The ship I took to shore, as well as the beach where we landed, were full of men and equipment to support the fighting. I asked around for the location of my unit, "Item" Company, Seventh Marines. A black truck driver pointed to the hills. I remembered vaguely that noncombatant African-American Marines volunteered wherever needed in combat or support, but this was the first time I had seen African-American servicemen. I wondered who they were and in what branch of the armed forces.

The dark-skinned men were working on the beach, stripped to their waists in the blistering, tropical sun, transferring heavy ammunition from landing craft onto trucks for delivery to the front lines. This task was extremely dangerous at any time, but during a battle, with enemy shells landing nearby, it was a heroic, thankless job that few of us wanted!

One of the men, the driver of a loaded ammunition truck, offered me a ride inland to the front lines. I accepted and climbed aboard. As the truck of explosive cargo bumped along the battle-scarred road, enemy shells crunched into the landscape nearby. I felt this selection of transportation was a dangerous choice on my part; fortunately, it was a short ride to the fighting area, and I reached my unit safely. I thanked the truck driver, wished him well and quickly disembarked.

When I reached our company command post, I located my top sergeant and reported for duty. He explained our battle assignment: "We are an understrength company, and our mission is to seize the ridge and mountains to our front. Gentlemen, get ready to earn your pay. That rocky, treeless mountain range is held by an elite, well-entrenched and hidden enemy who will defend this godforsaken place to their death."

The sweltering hot days and chilly cold nights added to the misery of this bloody assignment, which continued for weeks. Item Company's ranks grew thinner daily due to heavy casualties, rugged terrain and 115-degree heat.

Near a grim place we called "Death Valley," our company's advance was halted. We were pinned down in a deadly cross fire by a concealed enemy supported by mortars and artillery. We suffered heavy casualties and urgently needed reinforcements. I was a company runner of messages and reported the new losses and the dangerous situation to the top sergeant at the command post. The top sergeant radioed for additional troops, medical corpsmen, water, ammunition and as many stretcher bearers as he could get.

The word came back from battalion headquarters: "Negative! No reinforcements, no stretcher bearers, no help or supplies for the present! All support and reserve units are committed in an all-out battle throughout the island."

With a grim determination born of desperation, the top sergeant turned over his command to the next in line and, summoning another Marine and me, set out to find help. Our trio jogged in the blazing sun to several rear headquarters command posts seeking assistance, but none was available.

When we reached the beach area, a young African-American overheard our situation, walked up and immediately volunteered his platoon's services. "We are from a Marine ammunition depot company and have had some infantry training," he told us.

The top sergeant looked at the dark-skinned sergeant in surprise. The races were so completely segregated during this era that we had no idea who these African-American servicemen were. Suddenly, I recalled seeing and talking to the African-American troops on the beach when I first returned to battle a week earlier. Now, for the first time, I realized they were Marines!

Our perplexed top sergeant tried to discourage the non-combatant volunteers from coming, stating they were not trained or qualified for the intensity of this battle.

By now, the volunteers had heavily armed themselves and lined up behind their leader.

I heard our seasoned professional Marine top sergeant

say sharply, "Well, don't say I didn't warn you." But I know he welcomed their aid.

We all returned to the battle area. There was carnage everywhere. The top sergeant reported to the acting company commander and said, "Sir, I have a platoon of black—I mean a platoon of Marine volunteers who came to help!"

The commanding officer said, "Thank God! Thank you all for coming. Sergeant, get our wounded to safety and our dead out."

We watched in awe as the gallant volunteers did their job. While breaking through the surrounding enemy snipers, we saw more than one hold a casualty stretcher gently in one hand and, when necessary, fire an automatic weapon with the other hand.

One wounded Marine, probably the most bigoted man in our predominantly Southern unit, turned to me and said, "I'll never put Negroes down again. These men are angels—black angels."

The platoon of African-American Marine volunteers made many dangerous trips to our company area for the wounded. With each return trip from the rear, they brought badly needed ammunition, food and precious water. It was nightfall when the evacuation of all the wounded was complete. Then the volunteers moved into empty foxholes and helped fight off a night skirmish.

Finally, Item Company Marines were relieved from the gruesome mountain by a fresh U.S. Army infantry company. As the incoming soldiers passed what was left of our company on the road, the soldiers pointed at the African-American servicemen and hooted, taunting us, "Who are *those* guys in your outfit?"

Our senior sergeant bellowed, "Why, some of our best damn Marines—that's who!"

Edward Andrusko

Ernie Pyle's Last Battle

Fame and fortune had engulfed timid, wiry Ernie Pyle. His name was a household word. Millions loved him and prayed for his safety. He might well have rested on that pedestal. Yet, in March 1945, he found himself bidding good-bye to his beloved wife Geraldine, at the couple's modest home in their adopted city of Albuquerque, New Mexico. Once again, forty-four-year-old Ernie Pyle was off to war.

As a correspondent for United Features Syndicate, the Indiana native had been covering American GIs in the crucible of battle since the invasion of North Africa in 1942. There, the Pyle legend had burst into full bloom. In simple, gripping pieces, many done in foxholes, often under fire, Ernie had brought home all the fear, pain, horror, loneliness and homesickness that every GI felt. Those articles were the perfect supplement to the soldiers' own letters to loved ones.

Although he wrote of his own feelings and his own emotions as he saw boys killed and as he saw wounded boys die, he was merely interpreting the scene for the GI doing the fighting and bearing the brunt of the war. Ernie got people on the home front to understand that life in battle "works itself into an emotional tapestry of one dull, deadly pattern—yesterday is tomorrow and, O God, I'm so tired."

Ernie Pyle never made war look glamorous. He hated it. Rather, he wrote of the nobility of young men fighting for their country. When asked why he was there, his standard reply was: "A small voice came in the night and said go."

Ernie's first love was the infantry dogfaces—those who suffered the most and who took 90 percent of the casualties—and he shared their hardships in the front line and beyond. He was always on their side, putting into words in his columns what the GIs could not quite write. Ernie was the first to suggest the combat soldier deserved extra pay, not as reward—because there was no reward big enough—but as a sign that the foot soldier was something special.

Blown from a ditch by a German dive-bomber in North Africa, blasted out of a building at Anzio, almost killed by a strafing plane at St. Lô in Normandy, Pyle told of death, heartache and agony around him and he always "named names" of the boys and got their home addresses. Hundreds of thousands of combat troops, from star-spangled generals to infantry privates, knew him by sight, and called, "Hiya, Ernie!" when he passed.

In Europe, by late 1944, Ernie was a thin, sad-eyed man gone gray at the temples, his face lined, his reddish hair thinned. "I don't think I can go on and keep sane," he told his millions of readers. He started back home, with abject apologies to the GIs.

"You get to feeling that you can't go on forever without being hit," he would tell close pals. "I feel that I've about used up all my chances."

Meanwhile, Pyle's books, *Here Is Your War* and *Brave Men,* a collection of his columns, hit the bestseller lists. He was wildly acclaimed whenever he dared show himself in public, and he reluctantly journeyed to Hollywood to watch Burgess Meredith impersonate him in the film version of his books.

Ernie loafed awhile in his humble white clapboard cottage in Albuquerque. For hours, he would sit there in the veranda with Geraldine and stare silently across the lonely mesa. The front lines haunted him, beckoned to him. In January 1945, he felt that he had to go back but, this time, it would be to the Pacific.

"I'm going simply because there's a war on, and I'm part of it," he told Geraldine. "I've known all the time I had to go back. And I hate it."

So he went, winging out over the seemingly endless Pacific to embattled Okinawa, a final stepping stone to Japan. He stalked the enemy with Marine patrols and huddled with them under fire in foxholes. On April 8, a three-column photo in *The New York Times* showed Ernie, clad in full combat gear but carrying a batch of writing pads instead of a weapon, second man in a squad of Marines probing ahead of the lines.

A week later, Pyle was on Ie Shima, an obscure flyspeck of an island west of Okinawa. There, two Army divisions were locked in a death struggle with tenacious Japanese defenders who contested every yard of the bleak, rocky landscape. Before going to the front, Ernie Pyle felt a strange sensation.

"This will be my last battle," he confided to a fellow correspondent. "Sooner or later, a man's luck is bound to run out. You have just so many chances." Then he wrote George A. Carlin, his boss back in the States: "The boys are depending on me, so I'll have to stick it out."

On April 18, Pyle was jeeping to the front with Lieutenant Colonel Joseph B. Coolidge, commanding officer of a Seventy-seventh Infantry Division regiment.

Suddenly, a hidden Japanese machine-gun on a nearby ridge began chattering, and those in the jeep leaped for a roadside ditch as bullets hissed past them.

Two minutes later, Coolidge and Pyle raised up to look around. Another fusillade struck. Ernie fell over dead, a bullet in his head. A chaplain and four litter bearers edged up to the side and brought the correspondent's body behind the front lines.

In his command post, the hard-bitten combat veteran, Colonel Coolidge, fought back to hold his tears as he told newsmen of Ernie's death. "The GI has lost his best friend," Coolidge declared.

America was shocked by Pyle's death in battle. President Harry S. Truman said, "Nobody knows how many individuals in our forces and at home Ernie helped by his writings. But all Americans understand how wisely, how warmheartedly, how honestly he served his country and his profession."

"Taps" were sounded for Ernie Pyle at 11 A.M. on April 20 near the scene of the battle that was still raging on the remote Ie Shima. He was laid to rest alongside fallen soldiers who had loved him the world over because he had made himself one of them. The simple ceremony was characteristic of the life of the man who had confronted the Black Angel of Death in North Africa, Europe and in the Pacific.

The simple headstone on his grave read:

At This Spot
The
77th Infantry Division
Lost A Buddy
Ernie Pyle
18 April 1945

William B. Breuer

"Joe, yestidday ya saved my life an' I swore I'd pay ya back. Here's my last pair of dry socks."

7

COMING HOME

When you go home,
Tell them of us, and say—
For your tomorrow,
We gave our today.

J. Maxwell Edmonds,
epitaph on Second Division memorial, Kohima, Burma, 1944

Luther's Lumber

Fred Hill had not been in the service because when the war started in 1941, his parents had been in very poor health—his father with a bad heart and his mother with cancer. He was needed at home to care for them and operate the farm. It had been impossible to leave.

Yet when Luther, Fred's best friend since childhood, had flown over town in the B-17, and when the bodies of the Hobbs boys and Billy Martin had been shipped home, and when another local boy came home with hooks where his hands should have been, Fred had felt guilty. He felt he had not done his part for the war effort, and in his own eyes, he was diminished.

Luther had been home from the war four months now and worked at the Carnation milk plant in Mt. Vernon, where his wife, Jenny, also worked. Fred's parents had since died, and the farm was now his—his and his wife Maggie's. Fred proved to be a good farmer, and they prospered. They even had a nice car. Fred's father had bought a new 1941 Ford just before his first heart attack, and the car was now Fred's. To keep it looking new, Fred had recently built a garage.

This morning, Luther was in the little café next door to the post office waiting for the mail to be "put up." Fred was sitting across from him in the booth. They were discussing the war, which was still going on in the Pacific theater. Recruitment posters still lined the walls of the little café.

Today, Luther seemed depressed, and Fred asked him what was bothering him. "You seem down in the dumps, today, Luther," he said. "I can't see what could be bötherin' you. You came through the war without a scratch. You got a beautiful wife and a baby on the way. You got a good job. What's the problem?"

"Jenny's mother is in bad shape," said Luther. "We're going to have to take her in, and with the baby coming, we don't have the room."

"Can't build a room on?" asked Fred.

"No lumber available," said Luther. "I've tried here, Mt. Vernon, Springfield, Joplin, and there won't be any more shipments for the duration. Who knows how long that will be?"

"Tried Will's sawmill?"

"Yeah, but he just saws oak, and it's green. The baby'll be here in August, and we can't wait for the lumber to dry. Besides, you can't build a whole room out of oak, anyway."

"Wouldn't want to," said Fred. "Reckon the mail's up?"

"Probably." The two young men left the café and went into the post office next door. The postmaster had raised the door to the service window, signaling that the mail was in the boxes. Luther and Fred retrieved their mail and left—Luther to work at Mt. Vernon and Fred back to the farm.

That evening, Fred finished the milking and sat on the front porch with Maggie. "Days are gettin' longer," he said. "Man could get half a day's work done after five o'clock." They sat together on the porch until darkness fell, watching the heat lightning in the west.

When the wind started to rise, Maggie said, "Better put your pa's car up. Radio says rain tonight." Fred drove the car into the new garage and latched the door. He stood looking at the horizon, but not seeing it, for a long time. Then he went in the house to listen to the news of the war on the radio and shortly went to bed.

The next morning, Fred again drove his pickup into town for the mail. When he reached the café, Luther was there ahead of him.

"Still haven't found any lumber, I guess."

"No, I asked everybody at work, and nobody knows of any. I don't know what we'll do."

"I found the lumber for you," he said.

"You did? Where?" Luther was delighted.

"Fella I know. He'll let you have it free, you bein' a veteran and all. He doesn't seem to want you to know who he is, so I'll have to haul it in for you. It's good lumber, fir and pine, cut different lengths and got nails in it, but that's no problem. Tell you what—you get your foundation poured, and I'll bring you a pickup load every day and help you build it. We'll have it done before the baby gets here."

That's a friend for you, Luther said to himself as he drove to Mt. Vernon. That evening, he came home with sacks of cement in his pickup. He dug and poured the foundation, and when it was ready for the footings, he told Fred.

"Fine," said Fred, "I'll bring the first load over and be there when you get home from work."

Fred appeared every evening with a load of lumber, and the two men worked until it was too dark to see. Sometimes Maggie came, too, and the women sat in the house listening to the radio or talking about babies or Jenny's ailing mother, their sentences punctuated by the sound of the hammers outside.

Over the next few weeks, the new room took shape

and was finished and roofed. "Where did you get the shingles?" asked Luther.

"Same fella," answered Fred. "He's got all kinds of stuff." Luther didn't push. Lots of older folks liked to help out the young veterans anonymously. It was common.

It was done! The women fixed the room up inside and moved Jenny's mother in. The men went back about their business.

At supper one evening, Luther told Jenny he would like to do something nice for Fred and Maggie, since they had been so helpful with the new room. "I know," said Jenny brightly. "Maggie likes those big wooden lawn chairs like Aunt Birdie has in her lawn. Why not get them a couple of those?"

"Good idea," agreed Luther, and the next Saturday, he bought a couple at Callison's hardware store and loaded them into his pickup.

When he got out to Fred's farm, there was no one home, Fred and Maggie having gone into Springfield, shopping. *That's okay,* Luther thought. *I'll just put them in the garage in case it rains.*

He drove around the house and into the driveway that led to Fred's new garage.

The garage was gone. Only the foundation remained to show where it had been.

Luther put the chairs on the front porch and drove home, tears in his eyes. The two men are now in their mid-seventies, still the best of friends.

They never spoke of the incident. How could they? There was nothing to say.

Joe Edwards

The Cabbie

In March 1971, while serving in Vietnam as a combat engineer with the Eighteenth Engineer Brigade at Fire Support Base "Roberts," I received a severe head wound. Through a somewhat circuitous route, I ended up at the Walter Reed Army Hospital in Washington, D.C. After three operations to restore some of my eyesight, I was finally given my walking papers. I ached to return to my home in Atlanta, Georgia.

In preparation for leaving the service, I was transferred to Fort Dix, New Jersey, for discharge. At one of the many mustering-out meetings all departing soldiers attended, I was told that I might want to go home in "civvies" as the military uniform provoked a lot of outrage. I had never really considered myself very patriotic, and my wounds from a mortar blast hardly seemed heroic; yet I felt that I'd earned the right to wear my uniform, and I decided I'd do just that.

Departure day finally arrived. An Army bus drove a group of about a dozen men from Fort Dix to the airport in Philadelphia, Pennsylvania. Not all of us were Vietnam veterans, but when we stepped off that bus, it made no difference to the group of civilians, men and women, who seemed to know exactly where the bus was stopping. They stood waiting, a sort of reverse welcoming committee.

Physically, I was a wreck. Badly emaciated and weakened from my lengthy recovery time at Walter Reed, I was in no shape to face such a vitriolic crowd. They circled me, yelling and shaking their fists. No one spit, kicked or punched, but their loud words were hot against my face. Hurt and humiliated, I just stood there, shoulders slumped, duffel bag hanging limply from my fingers, unable to respond to a single question or accusation.

Then I noticed a small, elderly man slowly pushing his way through the irate horde. He made his way to me, and looking me right in the eyes, he picked up my duffel bag and asked, "Hungry?" Without waiting for an answer, he set off carrying my bag. The crowd parted as I followed the white-haired figure, who led us out the airport doors to a cab waiting at the curb.

The old man was an airport cabbie; more than that, he was the father of a Marine who had stepped on a land mine. He drove me to his red-brick row house, and we climbed the stairs to meet his wife. She greeted me warmly, as if I were a neighborhood boy returning home.

They introduced me to their son Tim by showing me his high school photos and the trifolded flag the Marines had presented them at his funeral. We sat down to eat our meal, and during grace, I found myself praying silently that there would be no more sons not coming home to eat at their parents' table.

The man drove me back to the airport, and he sat with me until my flight arrived. As I stood to board my plane, I hesitated, unsure if I should do what was in my heart. In the end, I decided to risk it. Standing very tall, I gave him my very best Army salute, then turned and walked on to my plane.

In 1990, when I went to visit the Wall in Washington, D.C., I looked up the Philadelphia couple's son. As I stood gazing at Tim's name carved in the smooth black surface, I wished I could have known the boy whose parents got his Purple Heart—the boy whose "welcome home" was given to me instead.

Robert L. Schneider

Back to the World

The Vietnam morning was like so many others: rainy. But it didn't matter, because for me, this day was different. Today, I was going home.

Dennis, a fellow U.S. Army infantryman who'd become one of my closest friends, stayed with me until the transportation came. We didn't talk much; we couldn't, because all the things we had meant to each other were about to end. When the truck pulled up, we silently shook hands and squeezed the other's shoulder. As the truck drove off, I watched Dennis hang his head and walk away.

It wasn't until we were ten miles down the road that I realized that I hadn't asked Dennis for his home address. It wasn't that I didn't care, but in my anxiety to go home, I just wanted to forget everything associated with the miseries of the war. I never saw Dennis again.

As we continued driving, an eerie sensation came over me. I felt the unearthly presence of GIs who had perished, some whose deaths I had witnessed, others I seemed to remember, though I couldn't understand how. As their faces flashed through my mind like a mournful roll call, the truck hit a bump, abruptly returning my thoughts to the more pleasant prospect of going home.

At the Phu Bai airport, I followed other homeward-bound GIs through a yellow archway reading, "DEROS AND ETS PERSONNEL REPORT HERE." I remembered looking jealously at this sign on other trips through Phu Bai. Now it was finally meant for me.

After completing some initial paperwork, we boarded a C-130 transport plane that brought us to our last in-country stop at Cam Ranh Bay for final processing of our records. It had been exactly one year since I had passed through this same replacement station, but it felt like a lifetime. The atmosphere was familiar. Small groups of clumsy new guys, dazed at being in Vietnam, gawked at me with the same awe that I once had for old-timers.

Every day, over two hundred homebound GIs from all over Vietnam converged at the replacement station, and although the processing was the usual maze of forms and long lines, the mood was surprisingly relaxed and upbeat. Though somewhat cocky, and with every reason to celebrate the end of our tour, we had yet to leave Vietnam. So we avoided doing anything rash that might delay our departure. Still, the spirit of the moment reflected on every GI's face. Glancing anxiously at the other men, I could see they all radiated the same excitement: "This is really it!"

Then as we watched in awe, the magnificent silver "Freedom Bird," a McDonnell Douglas DC-8, touched down. The plane, seemingly aware of its importance and audience, rolled to the end of the runway and majestically taxied back to stop directly in front of us. Never before had a symbol of American technology meant so much to me. The Freedom Bird, an angel descended from heaven, had come to take me home.

It seemed too easy, then, to just walk out and board the plane, but there was nothing else to do. As we crossed the tarmac, a tropical breeze blasted us with hot, humid air—a final reminder of what we were leaving behind. As I approached the passenger ramp, the navigational lights flashed brightly, and I floated up the steps as if I were in a movie. Smiling stewardesses greeted us at the door, and I dashed for a window seat with all the enthusiasm of a child.

As the seats filled, I looked out at the sand dunes of Cam Ranh Bay and wondered how such a beautiful country came to be so filled with trouble. Meanwhile, the excitement on board was building. GIs celebrated by shouting out military slang. "Short!" was the favorite, followed by "Take off! One round will kill us all!" Others yelled, "Hot LZ!"

As the plane's engines spooled up, our boisterous chatter dropped off to whispers. The aircraft nudged forward and taxied to the end of the runway, where it turned around and stopped. At that instant, all talking ceased, and time stood still while we waited for clearance to take off. Then, finally, the engines revved faster and louder as the freedom we had only dreamed of was about to begin.

The pilot released the brakes, and the plane lunged forward. The accelerating takeoff roll glued us to our seats. Rumblings and vibrations echoed louder until . . . we were *airborne!* The moment we lifted off, every GI let out a war whoop that outroared the aircraft itself. As we climbed out of South Vietnam's airspace, the men cheered with delirious joy. We were now safe from the war, with the plane aimed straight across the South China Sea toward the six-thousand-mile expanse of the North Pacific Ocean.

The mood on board was so relaxed that I slept for several long stretches. After the sun went down, with the backdrop of the engines' steady droning through the blackness, I imagined that the airplane was a spaceship bound for Earth. After all, we were going back to what could have been a completely different planet.

Several hours later, the "Fasten Seat Belt" sign blinked, signaling our descent. Everyone quickly found their seats and silently buckled up.

The plane's captain broke the silence, announcing that the shoreline of the State of Washington was directly ahead. We craned our necks toward the windows, straining for a first glimpse in over a year of our homeland. Suddenly a voice proclaimed, "I see lights! It's the world!"

A flurry of cheers, pointing fingers and bobbing heads confirmed that we were only moments away from landing.

"Cold LZ!" a lone voice yelled, exciting another round of cheers.

As the plane descended, the cabin was once again eerily quiet. Everyone sat still, sorting out the emotions racing through our minds. For a tense moment, it was as if every GI sent out the same silent prayer: "Please, God, let this be real."

Then the DC-8 touched down with a simultaneous thump, screech of tires and howling deceleration of reverse thrust. Before the plane had even slowed to ground-maneuvering speed, pandemonium erupted. The thrill of landing on American soil was celebrated with euphoric war whoops, tossed hats and the popping of air-sickness bags. GIs ran up and down the aisle, emotionally overwhelmed. Many shook hands, some hugged and more than a few wept. We were strangers by name, but as combat veterans, we were linked—savoring these final survival moments together.

"Gentlemen," said the captain. "This is my seventh return trip from Vietnam, and I never get tired of making the same announcement: 'Welcome home.'"

Arthur B. Wiknik Jr.

Wounded

In May 1969, I was an eighteen-year-old rifleman serving in Vietnam. One day, my platoon was assigned the relatively easy task of setting up road security. We would ride out on tanks, and two of us would be positioned every quarter mile to ensure that mines would not be placed between convoys.

I looked forward to a day of little activity and limited danger. I'd have time to write a letter home and to rest a bit from the days and nights we had just spent on patrol. It was a bright, beautiful morning. I was filled with thoughts of home and the joy that comes with just being young.

But a few moments after being dropped at my observation point, the flash of a grenade changed me forever. In one split-second explosion, I went from being a strapping young Marine to a crumpled, wounded casualty. As I lay on my back in the dirt, I looked down and saw my body riddled with shrapnel and broken bones. The pain was searing, and I was overwhelmed with fear.

Weapons were fired near me, and somewhere in the distance, I could hear the sound of my own voice screaming. It was a strange but familiar sound. I hadn't heard that cry since I was a child—grown men don't scream very often.

I was sure that the enemy soldiers would immediately come to kill me, finishing the job they'd begun. Thinking I would rather die standing, I managed to stand up, but my badly injured legs could only briefly support me. Before my legs buckled and I fell back to the ground, I saw two wounded Vietcong lying only a few yards away.

Several of the men in my platoon reached me almost immediately. One raised his gun to kill the two soldiers, and before I knew what I was saying, I cried out, "No! No! Don't do that! It's bad enough already." Somehow, the concept of "enemy" had disappeared, and we were simply three injured men lying in the road.

Then our Navy corpsman began to dress my wounds. Many times I had looked into the eyes of the wounded while struggling to keep my expression from betraying my shock and fear. Now it was my turn to hear words of comfort while I looked up into eyes filled with dread.

Even though my buddies were at my side, there wasn't a lot they could do to help me. My body had been horribly violated, and my mind was filled with a terror that couldn't be shared by anyone whose flesh was intact. The men in my unit and I had shared every hardship and many life-or-death experiences, but I had, in an instant, passed from their world of the whole to the new and terrifying realm of the wounded. I felt more isolated than I had ever felt before in my life.

While I lay in the dirt waiting for the medevac helicopter, my buddy Frank did an unexpected thing. He held my helmet in front of my face, forcing me to look at it. The camouflage-colored helmet cover was ripped to shreds. I saw that it had been only my helmet and a quick turn of my head that had saved my face, my eyes and probably my life.

When you are as messed up as I was at that moment,

you grasp at anything that can ease your fear. Seeing that helmet, believe it or not, made me feel a little better. All these years later, I am still grateful to Frank for helping me see my good fortune in the middle of the worst thing that had ever happened to me.

I spent the next seven months in a series of military hospitals undergoing grueling procedures to mend my broken body. Even with the morphine, I was in pain much of the time. Without bothering to ask, fate had taken me from their war in Vietnam and thrown me into a new, personal war, with my own body and mind serving as the enemy.

In those hospitals, in huge open wards, I met countless other young men who were recovering from devastating wounds. Many were so badly maimed that I knew I should count myself among the lucky.

When I was finally sent to a Naval hospital in the States, my parents and my girlfriend, Sharon, came to see me. When Sharon approached my bed, I whispered, "I love you." But I felt I had to let her know what the future might hold for us. "They may have to amputate my leg," I told her.

She didn't hesitate for even a moment before saying, "That's okay. It doesn't matter."

I turned my head away, struggling to maintain my composure in the face of such love. But as much as I wanted to, I didn't believe her. It wasn't okay.

When I was well enough to leave the hospital, I flew home. They had managed to save my legs, but I had lost a lot of weight, and one of my legs, was still in a cast. I was wearing my Purple Heart medal, but I knew I looked terrible, a bag of bones in a Marine uniform. Supporting myself on two canes, I made my way through the airport. At one point, I looked up and froze in horror.

Coming toward me were a mother, a father and a

muscular, fresh-faced young man in a new Marine uniform. They were obviously seeing him off. They also stopped abruptly and stared at me, the mother's hand flying up to her mouth in an attempt to stifle her involuntary cry.

I wanted to hide, to spare them the agony of what I'd been through, of what still lay ahead of me, but I also realized with surprise that I wanted to tell them it wasn't so bad. Maybe Sharon was right after all. I was alive. I was home! It was at that moment, I truly began to heal.

But all I said was a cheerful "Good luck, Marine." And turning to his mother, I said softly, "He'll be fine, Mom."

Then, smiling broadly, I continued down the concourse to meet my own waiting parents.

George W. Saumweber

Reunion on the Dock

It was a chilly December day in 1945. I stood, one of an expectant crowd, on a dock in Tacoma, Washington. Although the Red Cross ladies had given us steaming cups of coffee as well as thermal gloves to wear, we still huddled by the garbage-can fire, savoring its warm flames as they leapt up in the crisp sea air.

I reached into my pocket and pulled out the tattered letter that I must have read a hundred times, and read it once again. "The war is over. I'm coming home!"

Lieutenant Robert Marks, my husband, was alive and well, and coming home from Seoul. It had been so long, I still didn't know if I believed it.

The letter had been delivered to me in Seattle, less than fifty miles from Tacoma, where I was serving as company commander at the Ft. Lawton WAC Detachment. I'd been relieved and happy and excited all at once, and the girls in my company had shared my elation. Three long years of loneliness, sleepless nights and the dread of a "We regret to inform you" letter were about to end. Over and over, I'd had the thought, *What I wouldn't give to be there when Bob's troop ship, the* Oscaloosa, *pulls into dock!*

So I could hardly believe it when one of the ranking officers at Ft. Lawton pulled me aside and said, "We've arranged a surprise welcome for Bob in Tacoma. You'll be there when he steps onto American soil again for the first time."

The morning of Bob's return, my driver and I left Ft. Lawton so early that we arrived in Tacoma with hours to spare. I was waiting on the dock, dreaming of the future that Bob and I would share, when suddenly a tugboat made two short blasts with its horn, startling me out of my reverie. I watched as the tiny tugboats nudged the huge troop ship into the harbor, where it safely anchored.

The *Oscaloosa* was docked. My husband was home.

On board the ship, Bob's crewmates had kept the secret of our homecoming from him, so while I waited impatiently outside, Bob, deep in the hold, slowly and methodically packed his barracks bag. He was so absorbed in his task, he told me later, that he didn't even hear a page for him and was surprised when one of his buddies tracked him down and told him to report to his battalion commander.

"You're getting off the ship," Bob's commander told him.

"Just me?" a puzzled Bob asked.

"Just you," his commander replied. "Get your paperwork and gear together."

Bob gathered his things, wondering what was going on. As the gangplank was lowered, a large number of soldiers were all standing on deck, watching in silence. On the dock, my fellow officers and I strained to see, quiet with anticipation. The only sounds were water slapping against the ship and screeches from seagulls.

Suddenly the hatch opened and Bob—my Bob—emerged. He was thin, his skin orange from the medication he'd been given to ward off malaria. Still, my heart raced wildly. This was the moment I'd been awaiting for years, the moment when I'd run over to meet my husband, to hug and cry and laugh with him. But for some reason, I couldn't move. I was suspended in time, like a movie frozen midframe.

Bob walked slowly down the gangplank. Then he saw me, and time started again. Bob ran toward me, his bags tossed aside. He grabbed me, laughing, swung me up in his arms and covered my face with kisses. I hugged him again and again, tears of joy the only speech I could muster. The soldiers on deck went wild, cheering and chanting: "Mar-ga-ret and Bob! Mar-ga-ret and Bob!" They flashed the victory sign, and the band broke out into song: "It's Been a Long, Long Time."

We hugged so long that the people around us eventually smiled, shrugged their shoulders and returned to their tasks.

The Red Cross volunteers, fighting back tears, rushed out with steaming cups of coffee with real cream for us. Bob finally released his hold on me, took a sip and grinned. "This is the first good cup of coffee I've had in years," he said.

We nibbled at warm cinnamon doughnuts on the chilly dock, oblivious to anything but each other and our coffee and doughnuts. We touched hands and smiled with pure joy. Such simple, ordinary acts—they hardly warranted the delight they gave us. But my husband and I were together, you see, and it had been a long, long time.

Margaret Brown Marks

The Most Beautiful Man in the World

Private Joe Cohen was in the third bus that drew up before the entrance to Halloran General Hospital in Staten Island. Joe Cohen wasn't his name, but it will do. There were other Joe Cohens in the bus, of different names, religions, national origins. Some leaned on crutches, preparing to get out. Some clung to their seats, conserving every ounce of strength to the last minute. They were hollow-eyed, hollow-cheeked men, some with fresh bandages over old wounds. Private Joe Cohen's face was fearfully burned.

A chaplain in uniform, Aaron Blumenthal climbed in as the bus came to a stop. He welcomed the men "back to the United States and to the hospital." A band played military marches and Chaplain Blumenthal said he knew they had been through much suffering, as prisoners in Germany, but now that was behind them.

Now they were back in their own country, among relatives and friends, "and if there's anything any of us can do for you, we shall consider it a high privilege to be helpful." He said that many relatives waited for them here in the hospital and they would be able to see them soon.

In the tense silence that followed, crowding in with a

sort of physical weight you could feel, Joe Cohen said—as if to himself—"Gee, that's bad."

In the receiving ward later the chaplain made a point of shaking hands with the boy of the flaming red face, repeating the welcome he had already given to the returning "repatriates." The boy interrupted him impulsively.

"Look, chaplain," he said, "how can I find out whether my folks are here. And if they are, do I have to see them?"

"You don't have to," said the chaplain. "But—why not?"

The boy shrugged thin shoulders and said, "Look at me." Then he said, "It's all right. The way I feel about it, I'm lucky to be alive. I'm not worrying about myself. But I don't know. How's the family going to take this? How would, well, anybody take it? They told us about plastic surgery and later on, I guess, I'll be all right. But now . . ."

Gently the chaplain told him the miracle of plastic surgery was not performed in hours or days. It would take many months. Could he keep his family away that long? The boy—he seemed so young when you didn't look directly into his malformed face—said it wasn't only the family, but he didn't explain. He asked if the chaplain would speak to his dad . . . before his father saw him.

In a hospital corridor the elder Cohen asked, "Did you see my boy, chaplain? How bad is he?"

How do you answer a question like that, the chaplain asked himself. What words do you use? What intonation of voice? How do you go about telling the truth he must know, but without that shock that must go with the truth? Suddenly, the chaplain decided to hold back nothing.

"Your son," he said, "is very badly burned. Very. Otherwise the Nazis would not have permitted him to return. His face—"

He continued, describing the brutal details.

The father, his own face in his hands, moaned only, "God, God, God!"

"Yet all that," said the chaplain, "doesn't worry him. He knows about plastic surgery. He knows he'll be restored, almost to normal. He says, 'Thank God I'm alive,' but he doesn't know about you and his mother. He doesn't know how you two will take it."

"Can I see him?" asked the father. He promised, "I'll be all right. The boy's mother, she'd be all right, too. But there was a girl. If she breaks down, if she takes it wrong—that's what's worrying my boy—it will break his heart."

Father and son met that evening in the merciful shadows outside the hospital. "Thank God you're home, Son!" said the father. As they threw their arms about each other, the chaplain quietly closed a door and walked away. What more was said between them nobody else heard.

Private Cohen was pleased about the meeting with his father. "The old man's a great guy," he said. "I knew he could take it."

He knew, he said, that Mother would be all right, too. He had spoken to her by telephone. He had also spoken to the girl, told her she must not try to see him—ordered her to stay home until he was ready to pay her a call. He was obviously uneasy about that. Despite all his arguments, she hadn't promised to stay home and wait.

The next morning, there was a special ceremony in the hospital auditorium. In the presence of four hundred men, they presented awards to eleven of the repatriates. These were awards for outstanding heroism before they were made prisoners.

An officer on the platform called out the names one after another and read the citations. Sitting up in a front row, Joe Cohen glanced nervously now and then, over his shoulder. But there was too much of a crowd. Whether his parents—or the girl—were there, he couldn't see. The colonel's voice droned on. At last he called "Private Joe Cohen." Joe Cohen took his place beside the others, at a strict attention. The voice on the platform read on: "For extraordinary heroism in action against the enemy . . . ," "With complete disregard of his own safety . . . ," "Distinguished himself through his display of personal courage, dauntlessness and devotion to duty . . . ," "Reflects great credit on himself and the Armed Forces. . . ." The award: the Distinguished Service Cross.

The chaplain watched as the medal was pinned to Joe Cohen's jacket and Joe returned the colonel's salute. More names were called and more awards given. Standing at rigid attention, Joe Cohen wondered—he couldn't drive the thought from his mind—how he looked in his fresh uniform from the rear of the auditorium.

The ceremonies ended. The chaplain came up to shake hands with the boy, to tell him, "We're all proud of you." But Private Cohen hardly heard him. His eyes roved restlessly, searching, trying to pierce the auditorium full of soldiers and others, most of them now on their feet.

"Did you see my dad?" he asked.

At that moment a group of three broke through the crowd, and young Cohen saw them: father, mother—and the girl. For a fleeting moment the chaplain noted that she was slim and smiling with head held high, and in holiday dress, as if for a special occasion. An instant later, Joe Cohen had broken away from him and was racing down the aisle, while the girl was making her way swiftly, between the rows of chairs, toward Joe.

They met in the middle of the auditorium. Four hundred pairs of eyes were on them but they didn't care. The girl held him very close, never flinched as she looked into his poor, mutilated face and said over and over again, "Joe! Joe! Joe! You're the most beautiful man in the world!"

I. Kaufman
Condensed from American Jews in World War II

A Soldier Remembers

In 1987, while serving as the public affairs officer at Fort Bragg, I would frequently visit the local high schools to speak to the students about the Army. As a lieutenant colonel, I found it particularly rewarding to talk with the teenagers about the benefits of military service, if only for a few years of their lives.

During one of these visits, I reported to the secretary in the principal's office to let her know that I was here for the third-period civics class. I was a little surprised when she told me, "The principal would like to see you before you go to the class." Normally, in these small county schools, the principal was busy with a myriad of duties such as driver's education, administration, counseling and the like.

As I entered his office, I was greeted by a gentleman who appeared to be in his late thirties or early forties, and he welcomed me with a smile and a handshake. "You don't remember me, do you?" he queried.

I looked closely at the face again and could not recall where we may have met before. "No," I said. "I'm sorry, I don't."

"You were my company commander in basic training at

Fort Jackson in 1970," the principal said.

I again looked at the middle-aged face and had no recollection. We usually had 220 soldiers in each unit, and they all looked alike in uniform with short haircuts—and it had been seventeen years ago.

"Let me help you out," he suggested. "You gave me a three-day pass to go home and see my newborn baby." I immediately remembered the incident, if not the soldier!

"Yes," I said. "I remember now." It was the only three-day pass I had issued because the soldiers were on their way to Vietnam immediately after they finished training. But I knew if I did not let him go home to see his son and something happened to him, I would regret denying the opportunity he had to be with his family.

He stood up from his chair, walked around the desk and put his hand on my shoulder as we went down the hall to the classroom. "Come on, Colonel. I'd like to introduce you to 'the baby.' He's in your third-period class. By letting me go see him, you gave me a reason to stay focused and to come home safe from that war. Thank you, sir."

It was the most rewarding class I had ever given, and I had no problem telling the students about the bonds of friendship and the values that Army life can provide . . . and that can last a lifetime.

David R. Kiernan

Kids from Mars

A warrior I have been.
Now it is all over.
A hard time I have.

Chief Sitting Bull

Vietnam was two months and sixty nightmares behind me. I had frightened or angered all of my friends and family, so I got in my car and just drove away.

From Connecticut, I had zigzagged south till I found myself on some mid-Florida, two-lane byway with an empty gas tank and an empty wallet. It was time for my first experience with a pawnshop.

In Bartow, at about midstate, I found such a place. I had decided to sacrifice the almost new Akia reel-to-reel tape recorder I'd purchased while overseas. It had cost me $200 at a time when I was only making $215 per month. That amount included an extra $55 per month called "hostile fire pay," which works out to a little less than eight cents per hour to duck bullets. Not much, but I was grateful for the extra money all the same.

The pawnshop guy was willing to give me $15. He told me I'd be better off to drive to Florida Southern College in Lakeland and try to sell the Akia to some student. I took his advice and moved on.

The Mustang was breathing what gasoline vapor remained in the empty tank as I stopped alongside one of the large brick buildings on the FSC campus. I was expecting the worst. My experience with college kids since returning home had been entirely negative. I hated to put myself at the mercy of a collection of what I expected to be longhaired, sloppily dressed, self-important, spoiled brats.

Two young men approached me as I stood next to the car wondering what to do. They wore shirts with button-down collars, loafers, short hair and smiles. "We really like your car."

"Uh, thanks."

"Are you a student?" they asked politely.

To the casual observer, the three of us probably looked much the same: twenty-year-olds standing next to a high-powered convertible on a college campus. In fact, the differences were monumental. They were studying for exams and daydreaming of a bright future. I was wandering aimlessly and trying not to think about how hard it is to pry a weapon from a dead man's hand.

I explained that I wasn't a student and about my desire to sell the recorder. They asked to see it.

"Where did you get it?" The question was asked in an informational, not accusatory, tone.

"Vietnam." I waited for the clouds to form in their eyes.

The attitude of polite sincerity with which they had treated me never wavered. One of the students said he and his brother might want to buy the Akia and asked if I could wait while he located his sibling. I agreed.

The brothers and I agreed on a price of $100. They apologized profusely when they were only able to scrape together $90. Meanwhile, they and their friends had begun to ask me about my experiences in the war. To my surprise, their questions were not hostile. They were obviously founded in a genuine desire to obtain some first-hand impressions to compare with the torrent of government-filtered information provided by the newspapers and TV.

Our conversation went on for hours. I fielded questions from ten or so male students while we ate dinner together. Then they asked me if I would like to shower and spend the night in their dorm. Compared to bathing in a pond and sleeping in the Mustang, it sounded like a great idea.

Twenty minutes of hot water took away all the road dust and some of my anxiety. But more than the food and the shower, it was absolutely wonderful to talk to people who actually seemed to respect me for what I had done. I kept waiting for the other shoe to drop, for the return of a familiar reproach: "Killer. Fool. You should have known better." It never came.

The brothers' dorm room was crowded with shiny, inquisitive faces. The questions flew, several at a time, always polite and always well informed. I didn't realize America still had kids like this. I decided they were kids from Mars.

We talked till after midnight. I did my absolute best to be objective and impartial. They were amazed to learn that we were almost never allowed to shoot first. And that to do so could actually result in a court-martial. They were incredulous when I described going house to house trying to separate the good guys from the bad guys. I told them we did not—as had been reported—kill them all and let God sort them out. In America, in 1968, that was news.

They would have grilled me till the sun came up. I finally apologized and begged for some time to sleep. Everyone shook my hand and courteously retreated.

In the morning, they asked me to stay on. I was tempted. Perhaps here, surrounded by these kids from Mars, I would be able to leave my troubled memories behind. But, in the end, I decided to go. Richer—by a lot more than $90—I packed up my ghosts and said good-bye.

Joe Kirkup

The Tradition

Yesterday, the adrenaline had been thundering through my veins as I battled in a firefight against North Vietnamese regulars. Today, I was in a Ft. Lewis, Washington, NCO club, munching peanuts and chips and drinking a cold beer, my face still slightly hued with the black and green camouflage that had shaded my face the day before in combat. My extended tour of duty was over. I was going home. I should have been elated, but all I felt was dazed.

The flight home did nothing to improve my disorientation. My service in the Republic of South Vietnam had turned my young life upside down and backward. I hardly knew where I was or what I was doing. Even now, as an attractive stewardess tapped me cautiously on my shoulder, reminding me to fasten my seatbelt, I jumped, expecting to see the battle-hardened faces of the soldiers in my rifle squad fighting for their lives in a merciless jungle. I felt like I had deserted them, and I certainly didn't feel like I should be on this airplane.

The layovers at each airport only added to my confusion. We had all heard reports of protests against the Vietnam conflict, but either I hadn't thought much about them, or I thought I was so hardened by battle that nothing could bother me. But as I cast my eye over the "welcoming committee" of longhaired protesters, my blood ran cold with anger. *What did they know about fighting for your life in a jungle? And why were they screaming at me?*

By the time my parents and sister arrived to pick me up, I was psychologically overwhelmed. For three days, I did nothing but lie on my bed in my old room, staring at the ceiling and trying to sort out the pros and cons of coming home. Everything seemed so incongruous. Old high school friends called and asked me to cruise Main Street with them, and some former football teammates suggested we wear our letterman sweaters to a Friday night dance at a crosstown roller rink. All of it seemed empty, frivolous. Letter jackets? Roller rinks? How did that relate to silently stalking the Vietcong in the monsoon rain? I wasn't part of that crowd anymore, but if I didn't fit in there, where did I belong?

I stayed in bed, sweating through nightmares when I could sleep and showering several times a day to wash away the terror. But when I crawled back to bed, the horrors of combat were still with me.

Finally, one morning, my mom cracked my bedroom door and peeked in. "Permission to enter," she requested with a salute. I smiled faintly—the first time I had smiled since leaving Vietnam. Holding out her arm proudly, she displayed my freshly dry-cleaned uniform. My sister, Regina, marched in with a starched poplin shirt and necktie, and then my Dad, grinning sheepishly, carried in my spit-shined low quarters, which he had polished himself.

"What's this for?" I asked gruffly and sat up on the side of the bed. Regina ran up, gave me the shirt with a kiss, dropped the tie and scampered out of the room.

"Just don't you worry, dear," Mom said, bustling around the room. "You're going out with your father. He had your uncle Vito sew on your stars and things yesterday."

"Those are stripes, angel," Dad corrected her. He had been a company commander in the Philippines during World War II. "Stars are for generals and—"

"Well, Vince," she interrupted him, "Tony should be a general, you know. Now both of you get out of the house because I have a ton of things to do."

"Where we going, Dad?" I asked as I pulled myself out of bed. Dad looked hard at me but didn't answer; then he left me to get ready.

I showered, shaved and gave myself a twenty-five-point uniform check before leaving my room. Dad was waiting at the front door. I was startled by the serious expression on his face as he watched me come down the stairs. "Dad! Are you okay?" I asked.

But he only grinned. "Come on, General," he said, putting his arm around my shoulders. "Your grandpa took me out a few days after I came back from the Pacific. His father did the same when he returned from France after the First World War. I'm passing the family tradition on to you." He paused. "I pray to God that it ends today."

As we walked down the street toward the car, I noticed that my deep tan stood out among the winter-white New Yorkers. Again I felt conspicuous, as if I didn't belong.

Our destination was a veteran's service organization. An ordinary building, it didn't show much promise from the outside. Surely this wasn't the "tradition" that would make everything seem right again. Once inside, however, I was surprised. As Dad showed a burly bartender his metallic life membership card, he loudly greeted the men sitting at the bar by name. Everyone was lively and in good spirits; several waved at me as if I were their long-lost buddy.

Then Dad held up his hands for silence. "You guys

shared my worries for my son while he was in Vietnam," Dad said in a voice heavy with emotion. "Most of you already know Tony, but for those who don't, here is our newest life member."

Applause and hurrahs filled the room as Mr. Mizell, the post commander, hurried over to shake my hand. Soon, I was surrounded by a crowd of World War II and Korean War veterans slapping me on the back and welcoming me home.

Story after story unfolded that day as we drank together and shared our personal histories of war. My own father told me for the first time about the Bataan death march. My chest felt tight seeing the tears well in his eyes as he described the brutality he and his men had endured. Some veterans told of valor in Anzio, Iwo Jima, Omaha Beach, Guadalcanal, Midway, the Bulge and Bougainville. Others told tales of the Frozen Chosin, Pusan and the Yalu.

Then it was my turn to speak, and as I told about the bloody battles in the Ia Drang and An Lo valleys, the others listened to me attentively, nodding their heads or patting my shoulder in encouragement. As I talked and watched the men around me, I felt an inner calm come over me at last. I was surrounded by people who had experienced the same horrors of combat that I had, and they were now strong, noble Americans. Here were men worthy of my respect. They had found their place in this world because they knew they deserved it. I felt a shiver of pride pass through me as I realized that I, too, was one of these brave soldiers. I had earned the right to be here. And for the first time since I'd come home, the roaring confusion of battle and screaming protesters grew faint.

When we left that afternoon, we walked a little taller. Because my dad had had the wisdom to keep a time honored tradition, I was leaving the veteran's service organization full of self-respect and confidence.

I was home, where I belonged.

Antonio Camisa

[EDITORS' NOTE: *During Desert Storm, Antonio Camisa's son, Bryan, led an armor column of U.S. Cavalry swiftly across southern Iraq in pursuit of Saddam's elite republican guard. In May 1991, when Bryan returned home, Antonio bought him a life membership in the same veterans organization. Bryan's grandfather was proudly present at the post.*]

The Light

My family was a close-knit group, and my grandmother was the center of our universe. Although a stern disciplinarian, she ruled her children and her children's children with affection. We never doubted her love, even when she corrected us.

It was during the heat of World War II that her youngest son, my uncle Raymond, turned nineteen. Shortly after his birthday, he found himself in Italy fighting his way toward Berlin. A farm boy, he had never spent a night away from home until he shipped out for basic training. Homesick and scared, he slugged his way through towns, vineyards and woods, thinking of home and his family.

I remember the terrible day the Western Union car pulled up and a man got out. By the time the messenger walked up the sidewalk, all of us children were out on the porch, waiting silently for the news. Grandma moaned softly, not crying, but frightened. Grandpa stood next to her, his face grave. Grandma took the envelope in trembling hands and ripped it open. It was the longest wait of our lives as she began to read the message inside.

A wide grin spread across her face and she clutched

Grandpa's hand. "He's alive! Raymond's injured and coming home, but he's alive!" she cried.

There was much crying, dancing, hugging and cheering as we embraced one another.

The day Raymond got home, he looked so pale and tired, I thought we'd wear him out with our welcome. He was hard of hearing and still sore from his wounds, but he was in one piece and back with us. We pulled him inside, where we sat gathered around the table, while Raymond told us about the day he'd been injured.

"We had been fighting a battle for several days and were marching forward, bone tired, cold and frightened, yet happy that we continued to inch closer to the German border," he began. "It was late afternoon, and snow was on the ground. I was marching down a muddy, half-frozen road when an armored tank rolled by. Several of my buddies and I hitched a ride on it. We hopped on the tank, glad to rest for a short spell. We were laughing and talking when, out of the blue, a mortar round exploded around us.

"The next thing I remember is hearing Mama calling me to get up. 'Raymond, get up!' she shouted. 'Get up right now!'

"At first, I thought I was back home and she was calling me for school. Then I opened my eyes and realized I was in Italy. The world had gone totally silent. I knew I was deaf first, then I noticed the blood on my hands, where it had streamed down from my head.

"I was frightened and confused. My buddies and other soldiers lay dead all around me. I was in shock. I was disoriented and didn't know where the enemy lines were or where my troops had moved. By now, it had grown dark, and it was a night without stars. Panic set in because I couldn't hear. I felt helpless.

"Then Mama said, in her sternest voice, 'Raymond, go toward the light! Go toward the light.'

"Her voice sounded as clear as though she were standing over me. So I staggered down the road, confused, my head aching, too dazed to fully comprehend the danger, not even understanding what the light I saw might be. I hobbled around a bend in the road and fell into the arms of a medic.

"As soon as they checked me out, the medics evacuated me to a field hospital. They said that I was lucky to have caught them. They had already searched the area I was in for wounded, shipping them out first and then returning for the dead. Had I not regained consciousness and moved toward them, I'd have bled to death from the leg injuries before they found me."

Raymond stopped talking, and he and Grandma just sat there, looking at each other. No one spoke, and then my grandfather said loud enough for Raymond to hear, "Well, do you want to hear the rest of the story?" Raymond nodded, and Grandpa started telling what had happened here that same night.

"Your mama and I were asleep," he said, "when Mama awoke from a dream and shook me awake. 'Alston,' she said, 'something has happened to our boy. I dreamed he was calling to me for help. I thought he was a little boy again and he was crying, so I called to him to get up and come to the light so I could see what was wrong with him.'

"She got up and dressed, refusing to go back to sleep. All that day and for the next several days, your mama sat on the front porch waiting for the Western Union boy to bring us the telegram she knew was on the way."

The rest of us looked at Grandma in surprise, but Grandma wasn't paying any attention to us. She and Raymond just kept looking at each other, the tears running down their faces.

After the war, Raymond regained most of his hearing, married, and went on to live a long and happy life. Over the years, I heard him tell the story about Grandma and the light often. He always ended it by saying, "I was all the way over in Italy, stone deaf, but I heard her all the same.'Go to the light, Raymond,' she said. 'Go to the light.' I'll never understand how she did it, but it was my mama that saved my life that night. My mama and the light."

Patricia S. Laye

8

HONORING THOSE WHO SERVED

A nation reveals itself not only by the men it produces, but also by the men it honors, the men it remembers.

President John F. Kennedy, October 26, 1963

The Visit

The nation which forgets its defenders will be itself forgotten.

Calvin Coolidge

My dad, Angelo, was in the hospital in Tacoma, Washington. A former Marine and veteran of the Korean War, he was having his third knee-replacement surgery.

A long and very painful operation was going to be made even worse because Dad was going through it alone. There was no one to hold his hand, no familiar soft voices to reassure him. His wife was ill and unable to accompany him or even visit during his weeklong stay. My sisters and brother lived in California, and I lived even farther away, in Indiana. There wasn't even anyone to drive him to the hospital, so he had arrived that morning by cab. The thought of my dad lying there alone was more than I could stand. But what could I do from here?

I picked up the phone and called information for the Puyallup, Washington, Marine Corps recruiting station, where I joined the Marines ten years before. I thought that if I could talk to a Marine and explain the situation, maybe one of them would visit my dad.

I called the number. A man answered the phone and in a very confident voice said, "United States Marines, Sergeant Van-es. May I help you?"

Feeling just as certain, I replied, "Sergeant Van-es, you may find this request a little strange, but this is why I am calling. . . ." I proceeded to tell him who I was and that my father was also a former Marine and 100 percent disabled from the Korean War. I explained that he was in the hospital, alone, without anyone to visit and asked if Sergeant Van-es would please go and see him.

Without hesitation, he answered, "Absolutely."

Then I asked, "If I send flowers to the recruiting station, would you deliver them to my dad when you go to the hospital?"

"Ma'am, I will be happy to take the flowers to your dad. I'll give you my address. You send them, and I will make sure that he receives them," he replied.

The next morning, I sent the flowers to Sergeant Van-es's office just as we had planned. I went to work, and that evening, I returned home and phoned my dad to inquire about his surprise visitor.

If you have ever talked with a small child after that child has just seen Santa Claus, you will understand the glee I heard in my dad's voice. "I was just waking up when I thought I saw two Marines in their dress blue uniforms standing at the foot of my bed," he told me excitedly. "I thought I had died and gone to heaven. But they were really there!"

I began to laugh, partly at his excitement, but also because he didn't even mention his operation. He felt so honored: Two Marines he had never met took time out to visit an old Marine like him. He told me again and again how sharp they looked and how all the nurses thought he was so important. "But how did you ever get them to do that?" he asked me.

"It was easy. We are all Marines, Dad, past and present; it's the bond."

After hanging up with my dad, I called Sergeant Van-es to thank him for visiting my dad. And to thank him for the extra things he did to make it special: wearing his dress blue uniform, bringing another Marine along—he even took a digital camera with him. He had pictures taken of the two Marines with my dad right beside his bed. That evening, he e-mailed them to me so I could see for myself that my dad was not alone and that he was going to be okay.

As for the flowers, they hardly mattered, but I was glad for the opportunity to express my feelings. The card read: "Daddy, I didn't want just anyone bringing you flowers . . . so I sent the World's Finest. Semper Fi."

Tre' M. Barron

A Monumental Task

The willingness with which our young people are likely to serve in any war, no matter how justified, shall be directly proportional as to how they perceive the veterans of earlier wars were Treated and Appreciated by their nation.

George Washington

Everyone has had a dream. Some people dream of fame, some of political or military success. Some achieve their desire. Some do not.

More than twenty years ago, I had a dream that most people viewed as unattainable. It was to create a national memorial honoring Vietnam veterans: a memorial that would bear the names of the fifty-eight thousand Americans who died in the war—not to politicize about rightness or wrongness—but to honor service rendered by the veterans.

It would not be a government-sponsored edifice. It would be the "people's memorial," built only if individual Americans contributed the necessary funds.

In 1979, I was told that the dream and the plan were

both too radical to succeed. Yet in November 1982—just three years later—the national Vietnam Veterans Memorial was dedicated on the Mall in Washington, D.C., in the shadow of the Lincoln Memorial. Vietnam veterans, at long last, were recognized by a nation once too bitterly divided over the war to thank those who served.

Having been an infantryman in Vietnam, I knew first-hand about how Vietnam veterans felt. Many returned to be ostracized for serving in that controversial war. Many returned physically disabled, condemned to spend lives in wheelchairs. Others, with emotional problems or concerns about Agent Orange, returned to an indifferent and seemingly uncaring nation. Others never returned at all.

Vietnam veterans had not been treated well. It would certainly take more than a memorial to change this, but it could be a beginning.

The effort was not an easy one. I remember how my heart sunk when, on July 4, 1979, Roger Mudd announced on the *CBS Evening News* that only $144.50 had been raised for the planned national Vietnam Veterans Memorial.

The story, however, attracted the attention of the right people. One was Jack Wheeler, a West Point graduate with an M.B.A. from Harvard and a Yale law degree. Coincidentally, he had just completed a memorial effort at West Point. He assembled a group of extraordinary Vietnam veterans in Washington, D.C., and within a few months our organization, the Vietnam Veterans Memorial Fund, was moving at full steam.

One goal was crucial to success—approval to build on two acres near the Lincoln Memorial. We moved into the political arena and soon found that the United States Congress could be a rather difficult group to deal with. After eight months of exasperating effort, President Jimmy Carter signed the legislation into law at a ceremony in the White House Rose Garden on a hot July day in 1980.

Next we considered the design. The Memorial Fund held a competition and set four criteria: The design had to (1) be reflective and contemplative in character, (2) harmonize with its surroundings, (3) display the names of all who died or remain missing in Vietnam, and (4) make no political statement about the war. Of the 1,421 entries, one submitted by Maya Ying Lin, an architecture student at Yale, was the unanimous choice. Her design was a chevron-shaped, polished black granite wall to be built below the earth's surface. The winning design of the largest architectural competition in U.S. history was unconventional but beautiful because of its size, simplicity and the prominent display of the names of our war dead.

With the design chosen, the next hurdle was to find money to fund the project. The prospects of the massive effort to raise the $7 million needed for construction were not good. Previous efforts had not shown Vietnam to be a popular cause. Saving wildlife, conquering disease and funding political races were proven money raisers. But not Vietnam.

Yet the project gained momentum. Two large donations brought in $1.5 million. All at once, tens of thousands of individuals began contributing. The American Legion and Veterans of Foreign Wars sponsored fund-raising events. Individual Americans organized bake sales and yard sales.

Then controversy struck. The memorial's unique design became an object of angry debate. Suddenly we felt as if we were fighting the Vietnam War over again. In January 1982, twenty-seven members of Congress asked President Reagan to stop the memorial from being constructed.

Thanks to Senator John Warner of Virginia, a compromise was reached, incorporating a flag and a statue in the design. Political opposition subsided. The groundbreaking took place on March 26, 1982, and less than eight months later, America gave Vietnam veterans the homecoming they deserved.

Thousands of Vietnam veterans crowded the nation's capital for "National Salute to Vietnam Veterans," a week of reunions and reconciliations climaxing with the dedication of the memorial on November 13, 1982. Two years later, *Three Servicemen,* Frederick E. Hart's heroic-size statue, was dedicated on the memorial site, and a flagpole was added nearby. Finally, on Veteran's Day 1984, President Ronald Reagan accepted the memorial as a gift to the nation from the Vietnam Veterans Memorial Fund.

The Wall, which will forever honor the more than 2 million Vietnam veterans who served and sacrificed for their country, has become one of the most visited national shrines. It is a thing of beauty that one can only truly appreciate by experiencing its strength and power and by viewing one's own reflection in the names of those who fell in Vietnam.

I knew many of those who died in my infantry unit. I have found their names among the many thousands inscribed on the Vietnam Veterans Memorial. They will never see their memorial, but they will never again be forgotten.

The dream is now reality.

Jan Craig Scruggs

A Voice in the Dark

Airborne, Christmas 1969: Actress Connie Stevens was one of dozens who performed for the GIs overseas.

When Bob Hope said to me, "You've just got to come," I knew I would go to Vietnam to entertain the troops, even though I had two little ones, both under the age of two, at home. It was a difficult assignment for an entertainer. I had to perform in the jungle in the incredible heat. I certainly couldn't use my hair spray and look my best. I was who I was.

Between shows, when we were flying all over, we'd speak at night to the battleships from the plane. I remember flying over the ocean and falling dead asleep. Someone would wake me, and I'd go to the cockpit. Bob would say, "I'm talking to a ship that hasn't been home for months, they're out in the middle of the ocean and the speakers are on. Connie, why don't you talk to them?"

I'd hardly even be awake, but suddenly I'd be talking to twenty-seven hundred young men in the dead of night, over a black ocean. I'd just say, "Hi, glad to talk to you. Is it okay if I sing?" And I'd hear, "Yeah!" come back to me over the intercom. So I would sing some little a cappella song. I'd make up words about the way America should be feeling for them, what I thought their folks would say to them.

Whenever I stopped to think about the fact that I was talking to thousands of young men of all sizes, shapes, colors, trying to represent their mothers, their sisters, their homes, their country, it was just overwhelming. Especially since I couldn't see their faces, I was just talking on the loudspeaker—but the emotions reached all the way up to the plane. I'm sure mine reached to them, because I could hardly speak sometimes, I was so moved by the enormity of what I was experiencing. Even now I still run into someone every week that saw me in some jungle or heard my voice late one night, and they thank me.

They're still thanking me, when in fact we should be thanking them.

Connie Stevens

The Doorman

The year was 1945. World War II had blessedly and finally ended in Europe. Thousands of young men were moved from the battlefields to Paris. There they waited for the day they would be sent to the Pacific to once again risk their lives.

Every one of the soldiers was scarred from the horrors they had seen and of which they had been a part. Kindness, quiet and peace was the medicine necessary to heal their wounds, at least enough to pick up their guns once again.

My husband, Gene, was one of those men. Though he was decorated several times for bravery, war was foreign to his heart. Perhaps this was why he was particularly drawn to the French, who are people of tremendous personal warmth.

The hotel he was billeted in, Hotel Napoleon, was located in the heart of Paris. The elevator was a cage with pulley ropes, and the rooms were clean but simple. The hotel's most impressive feature was its doorman, Monsieur Jean Fratoni. His job was to stand outside the hotel and to open the doors for the guests. He would greet each visitor with *"Bienvenue à Paris"* ("Welcome to Paris"), spoken in his rich baritone.

Monsieur Fratoni was particularly kind to the American soldiers. He treated every young serviceman as a special friend, almost like a son. He remembered their names and was not above hugging them from time to time. They had liberated his country, and he loved them for it.

Happily, the war ended in the Pacific before the soldiers in Europe had to go. Instead, they were sent home. When they left Paris and Hotel Napoleon, many shared tearful good-byes with Monsieur Fratoni.

Forty years later, on his sixtieth birthday, Gene wanted to run the Paris Marathon, so we went to Europe. Gene hadn't been back since the war. Finally, with my emotional support, he was ready to see the towns he'd helped to set free; to travel the roads he'd walked while German soldiers on the hills on either side of the road had fired on them, picking the American soldiers off like flies; to visit cemeteries where so many of his buddies lay buried. It was a highly emotional tour, but the pinnacle was yet to come.

When we finally arrived in Paris, we went to register Gene for the upcoming marathon at an American-owned hotel. We thought we'd probably stay there as so many of the runners were doing. But then Gene had an idea: "Let's find Hotel Napoleon and stay there."

It sounded good to me. We got in the car, and after asking directions, we found it. But it was not at all what we expected. In 1945, it had been a simple hotel, definitely of the no-frills variety. Now Hotel Napoleon was one of the finest, most elegant hotels in all of Paris.

"Oh boy, it sure has changed. Must be very expensive." Gene said this softly, but there was something in his voice—I could hear how touched he was just being there.

Listening to my heart, I said, "Oh, but it's so beautiful,

and to think, you stayed in this very place all those years ago. Let's at least check it out."

We pulled the car up to the curb next to the hotel and sat there, just looking. Suddenly Gene drew in a breath and whispered, "Ohhhhh."

I watched as a very old gentleman bowed and opened Gene's door. *"Bienvenue à Paris,"* he said in a tremulous but rich baritone. Gene seemed suspended in time as he stared at the man's face. Finally, he stepped out of our car and stood facing the doorman.

I saw tears well in Gene's eyes as he placed his hands on the man's stooped shoulders. Swallowing hard, he said simply, "You were here during World War II, weren't you?"

The man nodded, holding his body very still. Gene continued, "So was I. I was one of the soldiers who lived at the Hotel Napoleon, and you were so kind to me. My name is Brody."

The old gentleman searched Gene's face and then threw up his hands and, with trembling arms, enfolded my husband, repeating over and over, *"Je me rappelle, cher ami.* I remember."

Finally, at Monsieur Fratoni's insistence, they gathered up the baggage and went inside. The hotel was very expensive, but they found us a tiny room with a bath that we felt we could afford. As we presented the clerk with our credit card, Monsieur Fratoni left us and went to speak briefly to an official-looking man. When we were taken to our room, it was not the "least room in the inn" but, rather, an elegant suite with antique furniture and priceless rugs.

When we said there was some mistake, Gene's friend shook his head. To Monsieur Fratoni, Gene was still the young soldier who had liberated his beloved France. The old gentleman just smiled and said, *"Seulement le mieux pour vous"* ("Only the best for you").

Jean P. Brody

The Cub Scout

It was a typical small-town Remembrance Day. While the majority of residents were enjoying a long weekend at the shore, perhaps a hundred of us gathered in Westmont, New Jersey, to listen to speeches by local politicians and watch aging veterans honor fallen comrades.

I had been dragooned into the VFW rifle squad. We stood sweltering in the sun while the speeches dragged on and wreaths were laid. There were six of us: three World War II vets in khaki, two present-day soldiers in Army green who happened to be husband and wife, and I in dark trousers, white shirt and an old Marine utility cap. All we needed was Norman Rockwell to paint the scene.

The squad commander was an Army vet who crisply snapped out orders. Of course, World War II was a while ago, so he was winging it on some commands. He ordered "Turn about" instead of "About face," for example, which hurt our parade-ground precision a bit. And as such small-town ceremonies often are, it managed to be both comic and touching.

I'm a sharp critic of rifle squads, but our three volleys weren't bad, considering we had never practiced. While kids scrambled to pick up the empty shells, we turned in the old M-1 Garands and thought about getting a cold beer at the post before heading home for the obligatory barbecue.

Drinking my beer, I found the funny-sad ceremony had put a lump in my throat. It brought back clear memories of the last time I served on a rifle squad honoring our dead, over thirty years ago.

* * *

It was in the spring of 1965, and Vietnam was heating up. I had been a young Marine private first class, full of "hot sand and ginger" in Kipling's words, working my way through a yearlong electronics school at the Marine Corps recruit depot in San Diego. My best buddy, Ron "Count" Pittenger, and I had already gone to our commander and volunteered for the infantry in Vietnam.

We didn't know we were volunteering for a war the politicians would have neither the will to win nor the will to end. Television pictures the '60s generation as long-haired hippies preaching "flower power," smoking pot and protesting a terrible war. Rarely do you hear that tens of thousands of kids from that generation believed in America, believed communism was a great evil and volunteered to fight in that war.

Lucky for us, our commander decided we should be studying electronics rather than carrying a rifle through a rice paddy. The skipper thanked us and sent us back to our duties. Vietnam would wait. I think we were equal parts disappointed and relieved.

A few weeks later, we had another chance to volunteer. We were between schools, and while waiting for classes to form, we were assigned various unpleasant duties. One morning, the company gunnery sergeant asked for volunteers for burial duty. I grabbed Count's arm and dragged him forward. We reported an hour later to the sergeant in charge.

I'd like to tell you we were motivated by a deep desire to honor the dead. The truth is, I was desperate to avoid another round of long hours walloping pots in the chow hall, where my most memorable accomplishment was cracking 120 dozen eggs for the cooks one morning. And I'd heard that burial detail was "skating" duty.

That's how the Count and I participated in over one hundred funerals in the next month. We worked at the national cemetery at Point Loma, California. It was easy duty, especially for the rifle squad. The big guys were assigned to be body bearers, carrying heavy coffins. All we had to do was stand straight, look sharp and fire three tight volleys from our seven rifles.

Most of the funerals were for old veterans, guys who had served in the First or Second World War. Often there was no one to see them off but the funeral director, the minister and us, rendering last honors on behalf of the nation.

When you're in ten or fifteen funerals a day, it quickly becomes routine. Of course, we took it seriously—we were Marines—giving every vet our sharpest effort. But we quickly stopped feeling sad. You can't grieve endlessly for strangers.

Then we buried the Cub Scout's dad.

We were told to look sharp because the next funeral was for a Marine who'd been killed in Vietnam. With the family was a Marine staff sergeant, most likely a buddy, assigned to help. The large crowd of mourners included the young widow and the son of the dead Marine, a Cub Scout in full uniform. He was perhaps eight years old.

When we fired our volleys, the seven rifles making a single crack, people in the crowd began to cry. The rifle fire always seemed to signal how final death was. Then we stood at present arms while our bugler played "Taps." He was a lance corporal permanently assigned to Point Loma, and he had blown "Taps" at several hundred funerals. No one has ever made it sound sadder.

While the bugle notes rolled down the hillside and the family grieved, the staff sergeant and the Cub Scout stood at the foot of the casket at rigid attention, saluting the tautly stretched flag. The tall Marine in dress greens stood motionless, his eyes fixed straight ahead. The small boy in blue gave his dad the Cub salute—the first two fingers of his right hand close together, just touching his eyebrows.

As they saluted, the boy turned his head slightly and looked up at the Marine. Then he quickly extended the other two fingers of his right hand as he turned his head back to gaze once more at the flag-draped casket. The young Cub Scout was now giving a perfect, open-handed Marine salute to his fallen Marine dad, honoring him as a soldier honors a soldier.

We held our position, but I wasn't the only Marine weeping openly. Finally "Taps" ended, the notes dying out over the sobbing of relatives. The body bearers folded the flag into the traditional triangle and passed it to the staff sergeant. He presented it to the Cub Scout and saluted. The boy accepted the American flag from his dad's grave and sharply returned the salute—in the open-handed Marine style. The mantle had been passed.

Slowly the family and friends drifted away, and we marched off. Another funeral was waiting.

Robert A. Hall

The Waiting Room

If a man had done his best, what else is there?

General George S. Patton

"It'll be about thirty minutes," the pharmacist told me as he slid a numbered tag under the thick glass window. I didn't care for this part of the VA hospital experience, sitting in the waiting room and pretending to read a magazine so that nobody bothered me.

I couldn't tell you what the magazine was, but waiting-room etiquette requires that each patient have one and appear to be giving it their attention. It's just something that one does to protect one's privacy when in the midst of strangers.

That's not to say that I wasn't aware. Although my eyes were staring blankly at the open periodical, I was very conscious of others in the waiting room, especially the conversation going on between two elderly patients sitting with their wives not far from where I sat. These guys obviously didn't know the rules.

They were talking about the coldest experiences of their

lives. The gentleman called "Slats" by his friend told about when he was a kid in North Dakota. He had walked to school one day when it was fifty-five degrees below zero and the tip of his nose had frozen. His wife politely reminded him, "It was cold in that bomber, too, wasn't it?"

"Oh, yeah," he reflected soberly. "I'd forgotten about that."

"That was a B-17, wasn't it?" his friend asked.

Apparently uncomfortable with the direction the conversation was taking, Slats answered in a low voice, "Yeah, Eighth Air Force.

"We had a thermometer on board," Slats continued quietly. "But it had been busted since our third mission. We were dressed for the cold, though, which really helped us out in the POW camp."

I was aching to get into this discussion. *I am sitting next to history,* I told myself as I stared at the magazine. *These guys saved the world, right over there, the little guy next to his wife, and the other fellow whose wife was almost asleep now. Did these guys know what they had done? Did they know back then what the odds were of their ever coming home again?* I don't know why, but these questions were burning inside me, and all I could do was stare at my magazine, because these were strangers and that's what you did in public.

"You were a tail gunner, weren't you?" Slats's friend asked.

"Yep, but we did a lot of damage from back there, too," Slats said as though defending or making excuses for tail gunners who were notorious slackers.

I'd had it! Forget decorum; I couldn't stay out of this any longer.

"Excuse me," I said, addressing Slats. "May I ask a question?"

Slats gave his friend a look as though to say, "Now we've done it. We've gone and disturbed this nice young man who was trying to read his magazine."

"Sure," he said.

I had to lay some groundwork here to let him know that I knew a little something about this, so I began, "The U.S. Army Tank Corps was sent to North Africa thinking they were the best-equipped and best-trained corps on earth. They were told that their tanks were invulnerable to anything the Germans had to shoot at them and that their guns could destroy German tanks with near misses. It wasn't until they were in combat that they discovered that the exact opposite was true." I didn't know of a delicate way to phrase my question, so I just asked, "Did you realize, at that time, what your odds were of ever coming home?"

"You look awfully young to have been in the world war," Slats said. "Were you in Korea? Vietnam?"

"Vietnam," I said, trying to put this aside. I was afraid he was trying to change the subject and evade my question.

"That was a bad deal there," he said sympathetically. "But to answer your question, yeah, we knew, but we tried not to think about it much. They let you go home when you flew twenty-five missions, but of all the thousands and thousands of B-17 crews that I know of, only about six or seven ever made their twenty-five missions.

"A lot of the guys in other crews were superstitious about it," he continued. "When they got to their twelfth mission, they'd call it "twelve-A." Then when they flew their thirteenth, they'd call it "twelve-B" and then go to fourteen. I used to tell them how stupid that was—that is, until we flew our thirteenth mission.

"I think we all knew inside that we'd probably never make it home again, but until that thirteenth mission, getting shot down was something that always happened to the other guy."

"But you knew and still went up?" I stated more than asked.

"I knew the odds of getting our twenty-five missions

were practically zero. I was also aware that the life expectancy of a B-17 tail gunner in combat was two and a half minutes, but we had to go. We were all that they had just then."

I nodded and retreated to the refuge of my magazine to contemplate what I had just heard. I was in the presence of a real hero, and I was too choked up to take advantage of it, to tap his personal knowledge, to exploit and revel in his memories. I just stared at the magazine.

"I'm not a hero," he said as though he'd been reading my mind, "but I knew one. Our pilot was a real hero." His voice was beginning to break. I looked up. His jaw trembled, and his eyes glistened as he fought to check his emotions.

"We never made it to the target on that thirteenth mission," he continued. "We were jumped by Jerrys and were shot up pretty bad. When we turned back, the fighters followed us and kept pounding us until they either ran out of ammunition or fuel or were shot down. It was just beginning to look like we were going to make it back when we ran into the flak. The navigator and I were too badly wounded to bail out.

Slats was looking at the ceiling now and blinking rapidly. "But the pilot crash-landed that plane with no engines, no landing gear and most of the tail section shot away. He saved the navigator and me, although the navigator died from his wounds. We were all captured because we stuck together, but we were all alive."

I stared defensively and silently at my magazine. I'd gotten a lot more than I had bargained for, almost more than I could bear.

Moments later, the pharmacist called him to the window. When he came back and helped his wife to her feet, he told his friend that he'd see him later, and then he looked over at me. He smiled, nodded and said, "Take care." I nodded and returned to the magazine I was holding.

Within minutes, I noticed someone standing in front of me waiting for my attention. I looked up to see that his wife had returned and was holding a copy of a newspaper from a nearby town that she had retrieved from the clinic waiting room. It was folded to show a quarter-page ad for the First National Bank, half of which was a black-and-white photograph of four officers and six enlisted men standing proudly in front of their B-17.

"This is my husband, Lowell, here," she said, pointing to a nineteen-year-old in a leather jacket. "And this is the navigator," she said, pointing to a not-nearly-as-handsome officer in the front row. "He died in Lowell's arms," she said. "I thought you might appreciate this."

She left while I stared at the photo. I wanted to thank her, but I was unable to speak. The eyes of the men in the photo were looking directly at me. They reflected the determination it would take to save the world but also betrayed the human frailty of which they were very much aware. "We were all that they had just then. . . ." They had been enough.

Michael Manley

Lowell “Slats” Slayton, standing far right, is the only living member of “Fridgen’s Pigeons,” whose B-17G Flying Fortress named “Homing Pigeon” was shot down over Germany on February 22, 1944. The Flying Fortress belonged to the 533rd Bomb Squadron, 381st Bomb Group of the Eighth Air Force.

Credit: Lowell Slayton.

Pie in the Sky

Never believe that a few caring people can't change the world. For, indeed, that's all who ever have.

Margaret Mead

Just prior to Veteran's Day in 1996, my wife and I drove to the new Colorado State Vietnam Veterans Memorial in our hometown of Pueblo, Colorado. It was the day the memorial was to be dedicated.

As I parked the car we could see that a crowd had already gathered. Hundreds of Vietnam veterans were quickly identified by their uniforms, hats or patches. It was also a "high profile" crowd including state legislators and virtually every one of our city officials.

From a distance I could see the three, eight-foot granite slabs that contained the names of the 620 Colorado men and women who had died in Vietnam. Above them flew the national colors, the flags of each branch of service and the POW/MIA flag. It looked just like the diagram Delbert Schmeling had shown me three years earlier. That thought caused me to cringe inside, first in embarrassment, then in shame.

My first impression of Delbert Schmeling had been that he was mentally handicapped. Delbert and his parents had attended a large celebration I had organized that included several Medal of Honor recipients. At the conclusion of the event Delbert had walked up to tell me how impressed he was with our program. "You know," he told me haltingly, "If you can put together something this big, maybe you can help me with a project I am working on."

Out of politeness, I invited him to call to make an appointment to discuss his project. "I will," he replied. To my surprise, he did, the very next week.

As I set coffee for the two of us on the desk in my office, Delbert began showing me pages of plans, designs and a list of names. He explained that it represented his dream for a local memorial to honor his brothers and sisters from Colorado who had died in Vietnam. The project had been started by the local chapter of the Vietnam Veterans of America (VVA), which disbanded shortly thereafter. By "default," Delbert became president of the nonexistent chapter and the sole hope for the future of the project. I appreciated the concept, but couldn't bring myself to believe in its viability.

As he talked, I studied Delbert. His appearance, the difficulty he had with speech and other mannerisms initially give one the impression that he may have been severely wounded in Vietnam. I thought to myself, *If a whole chapter of Vietnam vets couldn't get this done, there is no way Delbert will ever pull it off.*

Of course I didn't say that out loud; instead I went out of my way to be positive—the big brother offering encouragement while knowing "the kid" was dreaming of "pie in the sky."

That same afternoon Delbert opened up to me and

began to share a little about himself. His learning difficulties as a child left him far behind his classmates. He graduated from high school two years behind other people his age.

After finishing high school in 1967 Delbert felt the right thing to do was to serve his country. He volunteered to join the Navy, but they weren't interested in Delbert Schmeling. By November, however, the Army had enlisted Delbert and sent him to training. Ten months later he arrived in Vietnam. "I would have been there sooner," Delbert told me, "but I had to go through basic training three times."

Delbert never saw combat in the field, but for 365 days Delbert literally slept with his M-16 rifle, prepared for whatever may come. He tasted death, watched friends die in an explosion and fire on the base camp. On his last night "in country," the enemy reached out one more time. That night Delbert huddled in a bunker with other soldiers as a major rocket attack was launched against his position. Throughout the night he never knew from one minute to the next if he would be walking onto the "Freedom Bird" home the next day, or if others would be carrying his body in a bag to the belly of a cargo plane.

Delbert survived the night and came home. He tried to put his life back together, but Vietnam invaded his dreams. For fourteen years his inner demons plagued him time and again until Delbert finally broke down. After six months in a VA hospital, Delbert was diagnosed with post-traumatic stress disorder and was eventually determined to be 100 percent disabled.

Back home with his parents, Delbert struggled to survive the bad days and find a sense of purpose in his few good days. He found some comfort and understanding among fellow Vietnam Vets in the local VVA before the group disbanded. When they were gone, Delbert determined to follow through with the dream of building a memorial to all his Colorado brothers and sisters who had died in Vietnam.

When Delbert left my office that day back in 1993, my mind was flooded with a mix of emotions. I couldn't help but admire Delbert's courage and determination. Part of me wanted to reach out, to do what I could to help Delbert make the dream come true. The "rational" side of me was more inclined to spend my time on "more attainable" goals.

In the years that followed, Delbert would call or visit me from time to time. I'd pat him on the back, give him a few words of encouragement and then send him off to accomplish his mission—alone.

And that is exactly what Delbert had done. The kid who had so much trouble forming speech in normal conversation stood alone before the city council and city leaders to promote his project. He sat in front of local grocery stores for three years with a small glass jar to collect nickels, dimes and quarters to make the dream happen. He'd collect aluminum cans, visit businesses and solicit help wherever he could. He paced off an area allocated by the city council for a memorial site, dug up snow-covered dirt, and staked off areas for concrete masons and contractors. And now, just a week before Veteran's Day, the fruit of his labors had become a source of pride for our whole city. Delbert Schmeling had become, in his own simple way, a hero to all of us.

During the dedication of the memorial that day, I observed elderly mothers gently running their fingers across the engraved names of Colorado sons and daughters who had answered their country's call and paid the supreme sacrifice. Others left flowers, mementos and tears at the base of the three granite panels.

Since its dedication, seldom has a day passed that

Delbert has not visited the memorial. He tends the landscape, polishes the stone and regularly provides fresh flowers from his mother's garden. He is a daily volunteer at the local VA clinic, and he frequently drives the four-hour round-trip to take less fortunate veterans to the nearest VA hospital in Fort Lyons.

The man who I always thought of as a "kid brother" is proving to be the biggest of us all. I hope and pray that I can be half the man he is today.

Recently, while visiting with Delbert, he looked at me and said, "Doug, maybe you can help me with a project I am working on." I smiled inwardly and thought to myself, *Where have I heard those words before?*

"You know," Delbert said, "There is lots of space near the Vietnam memorial, and we need to do something to remember our Korean War Veterans. . . ."

Doug Sterner

A Daughter's Letter

Dear Dad,

My trip to the Wall was something I'll never forget. When you wrote me and asked me to make rubbings of your fellow soldiers' names for you, I knew that it was going to be something special, both for you and for me. And doing it alone was important to me. No kids, no husband, not even a friend. I didn't want the distraction of having anyone else there needing my attention.

I waited for a nice, sunny day—not too hot—and packed a lunch and took off on the metro. I walked through the streets of D.C. thinking about my quest. I was hoping that I had the right paper and the right pencils, and that my camera wouldn't flake out on me. When I arrived, I went straight to the registry to look up the addresses of the crew, which were easy to find. Then I headed toward the Wall.

Several students on field trips were standing around. I thought that this would keep me from doing my job, but as I approached each panel of the Wall that held a name I wanted, people just moved out of my way. I'm not sure if I said anything to them. Maybe they saw a certain look in my eyes that said I was there for a specific person. They were right to think so.

I came to the first panel, where I would find Thomas A. Davis's name. I located it quickly, and I had to sit down to do the rubbing as it was near the bottom of the Wall. I was nervous when I started. I wasn't sure that I had the paper lined up right, but as I dragged the pencil across the page, his name began to appear. I was really concentrating on the action so I could get it right for the rest, and that distracted me from the unhappy meaning of what I was doing.

The next one wasn't so easy. I found Thomas Duer a few panels down. He was within my reach, and I could stand and look at his name as if he were standing right there in front of me. But as I began rubbing, a sadness came over me. I thought about his age, twenty-five, and about what I was doing when I was that age. It seemed to me that I was only a kid at twenty-five, yet these men whose names I touched on the Wall never got any older than that. Never had children. Or if they did, never saw them grow up. Their parents must've gone out of their minds with grief over losing their boys. As I moved from name to name, thoughts like these kept going through my head, and I could hear people behind me, next to me and around me, all sharing those same feelings with the other people with them.

When I went to 14-E, where your crew is, I suddenly panicked. I couldn't reach anyone; they were all too high. I looked around for a tall person, then stopped. There was no way I was going to let some stranger do this. I had to do it! Only I was too short.

I began to cry, thinking I had failed you, when I saw a man who had a ladder. I was saved. I asked him to let me use it to trace my names off the Wall. He said he could do the rubbings for me, but he couldn't allow me to use the ladder. At first I fought him. I told him about my daddy, who went to Vietnam and whose friends died there: classmates and crew. I told him that this was something I had to do for him because it was the only thing I could do for him—I couldn't take it all away, and I couldn't help him with the pain; I said there are no words that can erase what my daddy saw and what he has to endure.

The man was so sympathetic, and he assured me that it would be okay if he did it, that the important thing was that I was there. I pointed out the names and watched him like a hawk, making sure he was doing it right. Of course, he'd been doing it awhile, so his came out better than mine. That was okay by me; I wanted it to be perfect.

After he was finished, he asked me a couple of questions about you, and I told him that you were over there twice but that I didn't know much more than that, except the names that I had on my letter from you. He told me that I was very lucky that you came home.

I told him that the way I see it, luck had little to do with it. You *had* to come home; you had to take care of us. You were meant to be my daddy, and you were meant to be around a long, long time.

But as I left the Wall, I remember thanking God that you did come home. I couldn't have stood there making a rubbing of your name; I'm not that strong.

I'm writing all this because if I tried to tell you, I know it wouldn't come out the same. I'm always hesitant to bring up Vietnam because I think it hurts you too much. I just hope you know that I'm always here for you and that I am very proud of you. I am so honored that you asked me to do this very special project for you. I will never know what it's like for you really, but I do often try to imagine.

Thank you for your service to our country, and thank you for being my daddy.

All my love,
Rani

Rani Nicola
Submitted by her father, George C. Miller

Former Enemies

Some years ago, while leading a church group on a tour of Pearl Harbor, I stood among the clergy and their spouses in the gleaming white-arched and covered memorial above the USS *Arizona.* One minister in our group, a man from Maine, had been there on December 7, 1941—the day the Japanese flew in to sink our Pacific naval fleet. He had not been aboard the *Arizona,* but his ship had also been hit. He described vividly the horror of being aboard the flaming and sinking vessel as bullets flew and bombs roared. As I listened, out of the corner of my eye, I noticed a Japanese tourist entering the memorial.

It was the man's fine clothes—long tie, buttoned sports jacket and shiny brown lace-up shoes—that initially attracted my attention. In Hawaii, professionals like lawyers, corporate executives, soldiers and ministers seldom, if ever, wear ties or jackets. Even network television news anchors wear open-collared aloha shirts. This man, dressed as he was, stood out.

Two women walked with him. The older one I took to be his wife, the other perhaps an older daughter. Both wore conservative dresses and fancy shoes. The man appeared to be in his sixties, and while he may have spoken English, I only heard him speak Japanese. In his left hand, he carried, almost shyly, an ornate and obviously costly multiflowered wreath about eighteen inches across.

Our group's veteran continued to speak as we clustered around him. He described being caught below deck: feeling disoriented as the ship took on water where he stood, fire coming from above and the smoke stealing his breath. His buddy lay dead at his feet as the young sailor struggled in the darkness to escape, fear and adrenaline propelling him to the surface. Everyone in our group was so engrossed in his story that no one, except for me, noticed the Japanese tourist and his family who walked quite near us.

As I watched, the tourist stopped, turned to his wife and daughter and spoke to them. They stood quietly, almost solemnly. Then the man straightened his tie, first at the neck and then near the belt, and tugged at the hem of his jacket. As if in preparation, he squared his shoulders, took a deep breath and then exhaled. Alone, he somberly stepped forward toward the railing at the water's edge above the sunken warship.

The other tourists swirled around him. From what I could see and hear, they were apparently all Americans. They were talking, laughing, looking, asking questions; some were listening to our minister's story, but none seemed aware of the tourist who had captured my attention.

I don't believe the Japanese man understood the minister's words. As I listened to one man and watched the other, the Japanese tourist came to the rail, bowed at the waist and then stood erect. He began to speak; I heard his words but could not comprehend them. From his tone and the look on his face, however, I felt their meaning. His manner conveyed so many things at once—confession, sorrow, hurt, honor, dignity, remorse and benediction.

When he had finished his quiet prayer, he gravely dropped the flowered wreath into the seawater—the same water the minister kept mentioning in his reminiscence—and watched as the wreath floated away on the tide. The man struggled to remain formal, to keep face, but his tears betrayed him. I guessed he must have been a soldier, a warrior of the air, whose own plane had showered the bombs and bullets that had torn through our soldiers, sinking their ships. It struck me that he had come on a pilgrimage of repentance, not to our government, but to the gravesite of those young men whose lives he had taken in the name of war.

Stepping backward one pace, the Japanese veteran then closed his eyes and bowed again, very deeply and very slowly from the waist. Then he stood tall, turned around and rejoined his family. His deed done, they began to leave. All the while, our minister veteran continued his narrative. He and the group were oblivious to the poignant counterpoint occurring behind them.

But I was not the only American to witness the Japanese man's actions. As I watched his family leave, I noticed another American step away from the wall on which he had been leaning. He was dressed casually and wore a red windbreaker with the VFW emblem on it. He had a potbelly and thinning hair, and he held his hat in his hand. I assumed the man was a World War II veteran. *Perhaps he had served in the Pacific,* I thought, *and is himself on a pilgrimage.*

As the Japanese family walked by him, the American stepped directly into their path, blocking their way. I immediately tensed, fearing a confrontation. The startled Japanese tourist, who had been deep in thought, stopped short, surprise and sorrow mixed on his face. His family, eyes on the ground, stopped abruptly, then crowded closer around him.

But the American simply stood at attention, once again a strong, straight-backed soldier. Then he raised his right hand slowly and stiffly to his forehead, saluting his former enemy.

The American remained in salute until the Japanese, with dawning understanding, returned the gesture.

As the tourists milled by, the two men stood as if alone, joined by their shared pain, glories, honors and memories, until the American, while remaining at attention, slowly lowered his arm and formally stepped backward one pace. The Japanese tourist, when his arms were both once again at his side, bowed formally to the man in front of him. To my surprise, the American returned the honor.

Neither said a word. Neither had to. Their solemn faces, wet with tears, communicated with each other in a universal language what never could have been said in words.

I watched as the two men, their reconciliation complete, went their separate ways, united in a way I had never imagined possible.

Reverend Peter Baldwin Panagore

9

HEALING

Let me not mourn for the men who have died fighting, but rather, let me be glad that such heroes have lived.

General George S. Patton, "Soldier's Prayer"

The Search for "Shorts"

It was the height of the Korean conflict, and nine-year-old Kim Jun Hawn, walking down a road near Taegu with his parents, had become accustomed to a country at war. As the steady drone of a fighter plane drew closer and closer, the mad dash for cover he made was automatic. And when, after the roar of the plane's guns had ceased and he could not find his parents again, his assumption was only natural: They were dead.

My father, Alan H. Stewart, was the supply sergeant in the 151st Combat Engineers in Korea from June 1951 until April 1952. When he came upon the little Korean boy, he felt an immediate attachment to the tiny, lonely figure. It was a bitterly cold winter, and my dad, feeling sorry for the boy, allowed him to live in his tent with him on the front lines, where Kim slept and ate for the duration of my father's tour of duty.

The soldiers nicknamed the little boy "Shorts," and his broad smile and tiny, bustling figure soon became a beloved sight in the unit. Every day, dressed in the military fatigues the soldiers gave him, he hurried about, doing errands and carrying water. He even did the men's laundry, squatting on the rocks of a nearby river. Occasionally, the soldiers gathered chestnuts from trees in the area and roasted them. Shorts helped to pass around the special treat with a huge, happy grin.

All the soldiers loved him, but my father was the one who was generally acknowledged to be his special protector and guardian. Dad even wrote home for schoolbooks so he could teach Shorts some English, and, eventually, Shorts was able to deliver mail to the right soldiers.

As my father's time of service drew to a close, he grew increasingly concerned for Shorts. Of course, Dad had known all along that he would not be able to take care of the little orphan forever—it was impossible to take Kim with him—and he worried how he and Shorts would handle the separation.

His worst fears were confirmed. Dad never was able to forget the day he left Korea, looking back at Shorts as a military jeep drove him away. Shorts cried and ran after him till he was out of sight. Dad felt as if someone had wrenched his own child away from him. Shorts was an orphan, again.

When he returned home, my father found out that the Korean government had gathered up all the children like Shorts and taken them to an orphanage in Seoul. It was what Dad had expected.

As a child, I loved to have Dad tell me the story about the little Korean boy called Shorts, but as I grew older, I realized that it hurt my father to talk about it; he would always leave the room with tears in his eyes. So I stopped asking Dad to talk about Shorts, but neither of us forgot about him.

Many years later, in November 1983, I watched a segment on the television show *20/20* on the reuniting of Korean families who had been separated during the war.

What a shame, I thought, *that I can't reunite my father with the little Korean boy he'd loved, too.*

But it had been more than thirty years. Shorts could be anywhere. Friends and family felt the same way: Don't even bother, they advised. It's impossible.

But I couldn't shake the feeling that it was the right thing to do. Undaunted, I sat down and wrote letters to the Korean embassy, the U.S. embassy in Seoul and the National Red Cross Tracing Service in Seoul. In each letter, I outlined all the information I had on Kim—which was precious little—and included a small photograph of the boy sitting on my father's knee. I knew it was a shot in the dark.

In the months that followed, I received the expected response: a few false leads, and then silence.

A year later, my father's phone rang in the middle of the night. Groggily, he picked it up, but for a moment couldn't understand the operator's garbled speech. Suddenly, Dad sat up; she was speaking Korean. There was a pause, and then a man's voice: "Sergeant Stewart, this is Shorts."

My father was speechless for a moment. Then the two men began to talk. Kim spoke in broken English, explaining the miracle of how he had happened to open the Seoul newspaper that he subscribed to and stumbled across the tiny picture of my father and himself embedded deep in the classifieds. The conversation was punctuated with long silences as both men, overcome with emotion, tried to find the words to describe their feelings. Before they said good-bye, Kim promised to send a letter soon.

When the letter arrived, there was no doubt in anyone's mind that we had found Shorts. He recalled events and people in the letter that only he and my father would know about. Kim's unknown life after the war unfolded for us. He had gone to Seoul as an orphan, only to discover that his parents had survived the airplane's gunfire on the road after all. They were reunited, and Kim was now a "successful man in my society and a schoolteacher at a middle school in Seoul." He sent pictures of his family—he had a wife and two daughters—and he wrote how much he would like the families to meet.

Two years later—thirty-three years after Dad drove away from Shorts—he was reunited with his "first son." As my father and mother came off the plane in Korea, a small, smiling man named Kim was there to meet them. They laughed and cried as they marveled at the changes the years had brought, and how circumstances had brought them back together.

One evening during their stay in Korea, as my parents were unwinding at their hotel, they heard a knock on the door. Opening it, they were greeted by a beaming Kim holding out a bag of fragrant roasted chestnuts. "I know Sergeant Stewart likes these," he said.

Taking the bag from Shorts and shaking his head, my father said, "You remembered *that*?"

"I remember everything," Shorts answered.

"So do I," my father said softly. "So do I."

There would be no more tears about the lost Korean boy. Despite a war that had been painful in so many ways, Shorts and my father had created memories that—at last—made them both smile.

Marta J. Sweek
Submitted by Jessie L. Stewart

Sergeant Alan H. Stewart and “Shorts” in Korea, 1951.

Credit: Stewart family.

Return to Hoa Quan Village

Thai Airways Flight 680 rumbled onto the runway at Tan Son Knut at 12:15 P.M. The trip had required much planning. It was 1993, and for Vietnam, the early 1990s were still the awkward, raw years—the dark days before the lifting of the embargo and the reestablishment of diplomatic relations that the nation's economy so desperately needed.

Ho Chi Minh City was alive with well-wishers on this bright, hot day. The locals still referred to the city as Saigon, showing their irreverence for the Communist government and harking back to better days, when the marketplace bustled with capitalism and enthusiasm.

My wife, Carolyn, and I had come to Vietnam to visit a village called Hoa Quan, where I had served during my tour of duty here. Back in 1969, as a lieutenant in charge of a five-man team of U.S. advisers, my job had been to accompany the 168th Regional Forces Company on all of their daytime patrols and night ambushes to help defend Hoa Quan Village from the Vietcong. My team not only fought alongside the South Vietnamese soldiers, but we also established relationships in the village with the elected officials and the monks at the pagoda. Our goal was to coordinate pacification of the area and preserve the freedom in Hoa Quan for which they so fiercely struggled.

The year 1969 had been one of the "hot years" for Vietnam combat. Together with 1968, it generated nearly half of the fifty-eight thousand names displayed in the quiet park off Constitution Avenue in Washington, D.C., the memorial most veterans now call the Wall. But South Vietnamese casualties during this period far exceeded our own. It had been my job during this time to be there for them, to call in air support, to bring in resupply and to be by their side when it was time to load them onto the medevacs.

When I'd left Vietnam in late 1969, I'd been uneasy about the civilians and soldiers that I'd left behind. Their situation was so hopeless, their losses so great—I felt that I was personally letting them down. This sense of failure had weighed heavily on my spirit for too many years.

Now, I was making this journey to bring my Vietnam experience "front and center," to deal with it, to get it behind me. I couldn't imagine that Vietnam could hurt me anymore, having already dominated my thoughts for nearly a quarter century.

The last leg of our expedition to Hoa Quan was by water. We approached the village, putt-putting along in the boat with four other men, part of an entourage we had accumulated in Ho Chi Minh City. Later, we found out they had been former Vietcong who were now government-paid "tour guides," a reward for their heroism during their American War.

After rounding a familiar bend in the canal, we passed what had been my living quarters at Hoa Quan, our "outpost," which had been nothing more than a triangular mud-walled fort surrounded by a moat. A new school stood where the old outpost had been.

At the center of the village, we had to check in at the Office of the People's Committee, a bombed-out French colonial building I recognized from 1969, when our 168th Regional Force soldiers rousted several VC out of the building with a grenade launcher.

Inside, we were introduced to the party chairman of Hoa Quan Village. In the old days, his post would have been the elected position of village chief. Now the job was a government appointment, held by a former Vietcong soldier named Vinh, whose right hand had been shot off during the war. He looked disdainfully at Carolyn and me, not liking this visit and the attention it brought from his superiors in Saigon. I sensed he also disapproved of the enthusiastic welcome we were receiving from the village people.

I explained that I had come to visit the village and the pagoda one more time, to rekindle friendships and to present the school with a gift of three hundred dollars. Finishing our interview with Vinh, Carolyn and I set out on foot for the short walk to the pagoda. I'd brought along a photo album with many pictures from 1969.

Being in Hoa Quan brought all my distressing memories back. I tried to shake them off, reminding myself, once again, of why I had come: I wanted to lay to rest the horrors that had occurred here and to see for myself that the people of Hoa Quan had no bitterness toward me or resentment for what we had tried to do there.

A crowd had now gathered around us, moving in unison as we arrived at the concrete slab in front of the pagoda. The monks greeted us as more people gathered, surrounding us and grabbing at the photo album. I felt the old pain stirring as I watched the crowd pass the photo album around. They pointed to the photos, chattering excitedly—identifying wives that had died fifteen years earlier, children who were now fully grown and others lost in the war. To my great pleasure, several remembered my team and smiled and shook my hand, thanking me for all the things we tried to accomplish in the village.

Then one of the young people began feverishly pointing to a picture of me with the platoon leader of the First Platoon, Thiêu Úy (Second Lieutenant) Hungl.

Lieutenant Hungl had been my counterpart at Hoa Quan for many months during my one-year tour. Hungl had repelled an attack on my life by a sniper in broad daylight, and Hungl's platoon had killed three Vietcong not one hundred meters from where I was now standing, the result of a failed ambush intended for the two of us. He had taken me on my first night ambush and taught me enough to keep my five-man team and me alive during what was the most terrifying and dangerous year of my life.

"This is my father," the young man said, pointing to Hungl in the picture. He had a twisted expression on his face.

"Your father?" I cried, "Thiêu Úy Hungl is your father? Where is he? Can we go see him? I'd love to talk to him!" I was beside myself with joy. I remembered now that Hungl's wife had been blessed with a baby boy in 1969. I realized with shock that the man standing before me was that baby boy.

"No," Hungl's son said, "we can't. He is dead."

"Dead?" I was stunned. "Dead?"

"He was shot," he continued, "killed by the Vietcong in January of 1970."

That was a month after I had left Vietnam.

I gazed at Hungl's son. He stood dressed in bright orange robes, the attire of his profession. The young man of twenty-four years had become a monk at Hoa Quan, a guardian of peace and freedom, a teacher of the peace-loving Buddhist faith.

"I want you to have this picture of your father," I said. "As a remembrance." I handed him the picture, and he took it reverently, silently, with both hands. "Your father was a guardian of freedom, a peace-loving man and a brave one."

Then, before I knew what was happening, we were embracing. We held each other and began sobbing like babies.

When I had left this village the first time, I had taken with me a restlessness and sadness that the years had done little to ease. When I left for the second time, I possessed an inner peace, a peace that remains to this day and that was given to me by the child of the man whose country we so desperately tried to free.

For me, the war was finally over.

Robert R. Amon Jr.

You're Never Alone on a Mission

"I've only seen one aviator killed since I've been here," my brother wrote in his last letter home, July 14, 1969. He had been in Vietnam for three weeks and was trying to reassure Mom. "You see, you're never alone on a mission. There's always somebody to protect you and get you out even before you hit the ground. I just don't want you to get upset because if I go down, I'd only be on the ground for about three minutes before they'd get me out of the area. We have what they call a 'downed bird alarm' in all of the hooches. Whenever a bird goes down, every bird here is airborne and en route to provide assistance in less than two minutes. That includes running to your aircraft, starting it and taking off. So you see, there's really nothing to worry about."

Then just a week later, on July 21, David's light observation helicopter was hit by a secondary explosion. He was the only one to survive the crash but died twelve days later, on August 3. He was nineteen.

I was only seven years old the day Mom, Dad and I saw David off at the airport on his way to Vietnam. One black-and-white Polaroid survives from that day: my mom smiling, heroically grasping two of her four kids, I, resentful of her hand clamping my shoulder, and my brother David, tall and proud in his "dress" tans.

David's death affected my family in ways that were hard for me to understand as a child. Mom cried and fought hard to get more details from the Army. Dad grieved more quietly, and my older brother and sister, who were twenty-seven and sixteen when David died, stopped talking about him. I learned very early that the Vietnam War was a subject that brought out strong and frightening emotions in people, a subject better left alone.

Yet I did remember my brother, a little. I remembered being told I was his favorite, remembered his letters that always ended, "Say hi to everyone and Julie." And I remembered vaguely how tall he looked in the flight suit with all the zippered pockets and how proud he was to model it for us in the living room the last time he was home on leave.

But as time passed, the name "David" came to mean the name on a marker in a cemetery, the color green, an insignia and some medals. It brought to mind the musty, overseas smell I will never forget, associated forever with the strange words "personal effects," a box of military letters and papers and a few photos.

Each time I stared into the face in those photos, I tried so hard to remember the tone of his voice, how long his fingers were, how his jacket felt. But I couldn't. To avoid the pain, no one talked about David, and, in fact, most of my best friends in high school never knew I lost a brother in Vietnam. The years went by, and I longed to find out more about him. I just didn't know how.

In September 1993, I visited the Moving Wall in Shakopee, Minnesota, and picked up a brochure on the Friends of the Vietnam Veterans Memorial and the In Touch program. I filled out the registration, and a few months later, I received my first response. The man who responded had not known my brother but opened a whole new world for me, sending me advice on where to continue my search, a membership directory of the First Cav Division Association and a Cav pin.

It took a few years for me to find the Vietnam Helicopter Crew Members Association and Pilots Association, and the Vietnam Helicopter Flight Crew Network, a group of 350 former helicopter pilots, crew chiefs, door gunners and other crew members who have an organized presence on the Internet and a strong bond. The first time one of them e-mailed me offering to help me find friends of my brother, it brought tears to my eyes when I read, "Your brother was our brother."

I began receiving e-mail from pilots sharing memories of their time in Vietnam with the First Cav and other units. Finally, after searching for three years for someone who knew David, a buddy of his from flight school, John Harris, contacted me. He told me about the funny times they'd shared, brawling on the bus on the way to the flight line, and the jokes they played on each other. At last, I was hearing the stories I never had a chance to hear.

Not long after, I received a note in the mail from a man who'd been in David's unit with him. "It's difficult to lose friends because the guys in C troop were closer than that, the bonds formed in combat are in many ways stronger than family," John Powell wrote. "The day your brother went down, I was flying the 'Big Bird' (Cobra) cover and was there until he was recovered. I never knew what happened to him until now."

On August 3, 1997, the twenty-eighth anniversary of David's death, I received my first phone call from Bob Tredway, his troop commander. I met Bob in person in Washington, D.C., that November. Since then, I've also met Luther Russell, who was the first pilot to the scene of the crash and who helped put David on the medevac.

Through contacts like these, by finding out where he was at the end of his life, I've been able to realize who David was up until then. I feel close to these men—brothers of my brother—my "new big brothers."

All those years ago, David had told us, "You're never alone on a mission." Now I knew it was true.

Julie Beth Kink

Sunglasses

In 1985, seventeen years after my tour in Vietnam, my wife and I made our first visit to Washington, D.C. I was finally ready to go to the Wall. I asked my wife if she would mind if I went by myself the first time. She readily agreed to give me whatever space I needed and said she would stay in the motel room, watching television until I returned. Our motel room was within walking distance of the Vietnam Veterans Memorial, so off I went, by myself.

Overwhelmed by the somber significance of the occasion, I forgot to take my camera with me, but I did remember to take my sunglasses, even though it was an overcast day. I knew I didn't want anyone else to see me if I couldn't contain my emotions.

It turned out to be everything people had told me it was. A solemn hush permeated the air for two hundred feet on all sides of the monument. People instinctively stopped talking as they entered the unlined boundaries of the outdoor sanctuary. At the Wall itself, I observed men and women of all ages. Some were lovingly tracing a name with their fingertips, others placed memorials at its base, and many simply stood and stared with a look that told me their thoughts were thousands of miles and many years removed from this place. I wasn't long in joining them.

After a volunteer showed me how to locate a name, I searched for and found name after name of those who fought beside me. Seeing their names etched in granite, I was glad I'd thought to bring the sunglasses. Tears stung my eyes. I felt my jaw clench and my stomach sink. For years, I'd hoped that maybe a mistake had been made and that my comrades-in-arms weren't really dead. Now, I couldn't escape the truth any longer—they were dead. Standing that afternoon in front of a wall of black granite sealed it for me. I could play no more mind games. My search for closure and peace demanded that I now deal with the facts.

After some time, when my jangled emotions began to subside, I stepped back a few feet. I wanted to gain greater perspective of the monument as a whole. I took off my sunglasses and began to pay closer attention to the other people who had congregated that day to pay their respects. As I looked from side to side, I had to laugh. All around me were middle-aged men, without their wives, wearing sunglasses.

Stephen C. Klink

The Honey Man

It was a living. We came every Sunday, my kids and I, to sell my handmade jewelry at the swap meet. Before sunrise each week, we were lined up with 150 other "swappers," people like me . . . fallen on hard times and finding a way to survive. While most folks were dressing for church, we were sharing Styrofoam cups of hot coffee, taking our places at the abandoned drive-in theater, setting out our wares. That's where we met the Honey Man.

I was just closing a much-needed sale of my handmade jewelry when Teddy, my toddler, smeared a viscous sweet matter on my corduroys with his two-year-old hand. "Bees make it," he said, beaming at me from under his sticky curls. He was holding a handful of plastic straws full of glistening golden honey. I turned to find Angie, my five-year-old daughter, sucking on one of the honey-filled straws.

"I hope you don't mind, ma'am." A bent sixty-something man was reaching out his hand. "It's all natural, won't hurt 'em . . . local honey from my own hives." His gnarled hand was slightly sticky when he firmly shook my hand.

"I'm Robin," I said, staring down his turquoise eyes, checking his character. As a single mother, I had to be cautious. But I saw only gristle, kindness and an untold story.

"Jake," he answered. "I'm parked just over there, if you need anything, ma'am." He turned a huge back with bent shoulders to me and walked away with a slight, almost unnoticeable limp, like an old injury that had been oiled with honey. Halfway to his booth—a display of honeycombs and diagrams of bees—he turned, as if he knew I was staring, and winked. Teddy and I laughed.

From then on, he became a part of our lives. Every Sunday, he unloaded his fold-up display from a yellow Volkswagen and set it up across from us in the old drive-in theater parking lot we used for the swaps. He wasn't much of a salesman—he simply gave out sample straws filled with his honey—but he never went home with leftovers. One taste and people were hooked. So were the kids and I, and not just to his honey. We were naturally drawn to Jake's quiet, unassuming manner and constant kindness to us.

We knew little about him. "I don't naturally talk about me much," he would say over coffee breaks and lunches during the next few months, and the only time a glimmer of his past peeked through was when I told him about my painful divorce. "The man had everything," he said, choking back tears and looking across to where my children were minding his booth. "What I wouldn't give . . ."

I saw my chance. "What about you, Jake?" I asked. "Where are your people?" He stared down into his coffee mug, but didn't answer. Finally, he looked up. "Tell you what. My peaches are ripe, and I make a honey cobbler that's to die for. Bring the kids around to my place. It's about time they met the bees."

The next Saturday, we bumped up a country road, following the map Jake had drawn. He emerged from a house he had built himself, carrying a pitcher of iced lemonade. He invited us to sit at the picnic table, and we ate his famous cobbler, surrounded by fruit trees with tinkling bells and carved wooden birds tied on their branches, flowers and beehive boxes.

Soon the kids were romping in the pasture with the baby goats, and I turned to the Honey Man, who had started on a long story about the bees, his favorite subject. "I want to hear about you, Jake," I interrupted. Jake rubbed his gray stubbled face and scratched the back of his thick neck. Then, reluctantly, he began to talk.

"You're too young to remember World War II. People were excited. We were all gonna go off to Europe and kill us some Nazis. My small unit was ambushed behind enemy lines. Only me left, with this hurt leg." He slapped his right thigh. "I don't know how I got to the farm. The old man must've found me in his field. He buried my buddies, and I believe he prayed over their bodies. Germans—they were supposed to be the enemy—but this man and his family, they were just people. I was slow to recover, and it must have been an awful risk keeping me in their house." He paused and wiped one of his large hands slowly across his face.

"The farmer had a niece. We were married by spring. Elizabeth wasn't the enemy. She was not fooled by Hitler's smooth words. We weren't legally married: just her uncle's family and me and a Bible, and a promise to love each other.

"Then news came that the war was ending, and my leg was healed. So I made my way back to my base camp and tried to negotiate with the commanding officer: I wanted to take my bride home with me. He put me off, assured me that it would all be processed after my return to the States. I tried to go back and say good-bye to Elizabeth, but it was crazy times; the war was ending, and Germany was being torn in two. I was threatened with a court-martial if I tried to crash the curtain.

"Court-martial! My heart was already in lockup! I'd left Elizabeth with her uncle's family. We thought she might be pregnant, and I knew she'd need me. I guess I was the only soldier who wasn't happy to be home. In the end, when the lines were drawn, the little farm and the woman I loved, fell on the east side of the line. People call it the Iron Curtain, but they don't know how cold and hard that iron is, not like I do."

My peach cobbler was looking blurry. Jake shifted his weight in the wooden chair. "I tried to find her," he said. "Uncle Sam couldn't help. In the end, I sent back my Purple Heart and all those medals, Bronze Star, the lot. They were nothing after losing Elizabeth.

"You should have seen her," he said, smiling. "Eyes as gray as cold steel, but when she'd smile, she'd light up the world. Her hair was a mop of yellow straw. Her skin was like the milk she got out of her uncle's cow each morning. I'm an old man now, and I wasn't much to look at then either. But she loved me; that I know. Wherever she is, she loves me still.

"Every year or two, I go to Germany and follow every lead I can, but every year, I come home alone. I'm getting tired, and I'm overdue to go again." Jake looked suddenly weary, and I worried that I shouldn't have reopened a painful wound. "Maybe if you and the young ones could pray for me. I need an angel to help me find her, 'cuz working alone has not been successful."

The next day, the Honey Man was not at the swap meet, and I worried some more. The kids and I made a point of mentioning Jake and his lost wife in our dinner prayers each evening. But the week slipped away from me, and I didn't get a chance to drive out and check on him. So I was elated when, the next Sunday, I saw his familiar yellow

Volkswagen lined up with the swappers. I was swamped at first and didn't get a chance to look for Jake. Then I heard him.

"Robin, I'd like to introduce you to . . . my people," Jake said, his voice husky. Taken aback, I looked up to see him flanked on either side by beautiful, identical, enormous blondes. "My daughters, Ute and Ingrid." They held out matching milk-white hands and smiled, apologizing for not yet speaking English well. There was no mistaking them. They had Jake's startling eyes, but they were taller than him, with big yellow beehive hairdos. I was speechless, looking from one woman to the other and then around for their mother.

Sensing my confusion, Jake spoke up. "They found me! The day after our visit, I was too low to come to the swap. Come Wednesday, when the doorbell rang, I tried to ignore it. But they'd come a long way and kept on ringing. When I finally opened the door, they didn't have to tell me who they were."

Elizabeth had recently died, the twins told him, but she had never given up on her lost husband, never doubted his love. "Your father is looking for us," she assured the twins as they grew up. "We should never give up on looking for him. He loves us."

Her insistence on that love was what had brought them overseas to find their father. Once Jake's daughters found him, they weren't losing him again. They moved into the home Jake had built for his long-lost bride, and they stayed there all together, surrounded by the fragrant trees, tinkling bells and humming bees. The war, with all its losses, was finally over for Jake, and, at last, the Honey Man took up living with his family.

Robin Lim

Just Like Me

"Twenty-seven, sir! A new company record!" my crew chief called over the intercom. A few minutes ago, we had been dispatched to the evac hospital from our base in Chu Lai, South Vietnam. One of our duties as an Army medevac helicopter crew, or "Dustoff" as we were called, was to pick up civilian casualties from the Army hospitals. We were to transport them to the provincial hospital at the city of Quang Ngai, about a fifteen-minute flight away. Some of the casualties were from gunshot wounds, booby traps, napalm burns from other war-related injuries, and some of them were from other illnesses and injuries common to Southeast Asia. While loading the UH-1H "Huey" helicopter, I noticed Vietnamese people of all ages, from the very young to the very old. When a family member was sent to the American hospital, the entire family went along, including the grandparents.

The helicopter had strained to maintain a hover prior to takeoff. The power was redlined as we struggled off the hospital pad and nosed out over the South China Sea. As we gained airspeed, I settled back. The hard part was over. Landing at the open field by the provincial hospital would be easy. "Okay, you take the aircraft," I told my copilot. "Be gentle. She's really heavy." Then, turning to the back, "Way to go!" I congratulated the crew. "It will be a long time before anyone breaks this record!"

We had a friendly competition going on in the company. It was a version of the old "See How Many People Fit in a Volkswagen" game, only our vehicle of choice was an Army Huey. The previous record was twenty-three. The crew of four could not be included in the count. It was a good thing Vietnamese were typically diminutive people. Surveying the cargo compartment, I could see people packed in like sardines. *Oh, well,* I thought, *it's only for a short time.* I was proud that I had been able to nurse such a heavy load off the ground. It took a gentle touch to get maximum performance.

The helicopter was so crowded that a young Vietnamese girl had to be seated on the end of the center console between the pilots' seats. I had actually bumped elbows with her as we were taking off. I noticed that in her arms she had what appeared to be a new baby wrapped in a blanket. It was common for the locals to send problem childbirths to the American hospitals for the superior care available. This was part of the so-called Winning the Hearts and Minds program the military had in place. This young mother met my eyes and gave me a small, shy smile. I reached over to the baby and lifted a corner of the blanket. "May I . . . ?" my eyes asked.

Her smile broadened to say, "Yes." She softly folded the blanket back so I could see her baby's face. Bright black eyes peered back at me from a beautiful little round face. I was captivated. I gently caressed the baby's exposed hand. Tiny fingers gripped my finger in the reflex response all babies seem to have. The mother held her precious bundle out to me. Though we could not talk, the communication was clear. I was taken aback. "Are you sure?" I looked the question at her.

"Yes! Yes!" Her vigorous nod and eager smile were easy to understand. Gingerly, I accepted her offer and cuddled the baby against me. The baby's soft warmth felt so good. How strange to hold the beginning of a new life, when my usual view of the back of the helicopter was of blood, broken bodies and the agony of war. The contrast was so extreme that it was almost unbearable. A tight feeling rose in my chest as we flew over the bomb-cratered countryside.

As we began our descent into Quang Ngai hospital, I reluctantly passed the baby back to Mom. Her beaming smile and the soft light glowing from behind her eyes spoke the universal language of love and pride. Her openness brought a rush of tears that I quickly hid behind the visor of my flight helmet. I believe she felt honored to see the American pilot tenderly holding her baby, but I was the one who was honored. She had given me a tremendous gift, perhaps one of the greatest I have ever received. I was moved and more than a little shaken. What started out as a lighthearted moment had suddenly become a momentous event. Her love, trust, pride and willingness to share spoke to me in a way I was completely unprepared for. These people were supposed to be inscrutable. We were taught during basic training and during flight school that our enemies were "gooks" and that they were different than we were. I remembered only too well the words of my drill instructor in basic training:

"What's the spirit of the bayonet?!" he would scream during drills.

"To kill!" We would scream back at him.

"To kill what?"

"To kill gooks, Drill Sergeant!!!" we responded.

The enemy was presented to us as less than human, which I suppose served a required purpose. It is easier to kill "gooks" than human beings, and in combat, one can't hesitate when it becomes necessary to kill. A second lesson we learned quickly was that no Vietnamese was to be trusted, because there was no way we could distinguish the "good" ones from the "bad" ones. Many times an innocent-looking child or grandmother tossed a hand grenade into a crowd of Americans or into a bus. I did not trust the Vietnamese, though I was rarely around any, other than our hut maids. To me, they were all "gooks" until proven otherwise.

Face to face with a young mother and her baby, I was forced to look at my callousness, and it hurt. These were real people, and they were just like me. The young mother could have been my sister, who also had a new baby—my namesake—whom I had not yet seen. From that point on, my view of the war was forced to change, a change that made the war even harder to bear. I saw the people and had compassion for their suffering. No longer were they just bodies in the back of the helicopter. Thank God for a young mother and her spontaneous gift. Thank God for God's message spoken in the universal language of love.

Jerold S. Ewen

Ebony and Ivory

In my role as a VA psychologist, I had organized a peer support group for older veterans still struggling with painful military memories. I prayed that it would help provide closure on this difficult chapter in their lives.

On the afternoon of our seventh meeting, I walked into the brightly lit group room. Sitting in a large circle were nine gray-haired World War II veterans, all of them living libraries with their own unique stories. This assembly of "senior citizens" was an interesting representation of the different branches of the service. On this particular day, several vets started discussing the realism in the movie *Saving Private Ryan.*

"One thing really bothered me," someone hesitantly remarked. All eyes turned toward the voice, waiting for an explanation. D. C., one of two African-American veterans in the group, shared that he only saw white soldiers in the film, even though many African-American men also fought for their country during World War II. He was worried the younger generations would not recognize the contributions of African Americans in American history—not realize that they, too, sacrificed everything and gave their lives for freedom and peace. Across the room, another dark face, somber and deeply wrinkled, nodded in agreement.

A faraway look came into D. C.'s eyes. He began describing what it was like to be a young black soldier during the days of segregation. He recalled completing boot camp and being on a train with hundreds of other young soldiers, chugging through the South, heading to the East Coast for the troops' deployment overseas. D. C. noted that the men were all tired, hungry and restless after being cooped up for so long. A stop for dinner was planned en route; a hot meal and change of scenery were eagerly anticipated by all. When the train started slowing down, everyone rose to get off at the upcoming station.

D. C.'s voice suddenly lowered. "Before the doors opened to let anyone out, this young lieutenant walked into our car, saying he had an announcement to make. He stated that he was very sorry but that all Negroes would have to stay on the train, assuring us that he would ask the white GIs to bring back some food. He explained that people in the area were very prejudiced and that it would be better if we just avoided potential problems by staying on the train." D. C. paused, then asked with a quivering voice, "Can you imagine how hard it was for that poor young lieutenant to have to stand up there and tell all of us colored soldiers that we couldn't get off the train?"

The room fell silent. *How many people,* I wondered to myself, *would be concerned about the lieutenant in that situation?* My admiration for D. C. deepened.

Finally, Leroy, the other elderly African-American vet, chimed in, sharing a piece of his own history. In 1944, the nineteen-year-old Leroy, wearing his military uniform, was sitting at the back of a bus, anxiously waiting for it to start and take him home for his few days of leave. Other passengers boarded one by one, filling the vehicle to capacity. Finally, the driver got on and headed down the aisle, collecting tickets. When he arrived at the rear, without even looking at Leroy's ticket, the driver told him that he was on the wrong bus and to get off.

Confused, Leroy asked where the bus was headed. When the driver told him, Leroy confirmed that it was his destination, too, displaying his ticket as proof. Again, without even looking at it, the driver repeated that Leroy was on the wrong bus and needed to leave immediately.

"But, sir," the young soldier responded politely, "I just paid six dollars and thirty-five cents for this ticket, so I know it's good. I'm going where you're heading, so this must be the right bus."

The driver responded firmly, "I am in charge, so I can decide whether or not you're on the right bus. Well, I've decided that you are on the wrong one, so get off now."

The other veterans in the room looked at Leroy sadly. This talented jazz musician was a soft-spoken man, an incredibly kind and gentle soul, undoubtedly now just an older version of the young soldier he once was.

He stared straight ahead and spoke once again. "There was this white passenger nearby who overheard the whole conversation. I can still see him. He was a really big man, wearing dark pants and a short-sleeved beige shirt. He stood up in the aisle. I thought he was going to make sure I didn't give the driver any problems and that I got off the bus without making a scene. There was nothing I could say, so I started collecting my gear."

Leroy slowly continued. "But that man, he said to me, 'Stay right there, soldier.' He turned to the bus driver and told him real calm like, 'This young man is serving in the United States Army. He is risking his life for our country. He has a perfectly good ticket, just like the rest of us. He is on the right bus. If he gets off, then the rest of us are going to get off. Aren't we, everybody?' By then, everyone had been looking at us and listening to what was going on. At first, I felt a little scared and even a little ashamed. No one moved or said a word. Then that man in the dark pants started gathering up his belongings and repeated to all the other passengers, 'If this soldier has to get off the bus, then the rest of us are going to get off, too. Aren't we?'

"Well, it was like a miracle. One by one, every single person on that crowded bus started picking up their things and standing, ready to walk off at a moment's notice. They all waited for the bus driver's response. Well, do you know that man didn't say another word? He just glared at me, grabbed the ticket out of my hand, walked back down the aisle, and got into his seat. All those other people just looked at me and smiled. There was no way that I could repay them. But mostly, I'll never forget that man in the dark pants who stood up for me."

Leroy's eyes were not the only ones that were bright with tears. He slowly scanned the circle of aging men and said softly, "I can't believe that I'm in this room today, talking like this with so many other veterans, sitting here next to each other, like black and white piano keys sit together to make one truly fine instrument. Once we were separated from one another—couldn't eat together, couldn't bunk together, couldn't even serve in the same units. I don't see the color of anyone's skin in this room. All I see are men like me, just other American veterans who all served our country, who have the same color blood."

Then Leroy reached out his right hand and took the hand of the man sitting next to him. John instantly did the same, and the gesture continued all around the room with Charles, Sam, D. C., Andy, George, Bill and Ron.

A peaceful silence filled the room, and it somehow seemed even more brilliantly lit than before. The men quietly exchanged smiles, untroubled by the emotional intensity and potential awkwardness of the moment. Finally, D. C. raised both arms high in the air, his strong dark hands still holding those of the men sitting next to him. He joyfully bellowed, *"Amen!"*

As if rehearsed, the others instantly raised their arms, too, simultaneously repeating, *"Amen!"* They broke into laughter, then stood and hugged one another.

Amen, indeed, I silently echoed. Some prayers are answered before our eyes.

Karen L. Waldman

10

REMEMBRANCE

Here rests the soul of our nation—here also should be our conscience.

Caspar W. Weinberger, U.S. Secretary of Defense
Veterans Day address at Arlington National Cemetery

Remembrance Day

Not in vain may be the pride of those who survived and the epitaph of those who fell.

Winston S. Churchill,
speech in House of Commons, 1944

He was very old now, but he could still hold himself stiffly to attention before the monument. His war, the one to end all wars, now just a fading part of history. Very few could remember firsthand the savageness of the ordeal that had sent millions of young men to their deaths. "Cannon fodder" they'd call them, sent before the guns to be mowed down and blown apart by chunks of metal that had decimated their frail bodies. The cream of a generation, almost wiped out. He was haunted by the faces of the boys he'd had to order into battle, the ones who'd never come back. Yet one nameless ghost was able to bring a measure of comfort to his uneasy mind. At the sound of the gun signaling the eleventh hour, he was mentally transported back to the fields of Flanders.

* * *

The battle had raged for over two hours, with neither side gaining any advantage. Wave after wave of soldiers had been dispatched from the muddy trenches and sent over the top. So many had died already that day that he decided he couldn't afford to lose any more men before reinforcements arrived. Perhaps they'd give the remnants a few more days of life. There came a slight lull in the battle, due to the sheer exhaustion of men on both sides. It was always the same.

There existed an unspoken agreement between the warring armies that they all be allowed some respite before continuing with the next onslaught. Time to catch one's breath, until it was taken away forever. During this interval, a young soldier came up to him requesting he be allowed to go over the top. He looked at the boy who couldn't have been more than nineteen. Was this extreme bravery in the face of the enemy, or was the soldier so scared he just needed to get it over with?

"Why would you want to throw your life away, soldier? It's almost certain death to go out there."

"My best friend went out over an hour ago, Captain, and he hasn't come back. He could be lying out there hurt. I must find him, sir." The pleading look in the young man's eyes touched him. But to let him go now would be to condemn him to death.

"I'm sorry, son, but I can't let you go out there. It would be suicidal." Forcefully he said, "Go back to your post, soldier. That's an order." The young man turned, his head hung low, and slowly made his way back.

The battle resumed its full fury, the guns pounding and acrid smoke stealing the little bit of fresh air that was left. Deafening explosions and showers of muddy earth hid the sight and sound of screaming men and horses.

It was nearly two hours before the next pause in the conflict. The captain rolled a cigarette between shaking fingers. The smoke could not even curl up to penetrate the foul air. As he looked through the haze that surrounded him, he saw a figure approaching. It was the young soldier. He'd come back again.

"Captain, please, please let me go out onto the battlefield," he begged. "I know my friend must be hurt and calling for me. I must go to him, sir. I must." There were tears in his eyes. It was as if this were the most important thing in the world to him.

"Soldier, I'm sorry, but your friend is probably dead. What purpose would it serve to let you sacrifice your life, too?"

"At least I'd know I'd tried, sir. He'd do the same thing in my shoes. I know he would."

He was about to order the boy back to the ranks again, but the impact of his words softened his heart. He remembered the awful pain he'd felt himself when his brother had died and he'd never had the chance to say good-bye.

"All right, soldier, you can go." Despite all the horror around them, he saw a radiant smile on the boy's face. It was as if a great weight had been lifted from his shoulders.

"Thank you, sir," said the soldier. As he watched him slip away, he heard him shout out: "God bless you, sir."

It was a long time before the guns fell silent, and each side was allowed to gather their dead and wounded. The captain remembered the young soldier. He had to know what had become of him. He looked through the piles of bodies. There were so many. Perhaps he should check the living, just in case. When he came to the makeshift hospital, he looked carefully through the casualties. With a shock, he soon found himself before the prone body of the soldier. He was alive, but mortally wounded. He knelt down beside the young man and gently laid a hand on his shoulder.

"I'm so sorry. I knew I was wrong to let you go."

"Oh, no, sir. I'm glad you did, and I'm glad you are here now so I can thank you. You see, sir, I found my friend. He was badly wounded, but I was able to comfort him at the end. As I held him dying in my arms, he looked me in the eyes and said, 'I *knew* you'd come.'" The young soldier gave one last gasp and slipped quietly into oblivion.

* * *

As the bugle sounded "Taps," the old captain, tears streaming down his face, envisioned once again the smiling face and heard the words, "God bless you, sir." Looking up, he could almost hear the stone monument calling out to him: "I knew you'd come."

Christine Ann Maxwell-Osborn

Let Them in, Peter

Let them in, Peter
They are very tired
Give them couches where the angels sleep
And light those fires

Let them wake whole again
To brand new dawns
Fired with the sun, not wartime's
Bloody guns

May their peace be deep
Remember where the broken bodies lie
God knows how young they were
To have to die

Give them things they like
Let them make some noise
Give roadhouse bands, not golden harps
To these our boys

And let them love, Peter
'Cause they've had no time
They should have trees and bird songs
And hills to climb

The taste of summer in a ripened pear
And girls sweet as meadow wind
With flowing hair

And tell them how they are missed
And say not to fear
It's gonna be all right
With us down here

John Gorka

[EDITORS' NOTE: *"Let Them in, Peter" was made into a song by John Gorka from a poem found in a hospital in the Philippines during World War II. The nurse who found the poem kept it all these years, and it was her daughter who sent a copy to John.*]

When Winter Was Warm

"Do you think I'm crazy?" Miss Lawrence would ask every time I visited her.

"Everyone is a little crazy in their own way," I would always answer.

I didn't belong in Miss Lawrence's house, but I couldn't help tagging along with my older brother when he did chores for the old woman.

Miss Lawrence paid my brother five dollars a week to chop wood for her little stove and to bring groceries when she needed something. I washed her few dishes and sometimes did her laundry.

Our mother would often send extra food with us, trying to put a few pounds on the tiny old woman's bones.

"Be sure you set out a plate for John; he might come home today," Miss Lawrence would say when I put the food on the table. She'd been setting an extra plate on the table for seventy-two years, waiting for John to return from World War I.

"John had hair the color of oak leaves in October. No one else ever had such beautiful hair. My own mother used to say it was a shame that such beautiful hair was wasted on a boy." Miss Lawrence would smile, and her wrinkles would deepen. "We were both seventeen when he left for the war. He promised we'd be sweethearts forever, and he promised he'd come home."

Those were the times I could almost see that seventeen-year-old girl. Miss Lawrence would smooth back her dry, white hair and tuck the wispy ends into the messy bun on top of her head. She'd been blond when she was young and had worn her hair in curls. Sometimes when she'd laugh about something, her eyes would sparkle again, just for an instant. That must have been how she looked when she was with John. I thought they must have been such a handsome young couple.

Everyone knew John had died somewhere in Germany during the bitter winter, but she would never believe it. Finally, people just found it easier and kinder to let her believe he was coming home.

Miss Lawrence never married, never had children. Over the years, her parents and sisters and friends had died, and now she was alone. Her only visitors were my brother and I and a nurse the county sent to her house once a month to check on her health.

Even in the summer, my brother still had to build a small fire in the potbellied stove before we left every afternoon.

"It's funny," Miss Lawrence said. "The weather used to be so different. When I was a girl, the winters were warm. John and I used to walk in the forest, and I'd slip my hand into his mitten. Sometimes he'd reach up and shake a branch and the snowflakes would fall down on us, but we never felt cold. I was never cold when I was with John. After John left, the weather changed, and I was never warm again."

As I listened to Miss Lawrence, World War I wasn't just something in a history book anymore. For my brother and me, it was something horrible that slaughtered thousands of young boys like John. The pain and loss and loneliness Miss Lawrence felt were just as fresh as if the war had happened yesterday.

I felt sorry for all the soldiers who were killed. I felt sorry for the soldiers who came home with wounded bodies and wounded hearts. But mostly, I felt sorry for Miss Lawrence and all the young women like her who waited for their sweethearts to come home.

No one talks about the girls who were left behind. They don't have a holiday and they didn't get any medals. But they were so very brave, and they were so terribly wounded.

One of the last times I visited Miss Lawrence she told me all her stories again, but this time she asked a favor.

"Will you make me a promise?" She laid her thin hand on my shoulder. "Will you promise me that you will never forget John? Someone has to remember John." Her voice trembled.

"I remember John had hair the color of oak leaves in October," I said. "And you were both seventeen, and you walked in the woods, and he shook the tree branches, and snow fell on you, and you were sweethearts forever."

"Yes. Yes." Sighing, she smiled sadly. "You do remember. Now someone else will always remember."

Storm Stafford

Stars and Stripes from Odds and Ends

It is the Fourth of July, and Pleasantville, Iowa, is staging its annual parade. People flock from neighboring towns to join in the celebration. American flags are flying everywhere, as they are in towns and cities all across America on this Independence Day. In the home of Keith and Billie Davis, their own Stars and Stripes are carefully displayed in the front window—for the first time in fifty-four years.

This isn't just any flag. This flag has a story. If you peer at the white stripes, which after all these years have become a bit dingy, you can make out twenty-five faded signatures. The blue of the flag is faded, too, but the red is as bright and brilliant as it was on those long-gone days in 1945. . . .

* * *

The war was just over. Staff Sergeant Keith Davis and the two dozen soldiers in his platoon had seen plenty of combat in the months before the end of World War II. They'd watched men die—friend as well as enemy—and they were thankful that, with Germany's surrender, those days were finally over.

Their new mission was to maintain order in a tiny German village populated by a few farmers and their families. It was a tedious time for that small group of soldiers, men from Alabama and California and Florida—a typical cross section of Americans—who wanted nothing more than to go home.

There wasn't much to do in the town. Just maintain order. And wait.

The thing was, something important was missing for these soldiers. This unit had no flag.

Every morning, military units around the world raise the American flag, and every evening, they gather again, salute and bring it down.

It didn't feel right not to have an American flag. This, they decided, would have to change.

The soldiers moved through the village, looking for help. They soon found a German seamstress—her name is long forgotten—and asked her to make their flag.

Perhaps not surprisingly, the woman was reluctant. She didn't want to do it, she told the men, and, besides, there was no material.

"We'll find some," they said.

And they did. The blue came from a villager's shirt, the white for the stars and the stripes, from a bed sheet. Red was a problem. Then somebody noticed a discarded German flag, the hated symbol of Nazism, the black swastika on a blazing banner of red.

The seamstress had her materials, and she agreed to do the job. She cut each of the white stars and carefully sewed them on the blue of the shirt; forty-eight stitched on each side of the flag. And then she cut and sewed the red strips along with the white of the bed sheet. Reluctant this seamstress may have been, but she took pride in her work; the result was a magnificent American flag.

Within days, the men in Davis's platoon were flying

their flag over their small headquarters. Each morning, they brought the Germans to the center of town and saluted as the flag was raised. Each night it came down. Daily, the flag kindled their pride in their country; it reminded them, in that strange land far from home, of what they held dear, of why they had fought this terrible war.

When the orders finally came and the soldiers prepared to head home, Davis had each man in the unit sign his name and hometown on the white stripes. Then he packed this remarkable flag away and brought it back to Iowa.

For over half a century, the flag was stored in a closet, wrapped in tissue paper, tucked inside a brown bag. Keith hardly mentioned it. His wife, Billie, would get it out once a year and air it out, turning it over gently in her hands. She would marvel at the skill of the seamstress, who had double-sewn the seams along the stripes with a finesse that even Billie, who had sewn all her life, felt she could not have matched.

Then, after all those years, when Keith's health started to fail, he began to talk about the unusual origin of their flag. And Keith and Billie agreed that now was the time for more people to hear about it and share in their memory.

So in 1999, for the first time since it was saluted and lowered for the final time that day in Germany, the fine flag made from odds and ends was put on display again.

People who stopped and inquired that day in Pleasantville learned how an old shirt, a bed sheet and an enemy flag had been transformed—changed into a symbol that had the power to cheer two dozen GIs in a lonely German village as a hard but lasting peace fell on Europe so many years ago.

John Carlson

Sweet-Pea Summers

Each summer in the late 1960s, my two sisters and I would ride the Greyhound bus from Arizona to Arkansas to stay with our father.

A World War II veteran, Dad had many medical problems, any one of which could cause many people to lose more than their sense of humor, but not him.

I have vivid memories of Dad waking us up in the morning. Before he'd put on his legs for the day (he had lost his legs after his discharge), his wheelchair was his mobility. Holding his cane, which was his extended arm, he would roll through the house yelling, "Up, up, up!" Get up and face the day! It's a beautiful day! Rise and shine!" If we didn't get up right away, he would repeat his song in rhythm with his cane hitting the end of our beds. This was no performance put on for our benefit; every day was truly a beautiful day to him.

Back in the sixties, there was no handicapped parking or wheelchair-accessible ramps like there are now, so even a trip to the grocery store was a difficult task. Dad wanted no assistance from anyone. He would climb stairs slowly but surely, whistling all the way. As a teenager, I found this embarrassing, but if Dad noticed, he didn't let on.

Once during a trip to the store, he found the three of us in the makeup department and began to look at makeup with us. He picked up a container of powder and started reading the label out loud. "'Leaves your skin soft and silky from head to toe.' Well, that leaves half of me out," he said, laughing. We had to laugh, too. He had a talent for finding humor in everything he did.

Those summers always ended too soon. He would drive us back to Arizona every year, stopping at the checkpoint for fruit and vegetables at the New Mexico-Arizona border. When asked if he had any fruits or vegetables, he would reply, "Just three sweet peas."

Our father has been gone for a long time now, but not the lesson that he taught us: You are only as handicapped as you let yourself be.

I know now, too late, that any one of his "sweet peas" would be proud to walk beside him—whistling—up a set of stairs. And be glad to wake to the sound of his voice, to rise and shine and see one of his beautiful days.

Susan Arnett-Hutson

In memory of Marian Segal Arnett Jr., World War II veteran, 1928–1970.

History

Lester Peskin is eighty-three, tall and fit. He wears his white hair combed back, and he has sharp eyes and a quick wit. Not long ago, after fifty years of practicing restaurant law in New York, he moved to Boca Raton, Florida. That was two years after Dorothy, his wife of almost fifty years, had died. His two daughters and four grandchildren still live up north.

Lester is alone but not lonely. He golfs and takes classes in the history of Judaism and the Old Testament. He even had a second bar mitzvah last year—he is, after all, thirteen years beyond the Bible's three score and ten.

Lester was young once and believed he would die young, as a lieutenant, a company commander in the 108th Regiment, Fortieth Division. He believed he'd die in the invasion of Japan scheduled for the fall of 1945.

But Lester came home whole, married Dorothy and settled down to law and family.

A couple of months ago, a large Japanese battle flag showed up at Grand Armée, a unique military memorabilia store near Lester's Florida home.

The flag had been taken at a Japanese surrender

ceremony in late August 1945 in Korea. It was signed by more than one hundred U.S. soldiers. It went home with a GI, then to his attic, then to his nephew's attic after the old soldier died. The nephew contacted Grand Armée and the transaction was made.

Soon after the flag arrived at Grand Armée, Lester and one of his daughters wandered in. They browsed. Lester noticed the flag and stood gazing at it.

Later he told his daughter he'd had the thought, *I signed a flag like that once.* But he supposed that a lot of Japanese flags were signed by a lot of U.S. soldiers.

His daughter studied the flag, too. Then looked up.

"Daddy," she said excitedly. "Look, there's your name."

And there it was, in the lower left corner of the flag: "Lt. Peskin, New York."

Waves of emotion capped by churning memories washed over the old soldier. He had lived an entire life between the day he'd signed that flag and the day he'd seen it again. Fifty-four years. So much time, gone so fast. When he could speak again, he told his daughter the story of that day in 1945.

Lester was more than just a signatory to the flag. He had been the commanding officer, the guy who'd taken the flag from a Japanese marine captain in a formal surrender ceremony at a small airbase at Pohang, on the east coast of Korea.

The Japanese captain outranked him and said he wouldn't surrender to Lester. Each man had his men behind him, watching, wary. Armed.

"You're gonna surrender," Lester told him. The translators went back and forth. The American didn't know who was saying what. For a long moment, the captain and Lester looked at each other. The captain surrendered.

The men of Lester's company signed the flag. Lester gave it to one of his men.

After the surrender, Peskin was promoted to captain and appointed military governor of the region. Six months later, he went home. He never again thought about the flag.

The war receded into a past Lester didn't want to visit. Later when his daughters begged him to tell them stories about the war, he left out the parts that would upset them. He knows his twenty-four-year-old grandson doesn't know much about the war, since nowadays they don't teach it in school.

That day in Grand Armée, Lester looked at the flag, worn, fading to yellow, framed under glass. Those guys on the flag? Most were probably dead. Their names, scribbled in pen and pencil, were still visible. But they, too, were fading away.

"It was a good outfit. They were good guys," he said quietly.

The war, that day in Korea, had become very real again, if only for a few minutes.

The moment passed. Lester took one last look at the flag and left, heading to his Old Testament class.

The flag had brought back the war for Lester, but for his children, it had made the war real for the first time. They knew now that Lester had been through things they had only read about or seen in films. It was time to honor their father and grandfather.

A few weeks later, a package arrived for Lester. It was the old battle flag, bought by his family. A surprise. Soon, his grandson plans to visit, to hear the story of the flag—and the history it represents—in person from a man who was there.

Paul F. Reid

Lester Peskin with the World War II Japanese battle flag he captured with his unit, an antitank company in the 108th Regiment, Fortieth Division. Peskin was the commanding officer, the man who took the flag from a Japanese marine captain.

Credit: Greg Lovett, Staff Photographer, The Palm Beach Post.

American Eagles

I met Geoff in the summer of 1995, when I was visiting the village of Portmeirion in Wales. Geoff appeared to be about my age, and I noticed him often as I walked about the area. Whenever our eyes met, we would smile at each other.

Once, as I walked toward the beach area, I saw him going in the same direction. When he saw me, he came over and began walking with me. We exchanged the usual pleasantries of introduction, and our conversation was routine until he asked if I had come directly to the U.K. from the States. When I answered that I had just come from Normandy in France, where I had been retracing the combat path of the Thirty-fifth Infantry Division in memory of someone very dear to me, I could tell that I had said something that affected Geoff deeply. He motioned for me to sit with him at a bench near the water. After a time, he began to speak in a voice filled with emotion, relating his own war story.

Like me, Geoff had been a young child during World War II. He'd lived in a small village in the interior of England, one that was of no strategic importance to the

Germans and, therefore, never touched by bombing. The effects of the war were felt in his village in other than the usual ways. Vast meadows near his home had been turned into tent accommodations for American GIs.

Everyone in Geoff's village had something to say about the Americans, not always complimentary, but the children worshiped them. To Geoff and the other boys his age, they seemed like gods. They were handsome, rugged, and, unlike the "stiff-upper-lip," reserved British men the boys were used to, the Yanks were extremely outgoing and friendly.

Geoff rode his bicycle to the GI encampment every day. He grew particularly fond of three of the GIs, young fellows who shared a tent together. They would give him chocolate and chewing gum, and on weekends, when he would run errands for them in his village, they would even give him coins. The gift he prized most of all, though, was the patch each man had given him. Three patches—just like the ones they wore proudly—all bearing the 101st Airborne Division emblem: the Screaming Eagles. Geoff and the GIs exchanged addresses, and the soldiers promised to keep in touch with the English boy when they returned to the States after the war.

One day when Geoff rode his bike to the American Eagles' campground, he found the meadow deserted. The field was so entirely bereft of men, tents and machines, it was as if they had never existed. He rode his bike home, told his mother and cried. He did not understand how they could vanish completely in the middle of the night.

Within weeks, the invasion began, and everyone in the village knew where the men had gone. Geoff was very excited about the role of the 101st Airborne. He sent letters to each of his GI friends by way of their home addresses in the States. Even now, he can still feel the awful sadness he experienced when he received word from the soldiers' families that each had been killed in action on June 6, in Ste. Mère Eglise.

This, he told me, was why he was so interested when I said I had been tracing the combat sites of the Thirty-fifth Infantry Division in memory of someone dear. Every sixth of June for the last forty years, Geoff has gone to the American Military Cemetery in Normandy and placed flowers on the graves of each of his three friends. It is a tradition he plans to continue for the rest of his life.

Two years after our talk by the beach, I visited Geoff at his home in England. He showed me the area of the encampment, still a lush green meadow. After dinner, as his wife washed the dishes, Geoff went to the attic and came down with an ordinary shoebox in his hands. When he opened it, I saw three patches with Screaming Eagles, looking as if they had never been touched.

"I don't show these to many people," Geoff said, "but I knew you'd understand."

He was right. I did.

D. W. Jovanovic

Windows for Remy

In war, resolution;
in defeat, defiance;
in victory, magnanimity;
in peace, goodwill.

Winston Churchill

On the afternoon of August 2, 1944, eight P-51 Mustangs of the U.S. 383rd Fighter Squadron were flying a sortie over France. As they approached the small, German-occupied town of Remy, northeast of Paris, they spotted a camouflaged train parked along a siding. The camouflage meant that the Germans considered the train important.

Four of the Mustangs zoomed to twelve thousand feet to provide high cover, while the rest peeled off in a trail formation and attacked the train with bursts of armor-piercing incendiary ammunition.

The train must have been carrying munitions, for during the last of five of these strafing runs, the train exploded. Smoke from the huge blast boiled up miles into the sky, and the shock wave from the explosion unroofed most of the houses in the village of sixteen hundred people. It also shattered the stained glass windows in the village's ancient church and killed a teenager more than half a mile away. The train was obliterated, leaving only a crater hundreds of feet long, ten feet deep and forty feet wide.

One of the American pilots, twenty-two-year-old Lieutenant Houston J. Braly Jr., was killed in the explosion when his Mustang was torn to pieces by flying debris.

Braly's plane crashed on the outskirts of town, bouncing through a small copse of trees, smashing through a low brick wall at a crossroads and finally coming to rest against a farmhouse.

Two teenagers, Marie Thérèse and her brother, François, ran from the house and pulled Braly's body from the burning wreckage within moments of the crash. Knowing the Germans would be searching for the body, they wrapped Braly in his parachute and hid him in the stable.

The Germans' initial search for Braly's body was unsuccessful. But soon afterward an anonymous collaborator informed them of the dead pilot's whereabouts. When the Germans found his body, it was covered with flowers from the villagers' personal gardens. This show of respect for Braly enraged the German commander.

The commandant initially refused to allow a funeral for Braly but relented on the condition that only four people could attend, including the parents of the teenager apprentice who had also been killed in the explosion. The commandant also decreed that villagers could place no more flowers on Braly's grave.

The villagers held Braly's funeral in the church—and flowers appeared on his grave. The German commandant ordered them removed. The next day, villagers placed four times as many flowers on the grave. The enraged commandant threatened to send Marie Thérèse and François to a slave labor camp, but he was eventually persuaded not to take action.

After the liberation, an unknown person who had scavenged a propeller blade from the wreckage of Braly's Mustang polished it to a high gloss, painstakingly engraved it with all the information found on Braly's dog tags—even down to the date of his last tetanus shot—and placed it at the grave. The blade served as his tombstone until after the war, when Braly's body was exhumed and returned to his family in the United States. The propeller remained as a memorial.

In 1995, more than fifty years later, some of the Air Force veterans of that day in 1944—along with Braly's surviving siblings—made a return trip to Remy.

There were many ceremonies honoring the veterans and Braly. Marie Thérèse and her brother, the two teenagers who pulled Braly's body from the wreckage of his plane, attended these ceremonies. In their mid-sixties, both vividly recalled the events of that long-ago day.

The former airmen were so moved by the way the French villagers had honored their fallen comrade, they decided to embark on one final mission: to restore the beautiful stained-glass windows in the town's thirteenth-century church. These windows, shattered in the blast, had been replaced with plain glass.

While the Windows for Remy project raised money from individual donors, the project's sponsors also worked with the French government to find a designer and artist who could fabricate reproduction windows that met strict French demands for historical authenticity.

It took five years, but the project was successful. In July 2000, over 150 Americans and hundreds of French citizens gathered in Remy for a day of ceremonies and parades. The climax came when the seven new stained glass windows in the Church of St. Denis were dedicated. The day ended with a fireworks display, followed by the lighting of the church windows.

The church windows were not the only windows that shone with light in Remy that night. In the home of Marie Thérèse, a single candle was lit next to the photo of Braly the Frenchwoman still keeps. This simple memorial speaks volumes about the sacrifice of one American pilot and what it meant to an entire village.

Frank Perkins

"JUST ONE MORE "CHICKEN SOUP" STORY BEFORE LIGHTS OUT, DRILL SERGEANT?"

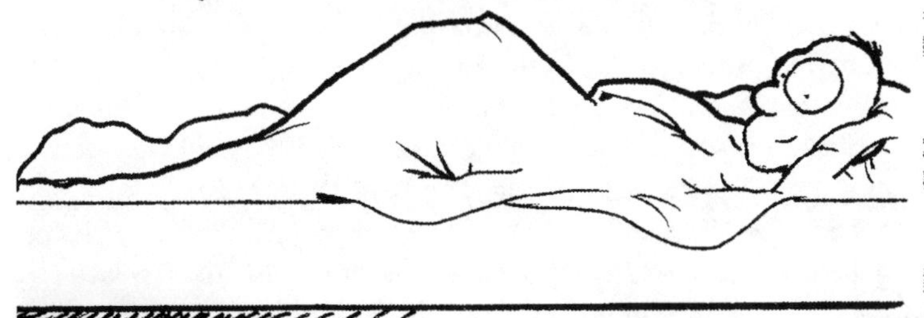

Reprinted with permission of Charles Wolf.

Who Is Jack Canfield?

Jack Canfield is one of America's leading experts in the development of human potential and personal effectiveness. He is both a dynamic, entertaining speaker and a highly sought-after trainer. Jack has a wonderful ability to inform and inspire audiences toward increased levels of self-esteem and peak performance.

He is the author and narrator of several bestselling audio and videocassette programs, including *Self-Esteem and Peak Performance, How to Build High Self-Esteem, Self-Esteem in the Classroom* and *Chicken Soup for the Soul—Live.* He is regularly seen on television shows such as *Good Morning America, 20/20* and *NBC Nightly News.* Jack has coauthored numerous books, including the *Chicken Soup for the Soul* series, *Dare to Win* and *The Aladdin Factor* (all with Mark Victor Hansen), *100 Ways to Build Self-Concept in the Classroom* (with Harold C. Wells), *Heart at Work* (with Jacqueline Miller) and *The Power of Focus* (with Les Hewitt and Mark Victor Hansen).

Jack is a regularly featured speaker for professional associations, school districts, government agencies, churches, hospitals, sales organizations and corporations. His clients have included the American Dental Association, the American Management Association, AT&T, Campbell's Soup, Clairol, Domino's Pizza, GE, ITT, Hartford Insurance, Johnson & Johnson, the Million Dollar Roundtable, NCR, New England Telephone, Re/Max, Scott Paper, TRW and Virgin Records. Jack is also on the faculty of Income Builders International, a school for entrepreneurs.

Jack conducts an annual eight-day Training of Trainers program in the areas of self-esteem and peak performance. It attracts educators, counselors, parenting trainers, corporate trainers, professional speakers, ministers and others interested in developing their speaking and seminar-leading skills.

For further information about Jack's books, tapes and training programs, or to schedule him for a presentation, please contact:

Self-Esteem Seminars
P.O. Box 30880
Santa Barbara, CA 93130
Phone: 805-563-2935 • Fax: 805-563-2945
Web site: *www.chickensoup.com*

Who Is Mark Victor Hansen?

Mark Victor Hansen is a professional speaker who in the last twenty years has made over 4,000 presentations to more than 2 million people in thirty-two countries. His presentations cover sales excellence and strategies; personal empowerment and development; and how to triple your income and double your time off.

Mark has spent a lifetime dedicated to his mission of making a profound and positive difference in people's lives. Throughout his career, he has inspired hundreds of thousands of people to create a more powerful and purposeful future for themselves while stimulating the sale of billions of dollars worth of goods and services.

Mark is a prolific writer and has authored *Future Diary, How to Achieve Total Prosperity* and *The Miracle of Tithing.* He is coauthor of the *Chicken Soup for the Soul* series, *Dare to Win* and *The Aladdin Factor* (all with Jack Canfield), and *The Master Motivator* (with Joe Batten).

Mark has also produced a complete library of personal-empowerment audio and videocassette programs that have enabled his listeners to recognize and use their innate abilities in their business and personal lives. His message has made him a popular television and radio personality, with appearances on ABC, NBC, CBS, HBO, PBS and CNN. He has also appeared on the cover of numerous magazines, including *Success, Entrepreneur* and *Changes.*

Mark is a big man with a heart and spirit to match—an inspiration to all who seek to better themselves.

For further information about Mark, write:

MVH & Associates
P.O. Box 7665
Newport Beach, CA 92658
Phone: 949-759-9304 or 800-433-2314
Fax: 949-722-6912
Web site: *www.chickensoup.com*

Who Is Sidney R. Slagter?

Sidney R. Slagter is the founder and president of Veteran Stories, Inc., a corporation dedicated to recognizing and honoring veterans from all wars and all branches of service. His goal is to preserve the memories of our country's greatest heroes so they can be passed on to future generations.

Born into a family of veterans, he developed a passion for military history at an early age, listening to his uncles' and cousins' tales of serving in World War II, Korea and Vietnam. He spends his time reading volumes of stories sent in by letter, e-mail and fax from all over the globe. He has appeared as a guest speaker on many television and radio shows, and he recently addressed the members and guests of the Medal of Honor Society in Pueblo, Colorado.

Sid's work has brought him into personal contact with thousands of our living heroes and their families, and his great honor is to share these amazing stories with the world.

Sid and his wife, Ilene, make their home in sunny Florida.

For further information on this and many other veterans' projects, you are invited to contact Sid at:

Veteran Stories, LLC
95 Uno Lago Drive
Juno Beach, FL 33408
Phone/Fax: 888-387-6373
E-mail: *remember@vetstories.com*
www.vetstories.com

Contributors

Everett Alvarez Jr., a distinguished Naval officer and government executive, is best known to the public as the first American aviator shot down over North Vietnam. He was taken prisoner of war on August 5, 1964, and held in North Vietnam for eight and a half years, until the general release of prisoners on February 12, 1973. In 1981, President Reagan nominated Alvarez as deputy director of the Peace Corps. President Reagan nominated him to be deputy administrator of the Veterans Administration and he assumed his post in 1982. A city park and two housing projects in California and Texas, a high school in his hometown of Salinas, California, and a Rockville, Maryland, post office have been named in his honor. Alvarez holds numerous military decorations, including the Silver Star, two Legions of Merit (with combat "V"), two Bronze Stars (with Combat "V"), Distinguished Flying Cross and two Purple Heart medals.

Robert R. Amon Jr. received the Bronze Star and numerous South Vietnamese decorations following his tour as a combat adviser in Vietnam. He is currently working on a book titled *Rice Roots,* based on a diary he kept during that year. Bob and his wife, Carolyn, live in New Jersey and have four children. Contact him at *amon@home.com.*

Edward Andrusko is a freelance writer who has written short stories and articles in a number of magazines, newspapers and books. Most of his narratives are about real people and events that touched their lives. After high school, he joined the U.S. Marines at the age of seventeen. Ed served four years—three years as a combat infantry rifleman. He and his wife, Gaynel, live and work in beautiful Boulder, Colorado. He can be reached at 303-939-8313.

Susan Arnett-Hutson lives in Roswell, New Mexico, with her husband of twenty-eight years. He is a Vietnam veteran and a recipient of the Purple Heart. They have four grown children and three grandchildren. Their youngest son is in the Marine Corps in Annapolis, Maryland. Susan keeps busy raising her granddaughter and remodeling her Victorian home.

Tre' M. Barron grew up in Richmond, California. She now lives in Indiana with her husband, Tony, and their son, Chris. After serving in the U.S. Marines, she went to work for the U.S. Army Corps of Engineers; she works at a lock and dam on the Ohio River.

Bernard Belasco is a retired school principal, eighty-four years of age, who gave away his snow shovels in Philadelphia and moved to Venice in sunny, warm Florida thirteen years ago. He spends his time volunteering for several civic groups, bowling and enjoying his hobby of amateur radio. He met his wife in Doc Ferguson's English literature class in 1939 when she borrowed a pencil from him. They have been married for fifty-seven years and still talk to each other.

Patricia Black's passion, now that she has the time, is writing. A senior newspaper occasionally prints her stories and observations. Her first attempts at writing were from a perch in her tree house, none of which was ever shown to anyone. Born in Des Moines, Iowa, she became a licensed pilot in 1945. Happily married for fifty-two years, she has four children, six grandchildren and two dogs. A ballet dancer and teacher, she has also made two skydiving jumps.

Susan Grady Bristol is a registered nurse and freelance writer who recently moved back to Omaha, Nebraska, after living in the Chicago area. The mother of three boys, she is active in school events, professional nursing organizations and church activities. She was born in North Platte, Nebraska, years after the World War II canteen closed. She learned about the canteen from a dear friend who was photographed as the troop train he was on stopped in North Platte.

Jean P. Brody is a national magazine columnist and writes two columns weekly for Kentucky newspapers. Her columns are all on the Internet. She teaches creative writing and is an active motivational and inspirational public speaker. She lives with her husband, their cat, Miss Aggie, and Willie T. Goat on their thoroughbred horse farm, the Jean and Gene Farm, in Winchester, Kentucky. Recently, they lost their beloved friend and companion, Guinney, a Newfoundland who was much more than a dog. Jean has published many dozens of short stories and articles, and *Braille Me,* a compilation of her published work. Her main work today is her research on miracles and her lectures on attitudinal wellness. She can be reached at the farm at 859-745-4779 or in the winter at their beach home on Perdido Key at 850-492-8815.

Robert E. Brooks Jr. received his bachelor of arts in 1974 and master of arts degrees in 1976 and 1985. He served in all branches of the armed forces between 1962 and 1986. Bob is a human services caseworker. Besides flying and collecting, he supports numerous veterans' activities and Constitutional issues.

Antonio Camisa served with the famed First Cavalry Division in the central highlands of South Vietnam. An infantry squad leader, he was wounded and decorated for valor. A graduate of South Georgia College, he is a research consultant and remains active in numerous veteran service organizations.

Barbara Sue Canale has written "Say Goodbye for Me," a women's fiction piece, based on the story "Too Young to Understand." She has also authored a book, *Our Labor of Love: A Romanian Adoption Chronicle.* Barbara volunteers in her church, the schools and community. She currently works as a freelance writer in Jamesville, New York.

John Carlson is a columnist at the *Des Moines Register.* He is a native of Oakville, Iowa, a graduate of Western Illinois University and was a Nieman Fellow at Harvard University. He served four years in the U.S. Air Force and was honorably discharged in 1971 with the rank of staff sergeant.

Watts Caudill was born in Washington, D.C., and graduated from West Point in 1964. He was the company commander of B Company, 1/18th Infantry from July 1967 to January 1968. He now lives in Manhattan, Kansas, and is a high school math teacher at Topeka High School.

The Chapel of Four Chaplains, established in 1947, is a national, nonprofit organization whose mission is to "encourage cooperation and selfless service among all people." For more information, contact: The Chapel of Four Chaplains, 1201 Constitution Ave., Philadelphia, PA, 19112. Phone: 215-218-1943; e-mail: *chapel@fourchaplains.org.*

Paul Charlillo is a retired construction worker. He has been married to Caroline for forty-five years. He is a father, grandfather, and great-grandfather. Serving with Company B, 151st Armored Infantry Battalion in Patton's Third Army, he received four Bronze Stars, the Combat Infantryman's Badge, numerous campaign ribbons, and the Presidential Unit Citation from President Harry S. Truman.

Akira B. Chikami, CMSgt (retired) is a former member of G Company, Second Battalion, Thirty-Eighth Infantry, Second Division. A prisoner of war in North Korea, he was captured on August 27, 1951, near Pia Ri, North Korea, and released on September 5, 1953. He wishes to recognize his fellow POWs and MIAs who did not return. He can be contacted at 713 Gilbert Rd., Winter Park, FL 32792-4632.

Susan M. Christiansen is the founder and author of the long-running VET FORUM advice column and the LOVVE support organization for veterans' loved ones. Susan is the recipient of the coveted Jefferson Award, the "Vet Center" Appreciation Award and the Red Cross Service Award. She resides in California, with the youngest of her four children and is currently working on her first novel. Contact her at *Svetforum@aol.com.*

Gene DuVall, born in Maryland, is a longtime writer, having begun with small poems as a child. He grew up in Rising Sun, Indiana, and entered service from Pennsylvania. While in the service, he had works published in the *Stars and Stripes.* Later work encompassed memoirs of Army days and of his own young family life. Often the subject of his writing is the beloved "other woman" in his life—his loving cat, Tinker. His works have been published in *Cat Fancy, Reminisce, American Legion* and *Grit.* A true writer in every sense, he labors ceaselessly putting down the depths of his memories and feelings.

David Eberhart is a retired Marine Corps line officer, judge advocate and former criminal trial lawyer. He is the author of five novels currently available from Pulsarbooks.com as trade paperbacks. Presently, he is an editor for Stars and Stripes Omnimedia. The flagship newspaper, the *Stars and Stripes,* is the oldest veterans' advocate publication in America, having roots that go back to 1877.

Larry Ebsch is sixty-nine years old and has been retired since January 2, 1996. He launched a career in newspapers (*Herald-Leader*) in his hometown,

Menominee, Michigan, in May 1955 and served as sports editor and general news reporter. Transferred to neighboring Marinette, Wisconsin (*Eagle-Star*), in 1962, he rose through the ranks to become managing editor. He served as executive editor when *Herald-Leader* and *Eagle-Star* merged into *EagleHerald* in July 1995, with a combined circulation of twelve thousand. Larry served with the U.S. Army Medical Corps during the Korean War, in 1952 and 1953 for fourteen months, including the Christmases of 1952 and 1953. He could not rotate home after one Christmas as scheduled because his military orders were lost. You can reach him at 521 6th Ave., Menominee, MI 49858.

Joe Edwards is a retired jazz pianist who turned to writing. His stories have been widely published in many countries, and he is the author of a collection, *The Red Mahogany Piano and Other Stories.* He may be reached at 1521 E. Whiteside, Springfield, MO 65804, or by calling 417-889-4257.

Diane Carlson Evans, R.N., served as a captain in the Army Nurse Corps during the Vietnam War. She led the ten-year effort to honor her sister veterans, culminating in the dedication of a bronze monument portraying three women and a wounded soldier at the Vietnam Veterans Memorial in Washington, D.C., in 1993. Diane is a mother, nurse, educator and advocate for veterans. To learn about the Vietnam Women's Memorial and the women who served during the Vietnam War or to order a replica of the memorial, please visit *www.VietnamWomensMemorial.org.*

Jerold S. Ewen lives in the western shadow of Wyoming's Big Horn Mountains. A husband of Kathy, father of three, grandfather of three and self-employed, he flew medevac helicopters in Vietnam. He likes to write, speak and tell stories. He loves God, family, his children, and Wyoming's hills and mountains. You can contact him at *jerrye@trib.com.*

Arnold Geier was born and raised in Germany, served in the counterintelligence branch of the U.S. Army in Europe, and is a retired insurance executive and prolific writer, with five published books and numerous articles to his credit. His latest book, *Heroes of the Holocaust* (Berkley, N.Y., 1998), features twenty-eight spellbinding, true accounts of human kindness, valor and altruism, and of miraculous forces that helped people survive in a society bent on genocide. The book is endorsed by Nobel Laureate Elie Wiesel, ADL National Director Abraham Foxman and religious leaders of all persuasions. *Heroes of the Holocaust* can be obtained from any bookstore or through major online booksellers (ISBN 0-425-16029-7). Mr. Geier can be reached at *Baldeagle99@mindspring.com.*

Sarah H. Giachino is a busy stay-at-home mother raising her two daughters, Olivia, age fourteen, and Victoria, age ten. Her husband, Nick, is an executive with Pepsi-Cola. She would like to honor her parents, Mary and Charles Hardman, by dedicating this true story to them: "They taught me to always believe in myself and respect our country. I would like to see my dad reconnect with any veterans who may have known him or served with him, by writing: Charles O. Hardman, 69 Clay Rd., Spencer, WV 25276."

John Gorka has truly hit his stride at the forefront of touring artists. *Rolling Stone* has called him "the preeminent male singer/songwriter of . . . the New Folk Movement . . ." His eighth recording "The Company You Keep" has been recently released on Red House Records and features John's version of "Let Them In."

John D. Governale was operations sergeant for Bravo Company, 299th Engineer Battalion. During Desert Storm, the company destroyed six thousand tons of Iraqi munitions at the Al Jazair Ammunition Supply Point. He has finally figured out he wants to be a writer when he grows up. He can be reached at 145 Ashton Rd., Norway, ME 04268; phone: 207-743-2057.

Kimberly Green is a senior at Bettendorf High School in Bettendorf, Iowa. She plans to attend Monmouth College in Monmouth, Illinois. She intends to major in history and secondary education. While studying writing and history, she spent time with Bob Brooks, her inspiration for this story. You can contact Kimberly at *fallscots2261@aol.com.*

Robert A. Hall is a U.S. Marine Corps Vietnam veteran. Following his service, he earned a degree in government at the University of Massachusetts, graduating in June 1972. That fall, he was elected to the Massachusetts State Senate, defeating an incumbent by a nine-vote margin. He served for five terms before retiring undefeated. While in the senate, he reenlisted in the Marine Reserves, serving an additional six years and rising to the rank of staff sergeant. Since leaving politics, he has managed professional associations. Currently, he lives in Oaklyn, New Jersey, with his wife, Bonnie.

Nick Hill joined the Marine Corps and went to boot camp after graduating from high school in 1977. Initially assigned to the infantry, he changed career fields as a sergeant to become an intelligence analyst. He served as an intelligence chief during the Persian Gulf War. Nick retired a master sergeant in 1997 and resides with his wife and two children in Colorado.

D. W. Jovanovic graduated from the High School of Music and Art in New York City, and received B.S. and M.S. degrees from the City College of New York. A musician and former psychiatric social worker, Jovanovic frequently volunteers for service activities for veterans of the Second World War.

David R. Kiernan, Colonel (U.S. Army, retired), graduated from Virginia Military Institute with a B.A. in English. He served on active duty for twenty-six years as an infantry officer and a public affairs officer. He is a paratrooper and a combat veteran who served in Germany, Vietnam, Saudi Arabia, Hawaii and Alaska, receiving three awards of the Legion of Merit and two Bronze Stars for his service. Kiernan received a master's degree from the University of South Carolina and after his Army career, served as a director of press operations and public information for the 1996 Atlanta Olympics. For the last five years, Kiernan has worked as director of strategic communications for MPRI, where he continues his interest in international and domestic mass communications.

Richard H. Kiley is a senior citizen living in a golf community in Vero Beach, Florida. He graduated from Georgetown University fifty years ago following three years of active Army duty in this country and in Europe. He is currently preparing a memoir of World War II experiences—*From Normandy to Dachau.*

Julie Beth Kink writes for a weekly newspaper in Stillwater, Minnesota, covering government meetings and features. She also is a public relations coordinator for a small adoption agency. She was born in Wisconsin (where her family lived during the Vietnam War), moved to Minnesota in 1972 and graduated from college in 1983.

Joe Kirkup is the author of over sixty nonfiction essays published in various periodicals and paperbacks, including *Reader's Digest, Chicken Soup for the Pet Lover's Soul* and *Chicken Soup for the Cat and Dog Lover's Soul.* A collection of Kirkup's essays, *Life Sentences,* can be purchased through *JoeKirkup.com* on the Internet or by calling 860-572-4423.

Stephen C. Klink is an ordained minister in the Christian Church, having served the last twelve years at Eaton Rapids Community Christian Church. He is also a frequent speaker at veterans' functions. Raised on a farm and not able to get it out of his blood, he lives on forty acres raising registered Belgian draft horses, longhorn cattle, a cat, a dog and a host of roller pigeons. Several years ago, his son chided him for his "nose to the grindstone" work ethic by saying, "Dad, you never do anything fun." After pondering his son's diagnosis of his lifestyle, he began to write for "fun." Steve has never written anything for publication before but presently has one book nearing completion, and some other writing will be included in an upcoming book by another author. He doesn't think he will let his son know how much work this "fun" has turned out to be. Steve can be reached at *sklink@voyager.net.*

Rabbi Paysach J. Krohn, Mohel, author and lecturer, has written *Bris Milah,* about the ritual of circumcision, and five delightful books of inspirational Jewish short stories, known as "The Maggid Series"—all published by Mesorah/Artscroll Publications, Brooklyn, New York. Contact him for his tapes and books at *krohnmohel@aol.com.*

Patricia S. Laye, author of seven novels and numerous short stories, and a frequent contributor to *Chicken Soup* books, teaches at writers' conferences and colleges throughout the south. She resides in Cuthbert, Georgia, where she is currently working on a novel. She travels worldwide exploring new settings for her novels.

Robin Lim was the absolute "Army brat." Her German-Irish-Native American father was blessed to meet her Filipino-Chinese mother while he was stationed at Camp John Hay Military Base in Baguio, Philippine Islands. Because her father, CW3 Robert A. Jehle, devoted his life to military service, she and her siblings saw a great deal of the world. Robin has seven astounding children and one granddaughter. She and her husband currently live in Asia, where she is a midwife. She is also the author of *After the Baby's Birth: A*

Women's Way to Wellness. Anyone interested in supporting her Healthy Mother-Healthy Baby foundation may contact her at *yayasan@aol.com.*

Sharon Linnéa is the producer of the Inspiration Channel at *Beliefnet.com* (where you'll find a lot more inspirational stories!). She and her husband, Robert Owens Scott, have two great, though slightly nutty, kids, Johnathan and Linnéa. Sharon has enjoyed being a freelance editor for several of the *Chicken Soup for the Soul* books, as well as being a staff writer for *Guideposts* and four other national magazines. Her most recent books are *Princess Kaiulani: Hope of a Nation, Heart of a People,* and *Raoul Wallenberg: The Man Who Stopped Death,* as well as the upcoming *Great American Tree Book* with Jeffrey G. Meyer. Sharon speaks often at writers' conferences as well as to schools on kids' needs for heroes. She can be reached at *Slinnea@warwick.net.*

Bill Livingstone, grandfather of four, is a native Los Angelino and retired urban planner who loves woodworking and thinking about the "meaning of life." He walks the beach below Santa Barbara's Shoreline Park every sunset while recalling stories for his memoirs. You can visit him at *wlivingstone@earthlink.net.*

Michael Manley, USN, 1965–1970, Assault Craft Unit One, Coronado/Danang, is a building maintenance mechanic. He is currently trying to peddle his first novel, *Blood Atonement.* He can be reached at *nothingdoing2@home.com.*

Ivan W. Marion spent three years and three months with the U.S. Army, of which two years and nine months were combat service in Africa, Sicily and Italy, from 1942 to 1945. He was a member of the 91st Cavalry Reconnaissance Squadron as a crew member of an M-5 Stuart light tank. His troops suffered heavy casualties, but he prefers to record the unusual and sometimes humorous situations that occurred during World War II. After the war, he spent most of his working years as an electrician in central upstate New York. His marriage to Eleanor for fifty-nine years (and still counting) has produced a son and daughter and three grandchildren. He can be reached at 904 Nancy Gamble Ln., Ellenton, FL 34222.

Margaret Brown Marks was a captain in the U.S. Army. Before that, she was a teacher in a one-room school. Later, she was a wife, a mother and, once again, a teacher. She has a master's degree in special education, four sons, five granddaughters and a million stories to tell. She can be reached at *Captainmarks@juno.com.*

Bill Mauldin served his country in World War II with the 45th Infantry Division and other outfits. He received the Purple Heart for wounds received in Italy. After the war he became one of the most distinguished editorial cartoonists in America, first for the *St. Louis Post-Dispatch* and later for the *Chicago Sun-Times.* He received the Pulitzer Prize for editorial cartooning in 1944 and 1959, as well as numerous other awards. He now lives in Santa Fe, New Mexico.

Christine Ann Maxwell-Osborn, originally from London, England, feels lucky to live in Calgary, Alberta, where inspiration for writing comes readily. Her first novel, *Rosie,* will be published in the summer of 2001. Now widowed, she lives with two dear old cats and is blessed to have the best son and daughter-in-law any mother could wish for.

Stacy Havlik McAnulty, aspiring author and dog trainer, lives in North Carolina with her husband, Brett. Currently, she works as a mechanical engineer in the aerospace industry. Stacy dedicates her story to her grandfathers, Joseph Jablanski and Frank Havlik, World War II veterans, and her father, John Havlik, a Vietnam veteran. Stacy can be contacted at *shbam@yahoo.com.*

George C. Miller is a retired warrant officer who served two years in Vietnam as an Army helicopter pilot. His daughter, Rani, who wrote the letter in the story, was three years old when he went to Vietnam. Though decorated for valor, he considers his wife, Kaye, as the true hero in the family. They live in Enterprise, Alabama. You can contact him at *millerg@ala.net.*

Emerson D. Moran's lifelong calling to write was postponed because of the Great Depression, World War II Navy service and a meatpacking career. His poignant essays and pointed op-eds began appearing in major newspapers in the 1970s. A native of Seneca Falls, New York, Moran, in his nineties, still offers commentary on the fullness of life over two centuries.

James R. Morgan was a helicopter pilot with A Company, Assault Helicopter Battalion, 101st Airborne Division. He served a tour of duty in Vietnam from December 1967 to December 1968. Jim was an air traffic controller for twenty-five years, and he now works for the Federal Aviation Administration testing air traffic systems. When he and his wife are not working, they can usually be found bicycling through Europe. He presently lives near Atlantic City with his wife of thirty-two years, Joan, and their golden retriever, Toby.

Jack Moskowitz was born and raised in Brooklyn, New York. Enlisting as an aviation cadet in 1942, he was sent to navigator school in Texas. Serving with the Eighth Air Force in England, his B-17 bomber, "Sleepy Time Gal," was shot down over Berlin on March 8, 1944. He was liberated by the Russians on May 1, 1945. Jack spent thirty-five years in the bakery business and eleven years with the Internal Revenue Service, and he retired in 1988. He has two sons and four grandchildren.

James F. Murphy Jr. is a professor who teaches writing and literature at Boston College and Massachusetts Maritime Academy. He is the father of six children and the author of four published novels. He holds an undergraduate degree from Boston College and two master's degrees. Professor Murphy is currently completing a novel—a journey—of the Korean War, in which he was a member of the Seventh Division, Seventeenth Infantry and the Honor Guard, Headquarters Company. He and his wife reside in Falmouth, Massachusetts, on Cape Cod.

Bill Newton Jr. began writing short stories as a student at the University of Houston, Victoria campus, in 1977. He is a six-year veteran of the U.S. Navy and a nine-year veteran of the U.S. Army. For seven years, Bill worked for the Gulf Bend Mental Health Mental Retardation center in Victoria, Texas. While manager of the Gulf Bend center in Cuero, Texas, he was very active in the Special Olympics and the local Boy Scouting program. He has one son, Clint, who is a poet, artist and musician. Bill currently lives with and takes care of his father in Marietta, Georgia, where he continues to write.

Captain Richard Oakley ended his military duty at Camp Dix, New Jersey, in February 1946. He once went "over the fence, AWOL" and hitchhiked to Montclair to be with his wife and nine-month-old daughter, meeting his beautiful child for the first time. His buddies sang out *"Here"* to cover his absence from the base. When he was sixty, his United Airlines flying career ended with a farewell party, and now, at age seventy-eight, his tennis game is improving.

Reverend Peter Baldwin Panagore graduated from Yale Divinity School, Yale University, M.Div., in 1986 and is presently serving the Congregational Church of Boothbay Harbor, Maine. He is a staff writer for *HOMILETICS Magazine,* Communications Resources, and leads international cultural immersion work trips for youth and adults. He relishes rowing an ancient Whitehall fourteen-foot or sailing a relic of a Beetlecat with his children, Alexa and Andy, on rural Linekin Bay amid the neighborly harbor seals and singing common loons. Peter is contently married to Michelle, who grows big orange pumpkins and delights in needlepoint.

Frank Perkins, sixty-six, is a retired journalist and Army officer who saw active and reserve service during the Cold War period. He has more than forty years' experience in broadcast and print journalism and currently writes a weekly military column for the *Fort Worth* (Texas) *Star-Telegram,* his hometown newspaper.

Walter F. Peters came home and married his high school sweetheart, took advantage of the GI Bill, got his master's degree and became an educator. Together, he and his wife raised four fine young men, and today they smile as they dance to "our" music, the music of the forties. It's been an incredible fifty-four years.

Thomas D. Phillips retired as an Air Force colonel after thirty-six years of enlisted and commissioned service. He led a detachment through a Red Brigades terrorist episode, served as director of the Air Force Personnel Readiness Center during Operation Desert Storm and commanded troops in Bosnia. He resides in Lincoln, Nebraska.

Thomas Lafayette Pool lives in Albuquerque, New Mexico, with his wife Donda. He is retired after over twenty years as a chiropractor and is now pursuing his next career as a writer. He and his wife look forward to traveling the world together, especially to Norway to visit their son and daughter-in-law.

Diana Dwan Poole joined the Army Nurse Corps in 1966. She spent two years at Letterman Hospital at the Presidio caring for Vietnam returnees. At age twenty-three, she went to Vietnam and served two voluntary tours at the Sixty-seventh Evac Hospital in Qui Nhon. She was head nurse of orthopedics, casualty receiving and triage. Diana is no longer in nursing but is active in Vietnam veteran activities. She is married to a Marine Vietnam vet, and she has two children. She resides in North Carolina.

Robert D. Reeves and his wife have five grown children and live in Washington, Illinois. Bob retired in 1982 from Caterpillar Tractor Company's tool design division after forty years of service to the company, which included the time spent in the U.S. Army. Before his induction into the armed forces, he had been with Caterpillar for only five months as a distributor in the tooling crib. He attended the University of Illinois at Champaign briefly, from 1940 to 1941, after having graduated from high school in Gridley, Illinois. He was raised with five brothers and sisters on a farm just outside Gridley. Robert can be reached at 425 Brookcrest Dr., Washington, IL 61571.

Paul F. Reid is a feature writer and restaurant critic for the *Palm Beach Post,* West Palm Beach, Florida. The *Post* is a member of the Cox Newspaper Chain. Reid's lifetime interest in history found expression at the *Post,* in stories he wrote about historian and Marine vet William Manchester, the Marines on Okinawa, downed fliers in Nazi-occupied Yugoslavia, forgotten vets of the Korean War, submarine warfare and many others. South Florida is home to the fastest growing vet population in the nation. These readers want their stories preserved for younger readers. Reid and two of his history-loving colleagues at the *Post,* Dan Moffit and Doug Kalajian, enjoy writing about vets, and only regret they will never be able to write all the stories of all the men and women who have served the country. Reid won the Cox Writer of the Year award in 1997 and the Cox Feature Writer of the Year award in 1998. He lives with his wife, Barbara and her son, Alex, in West Palm Beach.

Dr. Lester F. Rentmeester retired after thirty-one years in the U.S. Air Force, where he served mainly in developing and operating reconnaissance and intelligence systems. In 1954, he initiated the reconnaissance satellite (Eye in the Sky) system. After military retirement, he was the chairman of a graduate program at the Florida Institute of Technology in Melbourne, Florida. In collaboration with his wife, Jeanne Marie, he has written eight books and a dozen magazine articles.

George W. Saumweber grew up in St. Paul, Minnesota, and joined the U.S. Marine Corps when he was seventeen, two weeks after graduating from high school. In 1969, he was seriously wounded while serving in Vietnam as a grunt with the Fifth Marines. He married his high school sweetheart, Sharon, in 1971, and they have two children, Cheryl, twenty-one, and John, twenty. He has a business degree from the University of Minnesota and has worked for the Small Business Administration for twenty-four years.

Kenneth A. Schechter grew up in Los Angeles. Los Angeles H.S., UCLA (A.A.), U.S. Navy (Naval Aviator), Stanford (A.B.), Harvard (M.B.A.), Corporate

Business (Administrative & Executive), Insurance since 1968. Ken and Sue were married in 1955 and have three children, Jon, Anne and Rob, and five grandchildren. The Schechters live in Pasadena, California.

Robert L. Schneider lives in Oglethorpe, Georgia, with his wife, Ginger, and daughter, Rhiana. He's an apparatus engineer with the county fire department. He works with Vietnam veterans who are incarcerated.

Walter W. Scott, a retired twenty-year management consultant, also served as an administrator with the City of Philadelphia for eleven years and seven as executive director of a U.S. missionary society. "Wiggle Your Toes!" is a chapter from his book, *The Fighter Pilot and the Unseen Hand.* He has a Wharton School master's degree in government administration.

Jan Craig Scruggs is a wounded and decorated veteran of the Vietnam War, having served with the U.S. Army 199th Light Infantry Brigade. While researching Vietnam veterans for his master's degree, he had the idea to create a national memorial inscribed with the names of all American military who gave their lives in the Vietnam War. In 1979, Scruggs began the project using $2,800 of his own money. Despite controversy and numerous setbacks, the memorial was built and dedicated in November 1982.

Heather L. Shepherd resides in Ohio with her loving husband and four beautiful children, and is a poet and writer. Her current projects include a children's book, *Moon, Why Are You So Sad?,* and a poetry chapbook, alongside another Poet. "A Time to Heal" embraces the powerful magic of poetry to heal the victim within.

Barbara K. Sherer is an ordained Presbyterian minister who became a chaplain with the U.S. Army Reserves while serving a church in Stillwater, Oklahoma, in 1984. She entered active duty in 1992 and is currently stationed at Ft. Hood, Texas.

Storm Stafford is currently attending the University of Hawaii to get her M.F.A. in theater set design. She has written for *Seventeen* magazine and *Girls Life,* and recently sold her first novel, *Buttons and Beaus* to Precious Gems Romances. You can reach her at 1573 Kinoole St., Hilo, HI 96720.

Elgin Staples was discharged from the Navy in October 1945. He studied accounting and business administration under the GI Bill. At age seventy-seven, he still owns and operates his business, Staples Enterprises. His hobbies include gardening and sixteenth-century England. He can be reached at 1340 Marion Ave., Devore, CA 92407 or by calling 909-887-3550.

Doug Sterner is a decorated, two-tour Vietnam veteran who has dedicated his life to preserving and sharing American history. A recipient of the Congressional Medal of Honor Society's prestigious Distinguished Citizens Award, he is a popular author and speaker. He is considered one of the foremost historians on our nation's highest award for military heroism, the Medal of Honor, and operates one of the largest patriotic Internet sites, at *www.HomeOfHeroes.com.*

Marta J. Sweek lives in New Market, Indiana, with her husband, Mick. She is a buyer at Nucor Steel and has two children, Chris and Erika Craig. She can be reached at *mmsweek@wico.net.*

Barry Vonder Mehden, a fourth-generation Californian, was born in San Francisco in 1929. Entering the U.S. Army in 1950, he served in Korea and later in Berlin, Germany. He received numerous awards and decorations while in "Charlie" Company, Sixty-fifth Combat Engineers, attached to the Twenty-Fifth Division. Barry holds degrees from Oakland College, Boston University and Cornell University. Now retired, he is still active in the American Legion, Post #83, Merced, California, and VFW Post #9946 in Atwater, California.

Karen L. Waldman, Ph.D., finds working as a psychologist in a large veterans hospital extremely rewarding. She also enjoys music, nature, acting, writing, photography, traveling with her husband (Ken), and "playing" with their good friends, special relatives, and wonderful children and grandchildren (Alyson, Brian, Dave, Eric, Greta, Lana, Lisa, Tom). Her e-mail is *krobens@aol.com.*

Bill Walker logged over nine hundred combat hours in Vietnam as a helicopter pilot. He, his wife, Denise, and their children, Sara, Marisa, and Michael, live at 341 Shirley Ann Dr., Centerville, OH 45458. Bill is a sales representative and can be reached through the Lancer Web page at *www.members.tripod.com/dmussey/.*

Bruce Watson is a frequent contributor to *Smithsonian* and has also written for the *Los Angeles Times,* the *Boston Globe* and other publications. He is working on a book about A. C. Gilbert and his Erector Sets.

Tim Watts was born in Northern California, was raised in the Midwest and "fled to South Florida as soon as feasible." He was educated in community colleges, on the streets of Chicago and in the jungles of Vietnam. His stories and articles have been published in numerous magazines, newspapers and textbooks.

Ernest L. Webb enlisted in the U.S. Army in 1956 and served with both the Eighty-second Airborne and Eleventh Airborne Divisions. He subsequently attended West Point, graduated and served in the infantry. His assignments included two tours of duty in Vietnam.

Philip Weiner trained as a bombardier/navigator in World War II. He flew sixty-one combat missions over the North Italian Alps and Bremmer Pass. His awards include the Distinguished Flying Cross and the Air Medal with five oak leaf clusters. The author of "L'Inzecca: A Tale of Corsica", he now lives in Los Angeles, California with his wife, Edith. They have two sons, Rex and Kenneth, and three grandchildren, Carlos, Celia and Alice.

Arthur B. Wiknik Jr. served as an infantry squad leader with the 101st

Airborne Division from April 1969 to March 1970 and fought in the battle for Hamburger Hill. He frequently shares his wartime experiences in presentations at local Connecticut schools and civic organizations. Arthur is seeking a publisher for his memoirs of the humor, survivor mentality and the bizarre events of his Vietnam tour of duty. Contact him at *mucketman@juno.com*.

Ronald C. Williams served in helicopter duty during Vietnam from 1967 to 1968. He received his bachelor of arts from Brook Institute of Photography, Santa Barbara, California, and then began a twenty-year photography career in advertising based out of Nashville, Tennessee. Ron now resides in Missoula, Montana, living lighter and fishing more. He can be reached at 406-829-8039 or *ronwilliams.com*.

Jim Willoughby lives on the side of a pine-studded hill in Prescott, Arizona, with his wife Sue, a cat and two rowdy dogs. He writes and illustrates humor books for Arizona Highways and articles for numerous magazines, in addition to creating editorial cartoons for *The Daily Courier,* Prescott's prize-winning hometown newspaper.

Charles Wolf joined the United States Marine Corps in 1986 as an anti-tank assault man. A graphic illustrator in the Marines, his current duty station is Marine Corps Base, Kaneohe Bay, Hawaii. He enjoys cartooning and combat art. He credits his success to family, friends, fellow Marines, and loving wife Amy. He can be reached at *www.Toonville.com/sempertoons/*.

Benedict Yedlin was born in Brooklyn, New York, and attended Brooklyn College. When the United States entered World War II, he left college to join the Army Corps of Engineers and served as a photographic mapping technician before transferring to the Army Air Corps. Trained as a gunner and stationed in southern Italy, he flew most of his fifty combat missions in a B-24 named *The Buzzer.* After the war, he completed his college degree, married and joined his father's business building single-family houses. His son, Charlie, joined him, and the business expanded into a building, general contracting and property management company, the Yedlin Company, located in Princeton, New Jersey. In the 1990s, Mr. Yedlin turned over the operation of the business to Charlie and devoted his time to memoir writing, video production, traveling, and bicycling. He is a member of the 449th Bomb Group Association, the Fifteenth Air Force Association, the International B-24 Liberator Club and community service organizations. He produced *B-24 Bomber Crew,* a video of his crew's reminiscences of their experiences in World War II, broadcast on the History Channel and NJN. Ben also has two daughters, Jane and Nancy. He has six grandchildren. His second wife of twenty-one years, Nancy M. Yedlin, died in 1989.

Permissions

We would like to acknowledge the following publishers and individuals for permission to reprint the following material. (Note: The stories that were in the public domain or that were written by Jack Canfield, Mark Victor Hansen or Sidney R. Slagter are not included in this listing.)

Freedom Village. Reprinted by permission of James F. Murphy Jr. ©1993 James F. Murphy Jr.

The Code Talkers. Reprinted by permission of Bruce Watson. ©1993 Bruce Watson.

The Postcard. Reprinted by permission of Rocky Bleier and David Eberhart. ©2000 Rocky Bleier and David Eberhart.

That Old Man Down the Street. Reprinted by permission of Emerson D. Moran. ©1999 Emerson D. Moran.

The Harbinger and *The Watch.* Reprinted by permission of Bill Walker. ©2000 Bill Walker.

The Final Battle. Reprinted with permission of Simon & Schuster, Inc., from *Journey to Washington* by Senator Daniel K. Inouye with Lawrence Elliott. ©1975 Prentice Hall, Inc. ©renewed 1995 by Senator Daniel K. Inouye.

Wiggle Your Toes! Reprinted by permission of Walter W. Scott. ©2000 Walter W. Scott.

"Go, Gunfighter, Go!" From *My American Journey* by Colin Powell with Joseph E. Persico, ©1995 by Colin L. Powell. Used by permission of Random House, Inc.

Against the Odds. Reprinted by permission of Elgin Staples. ©2000 Elgin Staples.

The Rescue. Reprinted by permission of Robert E. Brooks Jr. and Kimberly D. Green. ©1999 Robert E. Brooks Jr. and Kimberly D. Green.

Sergeant Mills. Reprinted by permission of John D. Governale. ©1995 John D. Governale.

The True Face of Humanity. Reprinted by permission of Thomas Lafayette Pool. ©1999 Thomas Lafayette Pool.

One Hell of a Plan. Reprinted by permission of Ron Williams. ©1999 Ron Williams.

The Altar Boy. Reprinted by permission of Richard H. Kiley. ©2000 Richard H. Kiley.

The Vision. Reprinted by permission of Paul Charlillo. ©1994 Paul Charlillo.

Boom Boom. Reprinted by permission of James R. Morgan. ©1998 James R.

Morgan.

Prepare to Ditch. Reprinted by permission of Jack Black and Patricia Black. ©2000 Jack Black and Patricia Black.

Christmas in Korea. Reprinted by permission of Larry Ebsch. ©1999 Larry Ebsch.

Help from an Unexpected Source. Reprinted by permission of Dr. Lester F. Rentmeester. ©2000 Dr. Lester F. Rentmeester. Condensed from an article in *Voyageur* magazine, Green Bay, WI, December, 2000.

Blind and Alone over North Korea. Reprinted by permission of Kenneth A. Schechter. ©2001 Kenneth A. Schechter.

Do Not Resuscitate. Reprinted by permission of Diane Carlson Evans. ©2000 Diane Carlson Evans.

Colonel Maggie and the Blind Veteran. Reprinted by permission of Susan M. Christiansen. ©1987 Susan M. Christiansen.

The Stuff They Don't Give Medals For. Reprinted by permission of Tim Watts. ©1989 Tim Watts.

The Valley. Reprinted by permission of Barry Vonder Mehden. ©2001 Barry Vonder Mehden.

The Mitzvah. Reprinted by permission of Arnold Geier. ©1945 Arnold Geier.

Nurse Penny. Reprinted by permission of Ernest L. Webb. ©2000 Ernest L. Webb.

The Four Chaplains. Reprinted by permission of The Chapel of Four Chaplains. ©1947 The Chapel of Four Chaplains.

My Most Memorable Christmas. Reprinted by permission of Gene DuVall. ©1993 Gene DuVall.

To Any Service Member. Reprinted by permission of Nick Hill. ©2000 Nick Hill.

Now I Lay Me Down to Sleep. Reprinted by permission of Diana Dwan Poole. ©1998 Diana Dwan Poole.

Hot Lips. Reprinted by permission of Philip Weiner. ©1995 Philip Weiner.

Lord of the Chinese Flies. Reprinted by permission of Akira B. Chikami. ©1998 Akira B. Chikami.

A Show of Strength. Reprinted by permission of Ivan W. Marion. ©1998 Ivan W. Marion.

Stalag Las Vegas. Reprinted by permission of Robert D. Reeves. ©1990 Robert D. Reeves.

The Greatest Compliment. Reprinted by permission of Thomas D. Phillips. ©2000 Thomas D. Phillips.

Operation Chow Down. Reprinted by permission of Richard Oakley. ©2000 Richard Oakley.

Amina's Way. Reprinted by permission of Barbara K. Sherer and Sharon Linnéa. ©2000 Barbara K. Sherer and Sharon Linnéa.

Morse Code. Reprinted by permission of Bernard Belasco. ©2000 Bernard Belasco.

The Twelfth Man. Reprinted by permission of Rabbi Paysach J. Krohn. ©1999 Rabbi Paysach J. Krohn. Condensed from *Along the Maggid's Journey.*

Bob "March Field" Hope. Reprinted by permission of Bob Hope and Melville Shavelson. ©1990 Bob Hope and Melville Shavelson.

A Flag of Any Size. Reprinted by permission of Stacy Havlik McAnulty. ©2000 Stacy Havlik McAnulty.

Too Young to Understand. Reprinted by permission of Barbara Sue Canale. ©2000 Barbara Sue Canale.

I Have the Coffee On. Reprinted by permission of Susan Grady Bristol. ©1999 Susan Grady Bristol.

The "Super-Gunner." Reprinted by permission of Benedict Yedlin. ©1999 Benedict Yedlin.

Love Letters. Reprinted by permission of Sarah H. Giachino. ©2000 Sarah H. Giachino.

The Gift of Hope. Reprinted by permission of Bill Livingstone. ©1996 Bill Livingstone.

A Joyful Noise. Reprinted by permission of Everett Alvarez Jr. ©2001 Everett Alvarez Jr.

More Than Brothers. Reprinted by permission of William C. Newton and Bill Newton Jr. ©1999 William C. Newton and Bill Newton Jr.

Honor Bound. Reprinted by permission of Jack Moskowitz. ©2000 Jack Moskowitz.

Combat Boots. Reprinted by permission of Watts Caudill. ©2000 Watts Caudill.

The Nine Days. Reprinted by permission of Walter F. Peters. ©1999 Walter F. Peters.

Grandpa's Apple Pie. Reprinted by permission of Heather L. Shepherd. ©2000 Heather L. Shepherd.

Fellow Marines. Reprinted by permission of Edward Andrusko. ©1998 Edward Andrusko.

Ernie Pyle's Last Battle. From *Unexplained Mysteries of World War II* by William B. Breuer ©1997. Adapted by permission of John Wiley & Sons, Inc.

Luther's Lumber. Reprinted by permission of Joe Edwards. ©1999 Joe Edwards.

The Cabbie. Reprinted by permission of Robert L. Schneider. ©2000 Robert L. Schneider.

Back to the World. Reprinted by permission of Arthur B. Wiknik Jr. ©1999 Arthur B. Wiknik Jr.

Wounded. Reprinted by permission of George W. Saumweber. ©1999 George W. Saumweber.

Reunion on the Dock. Reprinted by permission of Margaret Brown Marks. ©1999 Margaret Brown Marks.

The Most Beautiful Man in the World. Excerpted from *American Jews in World War II: The Story of 550,000 Fighters for Freedom* by I. Kaufman, ©1947. Reprinted by permission of I. Kaufman.

A Soldier Remembers. Reprinted by permission of David R. Kiernan. ©2000 David R. Kiernan.

Kids from Mars. Reprinted by permission of Joe Kirkup. ©1992 Joe Kirkup.

The Tradition. Reprinted by permission of Antonio Camisa. ©1999 Antonio Camisa.

The Light. Reprinted by permission of Patricia S. Laye. ©2000 Patricia S. Laye.

The Visit. Reprinted by permission of Tre' M. Barron. ©1998 Tre' M. Barron.

A Monumental Task. Reprinted by permission of Jan Craig Scruggs. ©2000 Jan Craig Scruggs.

A Voice in the Dark. From *Newsweek,* 3/8/99 "A Voice in the Dark" by Connie Stevens ©1999 Newsweek, Inc. All rights reserved. Reprinted by permission.

The Doorman. Reprinted by permission of Jean P. Brody. ©1998 Jean P. Brody.

The Cub Scout. Reprinted by permission of Robert A. Hall. ©1997 Robert A. Hall.

The Waiting Room. Reprinted by permission of Michael Manley. ©1999 Michael Manley.

Pie in the Sky. Reprinted by permission of Doug Sterner. ©1999 Doug Sterner.

A Daughter's Letter. Reprinted by permission of George C. Miller. ©1999 George C. Miller.

Former Enemies. Reprinted by permission of Reverend Peter Baldwin Panagore. ©1998 Reverend Peter Baldwin Panagore.

The Search for "Shorts." Reprinted by permission of Marta J. Sweek. ©1984 Marta J. Sweek.

Return to Hoa Quan Village. Reprinted by permission of Robert R. Amon Jr. ©2000 Robert R. Amon Jr.

You're Never Alone on a Mission. Reprinted by permission of Julie Beth Kink. ©1999 Julie Beth Kink.

Sunglasses. Reprinted by permission of Stephen C. Klink. ©1999 Stephen C. Klink.

The Honey Man. Reprinted by permission of Robin Lim. ©1997 Robin Lim.

Just Like Me. Reprinted by permission of Jerry Ewen. ©1998 Jerry Ewen.

Ebony and Ivory. Reprinted by permission of Karen L. Waldman. ©2000 Karen L. Waldman.

Remembrance Day. Reprinted by permission of Christine Ann Maxwell-Osborn. ©1999 Christine Ann Maxwell-Osborn.

Let Them in, Peter. Based on an anonymous poem with additional words by John Gorka. ©Blues Palace Music. 1989 ASCAP.

When Winter Was Warm. Reprinted by permission of Storm Stafford. ©1998 Storm Stafford.

Stars and Stripes from Odds and Ends. Reprinted by permission of John Carlson. ©2000 John Carlson.

Sweet-Pea Summers. Reprinted by permission of Susan Arnett-Hutson. ©2000 Susan Arnett-Hutson.

History. Reprinted by permission of Paul F. Reid. ©2000 Paul F. Reid.

American Eagles. Reprinted by permission of D. W. Jovanovic. ©1997 D. W. Jovanovic.

Windows for Remy. Reprinted by permission of Leslie F. Perkins. ©1999 Leslie F. Perkins.

Chicken Soup for the Soul®

Improving Your Life Every Day

Real people sharing real stories—for nineteen years. Now, Chicken Soup for the Soul has gone beyond the bookstore to become a world leader in life improvement. Through books, movies, DVDs, online resources and other partnerships, we bring hope, courage, inspiration and love to hundreds of millions of people around the world. Chicken Soup for the Soul's writers and readers belong to a one-of-a-kind global community, sharing advice, support, guidance, comfort, and knowledge.

Chicken Soup for the Soul stories have been translated into more than 40 languages and can be found in more than one hundred countries. Every day, millions of people experience a Chicken Soup for the Soul story in a book, magazine, newspaper or online. As we share our life experiences through these stories, we offer hope, comfort and inspiration to one another. The stories travel from person to person, and from country to country, helping to improve lives everywhere.

Chicken Soup for the Soul®

Share with Us

We all have had Chicken Soup for the Soul moments in our lives. If you would like to share your story or poem with millions of people around the world, go to chickensoup.com and click on "Submit Your Story." You may be able to help another reader, and become a published author at the same time. Some of our past contributors have launched writing and speaking careers from the publication of their stories in our books!

Our submission volume has been increasing steadily—the quality and quantity of your submissions has been fabulous. We only accept story submissions via our website. They are no longer accepted via mail or fax.

To contact us regarding other matters, please send us an e-mail through webmaster@chickensoupforthesoul.com, or fax or write us at:

Chicken Soup for the Soul
P.O. Box 700
Cos Cob, CT 06807-0700
Fax: 203-861-7194

One more note from your friends at Chicken Soup for the Soul: Occasionally, we receive an unsolicited book manuscript from one of our readers, and we would like to respectfully inform you that we do not accept unsolicited manuscripts and we must discard the ones that appear.

Tough times won't last, but tough people will. Many people have lost money, jobs and/or homes, or made cutbacks. Others have faced life-changing natural disasters, or health and family difficulties. These encouraging and inspirational stories are all about overcoming adversity, pulling together, and finding joy in a simpler life. Stories address downsizing, resolving debt, managing chronic illness, having faith, finding new perspectives, and blessings in disguise.

978-1-935096-35-1

Life begins again at 60! Crossing that magic age might bring a few new wrinkles but also new experiences, and this book celebrates all the fun and wonder of getting older. Readers will revel in these 101 new stories by other dynamic older singles and couples who are actively enjoying their "senior years!" Filled with humorous and fun adventures of love, family, travel, careers, and new pursuits, this book will delight and invigorate readers.

978-1-935096-71-9

You cross the magic sixty-year mark and still feel young at heart, despite a few new wrinkles. This book focuses on the wonders of getting older, with many stories about dynamic older singles and couples finding new careers, new sports, new love, and new meaning in their lives. This inspiring, amusing, and heartwarming book includes the best 101 stories for today's young seniors from Chicken Soup for the Soul's library. Printed in a larger font.

978-1-935096-17-7

A parent becomes a new person the day the first grandchild is born. Formerly serious adults become grandparents who dote on their grandchildren and find new delight in life. This new book includes the best stories on being a grandparent from Chicken Soup for the Soul's library. Everyone can understand the special ties between grandparents and grandchildren -- the unlimited love, the mutual admiration and unqualified acceptance. Printed in a larger font.

978-1-935096-09-2

Every cloud has a silver lining. Readers will be inspired by these 101 real-life stories from people just like them, taking a positive attitude to the ups and downs of life, and remembering to be grateful and count their blessings. This book continues Chicken Soup for the Soul's focus on inspiration and hope, and its stories of optimism and faith will encourage readers to stay positive during challenging times and in their everyday lives.

978-1-935096-56-6

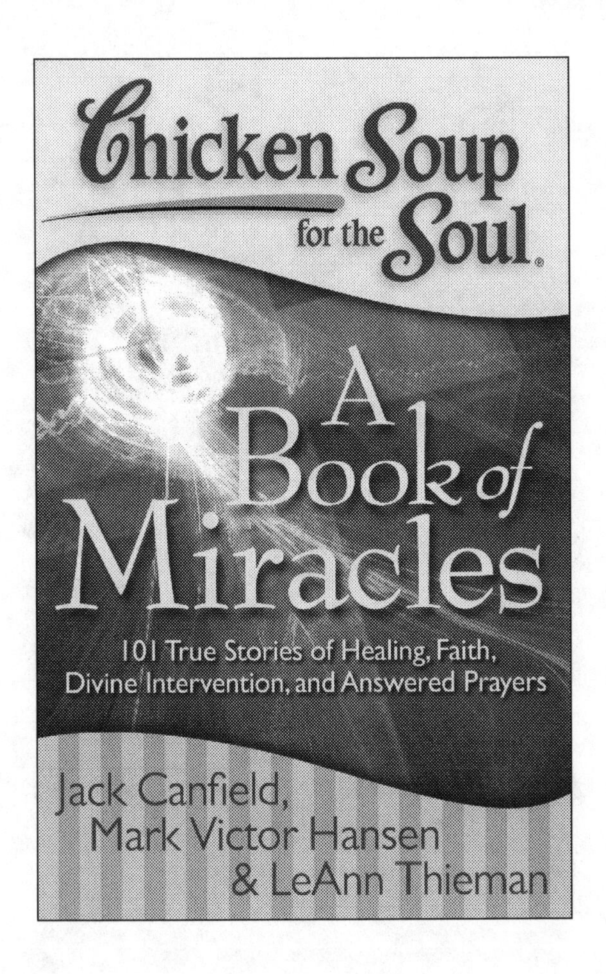

Everyone loves a good miracle story, and this book provides 101 true stories of healing, divine intervention, and answered prayers. These amazing, personal stories prove that God is alive and active in the world today, working miracles on our behalf. The incredible accounts show His love and involvement in our lives. This book of miracles will encourage, uplift, and recharge the faith of Catholics and all Christian readers.

978-1-935096-51-1

We all need help from time to time, and these 101 true stories of answered prayers show a higher power at work in our lives. Regular people share their personal, touching stories of God's Divine intervention, healing power, and communication. Filled with stories about the power of prayer, miracles, and hope, this book will inspire anyone looking to boost his or her faith and read some amazing stories.

978-1-935096-76-4

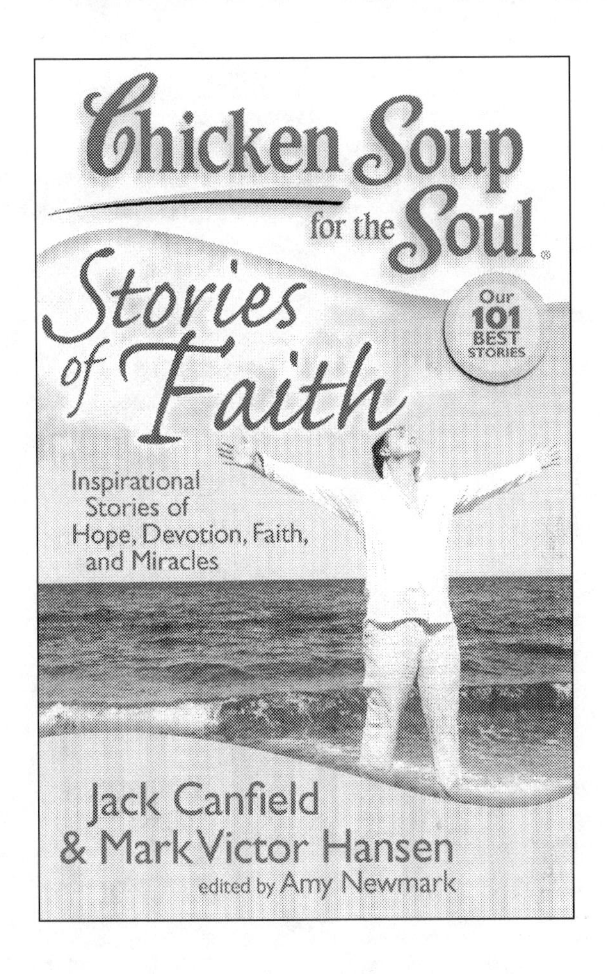

Everyone needs some faith and hope! This book is just the ticket, with a collection of 101 of the best stories from Chicken Soup for the Soul's past on faith, hope, miracles, and devotion. These true stories, written by regular people, tell of prayers answered miraculously, amazing coincidences, rediscovered faith, and the serenity that comes from believing in a greater power, appealing to Christians and those of other faiths—anyone who seeks inspiration.

978-1-935096-14-6

Chicken Soup
www.chickensoup.com
for the Soul